D1528780

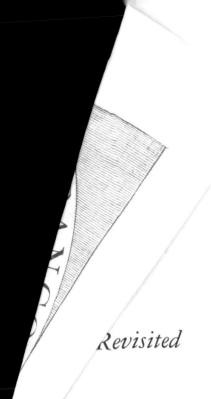

Revisited

Twayne's World Authors Series

French Literature

David O'Connell, Editor

Georgia State University

TWAS 837

M. FRANÇOIS RABELAIS DOC. EN MEDECINE.

Les Oeuures de M.F. Rabelais D. en Medeſine
ou eſt contenue lhiſtoire des faiᵗ heroiques de
Gargantua et de ſon fils Pantagruel.

M. aſne. fe.

FRANÇOIS RABELAIS

Rabelais Revisited

Elizabeth Chesney Zegura and Marcel Tetel

Twayne Publishers • New York
Maxwell Macmillan Canada • Toronto
Maxwell Macmillan International • New York   Oxford   Singapore   Sydney

Rabelais Revisited
Elizabeth Chesney Zegura and Marcel Tetel

Twayne Publishers
Macmillan Publishing Company
866 Third Avenue
New York, New York 10022

Maxwell Macmillan Canada, Inc.
1200 Eglinton Avenue East
Suite 200
Don Mills, Ontario M3C 3N1

Library of Congress Cataloging-in-Publication Data

Zegura, Elizabeth Chesney
    Rabelais revisited / by Elizabeth Chesney Zegura and Marcel Tetel.
        p.   cm. — (Twayne's world authors series ; TWAS 837. French
    literature)
    Includes bibliographical references and index.
    ISBN 0-8057-8294-X
    1. Rabelais, François, ca. 1490–1553?—Criticism and
interpretation.   I. Tetel, Marcel.   II. Title.   III. Series:
Twayne's world authors series ; TWAS 837.   IV. Series: Twayne's
world authors series.   French literature.
PQ1694.C54   1993
843'.3—dc20   936761
                                                                       CIP

The paper used in this publication meets the minimum requirements
of American National Standard for Information Sciences—Permanence
of Paper for Printed Library Materials. ANSI Z3948-1984. ∞™

10 9 8 7 6 5 4 3 2 1

Printed in the United States of America

From E.C.Z.
to
K.E. and S.L.Z.

From M.T.
to
F.M. and J.G.

Preface

To revisit Rabelais is to see him differently, in part because the possibility of other readings is inscribed within his polyvalent text, and in part because our own critical perspectives are constantly changing. The past 30 or 40 years have witnessed multiple innovations in the field of literary criticism, as structuralism and aesthetic formalism, deconstructionism and semiotics, psychoanalysis and gender studies have enriched traditional Rabelais scholarship with alternative ways of reading the text. These new methodologies have by no means solved the Rabelaisian puzzle, but they have made us increasingly aware of the multiple ways in which words, literary forms, and linguistic tokens can signify, thereby enhancing both our enjoyment of the text and our recognition of its tensions and countercurrents.

That these tensions and countercurrents are a function of exchange, and that exchange is important in Rabelais, has been suggested by numerous critics during the period in question. We owe some of the earliest and most influential analyses of dualities in the Pantagrueline Tales to the Russian formalist Mikhail Bakhtin, whose controversial view of a dialogic or polyphonic Rabelais, steeped in market elements, gained favor at a moment when formal studies of the Pantagrueline Tales were already beginning to grapple with textual ambiguities and tensions. Grounded in an understanding of the Renaissance, which was teeming with dialectical forms and contradictory social and philosophical manifestations, these studies recognizing stylistic and thematic polyvalence in Rabelais have been cross-fertilized in recent years by theories of communication, representation, and symbolic exchange that emphasize the same tension between origins and originality, reference and referent, words and things, that we see in the Pantagrueline Tales. This interest in linguistic exchange has been paralleled in recent years, primarily in historically based criticism, by a growing recognition of the importance of monetary elements and economic language in Rabelais, whose writings are coeval with sweeping changes in the European economy at what was arguably the dawn of a new economic order.

Taken in isolation, each of these specialized approaches to exchange in Rabelais offers invaluable insights into important facets of the Pantagrueline Tales. Yet what becomes clear as we attempt to delimit the elements of exchange in Rabelais is the manner in which they all converge, in part because both money and words are symbolic tokens prone to two-sidedness, inflation, and devaluation, and in part because commerce with alterity or otherness necessarily structures the epic and humanistic voyage. Taken in its broadest sense, exchange permeates virtually every major episode and component of the Pantagrueline Tales, providing an excellent springboard for a broad-based overview of the text encompassing style and structure, themes and characterization, aesthetics and epistemology. To trace the development of exchange in Rabelais is to see episodes as diverse as Gargantua's letter to Pantagruel, Epistemon's hell, the Picrocholine War, and the marriage question in a new and unifying light. By virtue of its dialogic nature, moreover, exchange also provides a point of access to the text's puzzling dualities, which have dominated Rabelais studies in recent decades. Given the fascination with exchange during Rabelais's era as well as today, finally, this composite approach allows us to elucidate the text with both historical insights and modern critical theory. Ideally this pluralistic reading will offer something new to specialists and nonspecialists alike, who will find in Rabelais not just an artist long dead but a kindred spirit grappling with problems that still beset us, including economic instability, epistemological uncertainty, linguistic inadequacy, and religious ferment.

Because of the diverse readership for which this volume is intended, and because recent American translations were unavailable at the time this study was begun, we have quoted from the Jacques LeClercq translation of Rabelais, first published in 1936 in a Modern Library edition that combines clear language with general stylistic fidelity to the original text. Unlike most alternative versions in English, the LeClercq translation frequently incorporates into the text explanations of terms unfamiliar to modern readers, a practice that has obvious advantages and disadvantages. On the one hand, it makes what is undeniably a difficult text more accessible to nonspecialists; but on the other hand, this "overtranslation" tends both to perplex literary purists and to reduce the play of dualities and ambiguities upon which so much modern criticism hinges. In an effort to address this problem, we have provided our own literal translation in cases where LeClercq is unclear, imprecise, or misleading. The reader may also wish to consult the more recent translations by Burton Raffel and Donald Frame (see the Selected Bibliography). Scholars requiring even more precision, or desirous of capturing the full flavor of Rabelais, are encouraged to sudy the original French text: for ultimately the Pantagrueline Tales are as "peerless" and "incomparable" as their long-ago hawker first boasted.

To simplify references and facilitate the reader's access to them, the following abbreviations are used after quotations: *P* (*Pantagruel*), *G* (*Gargantua*), *TB* (*Third Book*), and *FB* (*Fourth Book*). The roman numerals after these abbreviations refer to the chapter number, and the arabic numerals designate the page number. Because of doubts regarding its authenticity, the *Fifth Book* is not included in our discussion.

Chronology

1494   The probable date of François Rabelais's birth, although some literary historians have pushed it back as far as 1483. Born at La Devinière, a family property near Chinon, where his father, Antoine Rabelais, was a lawyer.

1511   Possible date for his entry into a monastery of the Franciscan order at Fontenay-le-Comte.

1525   Passes to the Benedictine Order with the hope that he can pursue his humanistic studies more freely.

1527–1530   Peroid during which his natural children Junie and François are probably born, the fruit of Rabelais's liaison with a Parisian widow.

1530   Registers on 17 September at the school of medicine of the University of Montpellier. Receives his bachelor's degree in medicine on 1 November.

1531   Gives lectures from 17 April to 24 June on Hippocrates and Galen. Toward the end of the year goes to Lyon.

1532   Nominated doctor at the hospital of Hôtel-Dieu in Lyon on 1 November. *Pantagruel* first appears in print, possibly at the Lyon fair in November. In late 1532, or early the next year, the *Pantagrueline Prognostication* and the *Almanac for the Year 1533*, are published.

1533   *Pantagruel* is censured by the Sorbonne on 23 October. Leaves for Italy on 8 November as personal secretary and doctor to Jean du Bellay, Bishop of Paris.

1534   Remains in Rome during February and March. Returns to Lyon in May. *Gargantua* is probably published sometime around August.

1535   Makes second trip to Rome with Jean du Bellay, who is appointed to the college of cardinals in May.

1536   Returns to Lyon in July and then departs for Paris with Cardinal du Bellay, who is in charge of fortifying the capital against Charles V.

1537   Receives M.D. degree at Montpellier. Dissects the body of
        a hanged man.

1538   Rabelais's third illegitimate child, his son Théodule dies,
        at the age of two.

1540   Goes to Turin with Guillaume du Bellay, Sieur de Langey
        and the cardinal's eldest brother.

1542   Returns to France in December with Langey, who will die
        before reaching his destination.

1543   The Sorbonne again censures *Gargantua* and *Pantagruel*.

1545   Francis I licenses Rabelais to publish another work.

1546   The *Third Book* is published. In spite of the license, a new
        censure forces Rabelais to seek refuge in Metz, where he
        practices medicine.

1547   Returns to Paris, then leaves for Rome in July with Jean
        du Bellay. While passing through Lyon, he gives the first
        11 chapters of his *Fourth Book* to the publisher.

1549   In September sends back to the French court his *Scio-
        machie*, a description of the festivities in Rome celebrating
        the birth of Louis, the second son of Henry II.

1550   Receives an official license for the *Fourth Book*.

1551   Through the auspices of Cardinal du Bellay, obtains the
        vicarship of two parishes and financial security.

1552   The *Fourth Book* is published. The Sorbonne renews its
        harassment in March.

1553   Resigns from his two vicarships. Dies sometimes around
        April.

1562   *L'Isle Sonante* (*Ringing Island*), usually attributed to Rabe-
        lais, is published.

1564   Supposedly written by Rabelais, a *Fifth Book*, whose first
        16 chapters compose the episode of Ringing Island, is
        published.

Chapter One
Change and Exchange

François Rabelais hawked his *Third Book* (1546) by claiming the text would never run dry. "Our barrel will prove inexhaustible," he tells us, comparing his book to a bottomless cask of wine that is "lively at the source and of perpetual flow . . . a veritable cornucopia of merriment and mockery" (*TB*, Prol., 298–99).[1] That the prognostication holds true today, not just for the *Third Book* but for the entire Rabelaisian text, is a tribute to the good doctor's special brand of alchemy, which within the crucible of the fiction combines ingredients so diverse that they never stop interacting. To catalog this hodgepodge of ingredients, which we often label macaronic, would be to catalog the Renaissance itself, a syncretic period of socioeconomic and intellectual ferment that was afloat with heterogeneous philosophies and cultural manifestations. In both the text and the world it represents, humanism is coeval with Scholasticism, a regressive fascination with origins is counterbalanced by progressive attempts at originality, Platonism and Aristotelianism coexist with witchcraft and necromancy, and utopian treatises advocating shared values and property are inscribed against a backdrop of petty tyranny, theft, and vandalism.

The result is a rich but volatile admixture of contraries that yields new complexities with each successive taste, as signifiers recombine like atomic particles in new molecular configurations. No reading is ever quite identical to its predecessor, for instead of ironing out semantic wrinkles and reducing the play of signifiers, each taste and each aftertaste from the "cornucopian text" at once challenges our old interpretive paradigms and restructures our image of the author.[2]

The Textual Enigma

Five centuries after his birth, the "real" Rabelais still eludes us. Instead he remains what he has always been: a tantalizing enigma, a puzzle whose pieces do not quite fit. Moreover, among the readings that have been proposed through the years, some provisionally and others positivistically and reductively, there is little consensus. Indeed, our interpretations taken collectively are as contradictory and often as puzzling as the Pantagrueline Tales themselves. Gilbert Ducher, known as Vulton (1538), hailed his fellow humanist as the "supreme master" of Renaissance letters; Pierre Boulanger (1587) marveled at his "refined genius"; and Anatole France (1889) called him "the miracle of the sixteenth century." In his *Théotimus* (1549), however, Gabriel du Puy Herbault labeled Rabelais "an impure and corrupt man" possessing the gift of gab but very little common sense, and John Calvin (1555) placed Maître François among the lowly ranks of "mad dogs" whose literary output is garbage.[3]

Clearly the slurs upon Rabelais by Calvin and du Puy Herbault must be taken with a grain of salt: functioning first and foremost as religious polemic, they constitute return volleys in a rhetorical battle between Rabelais, the Calvinists, and the Sorbonne during an era of profound upheaval in the Church. As any teacher of Rabelais knows, however, the basic negativism of both Calvin and du Puy Herbault finds adherents even today. Counterbalancing the aficionados who find Rabelais sublime, a Gargantuan artist rivaling Shakespeare in his use of language and the breadth of his inspiration, are detractors so antagonized by his ebullient scatology that they consider him a second-rate pornographic writer. For all those who see in him the embodiment of Renaissance reason, which exuberantly challenged the medieval *episteme* with its normative values and closed corpus of knowledge, there are detractors who deplore his exploration of madness and his nonsensical breaches of logic. Depending upon the metatext one reads, Rabelais may be labeled feminist or antifeminist, atheistic or evangelistic, profoundly original or a plagiarist of the worst sort.

What emerges from this fractured spectrum of readings is a profoundly dichotomous Rabelais, whose emblem might well be the two-colored man of the *Third Book* prologue (*TB*, Prol., 297), or Gargantua's two-headed androgyne (*G*, VIII, 28), or even the reversible Silenus box (*G*, Prol., 3–4), which turns into its opposite when examined closely. Even for his contemporaries, the object of this controversy was not so much Rabelais the man, an eminent physician and classicist, as the corpus of his fictional writing: *Pantagruel* (1532), *Gargantua* (1534), the *Third Book* (1546), the *Fourth Book* (1552), and a partially finished *Fifth Book*, the disputed origins of which have fueled the controversy surrounding Rabelais.[4] As for the four authenticated books, which revolve around the adventures of Gallic giants who double as Renaissance men, they are a brilliant but disjointed combination of lists, enigmas, epic feats, burlesque comedy, topical satire, fantasy, folklore, philosophy, pedagogy, theology, and scatology, all grafted onto the Gargantua legend. Almost impossible to classify generically, this magnum opus yields glimpses of a Rabelais who is by turns pious and irreverent, earthy and refined, regressively misogynist and progressively androgynous.

All literature is ultimately ambiguous, to be sure, owing to the inherently double or plural nature of figurative language and discourse. We as readers further fragment textuality with the biases, sensitivities, and expectations we bring to the reading experience. Even given these caveats, however, antinomies and unresolved enigmas are so prevalent in Rabelais that they arguably constitute the *substantificque mouelle* or "marrow" of his fiction. Admittedly a good number of the loose ends that puzzle readers today are learned puns and inside jokes to be deciphered by Rabelais's fellow humanists, enamored of Platonic duality and allegory, who delighted in intellectual games.[5] Similarly, Rabelais's penchant for contradiction can be partially explained as a function of the pro and contra logic of Scholastic reasoning, which still prevailed at the Sorbonne during Rabelais's lifetime, and his abrupt shifts from high to low style have been convincingly linked to the upside-down worlds of carnival and the feast of fools, where aristocrats were mocked and idiots venerated.[6] While each of these historical insights adds immeasurably to our appreciation of particular facets of Rabelais's writing, none comes close to accounting for the massive depth and breadth of polyvalence in the Pantagrueline Tales. Given the conjunction between these textual bipolarities and those in the culture at large, it seems likely that the systemic all-prevasiveness of Rabelais's ambiguity reflects the divided consciousness of an era in transition.

If it is difficult to pin Rabelais down, it is because he is never stationary. His world, both fictional and historical, is dominated by the forces of change. Aside from the minimal amount of sleep they require, the giants populating Rabelais's fiction, who owe their stature to an inherited mutation, are constantly on the move: eating, growing, studying, reproducing, inventing, playing, traveling, defecating, asking questions, working, and warring. In typical Renaissance fashion, even the education of the heroes is predominantly peripatetic, taking them outside the classroom to fields and meadows in the *Gargantua*, to neighboring university towns in the *Pantagruel*, to experts from multiple disciplines in the *Third Book*, and to a series of foreign countries in the *Fourth Book*.

At the beginning of *Pantagruel*, this movement seems overwhelmingly progressive: in his celebrated letter (*P*, VIII), Gargantua places his son's education and growth under the hubristic emblem of humanistic advances, the much-heralded transition from darkness to light that is a commonplace of Renaissance writing. Further reading, however, reveals that Rabelais's world is not only expanding diachronically; on a synchronic level, it also gyrates wildly on its axis, rather like the cyclical wheel of fortune and reversible world upside down that inform so much of the Rabelaisian text. This is because change permeates not just the themes and action but also the discourse itself of Rabelais's novel. The narrator is shifty, the logic dialectical, the discursive mode dialogic, and the language ambiguous, filled with plays upon words and multiple entendres that leave the reader vacillating between two or more interpretations.[7]

Far from gratuitous, the protean instability of Rabelais's narrative is in large measure a function of exchange, which denotes the substitution or trade of one thing for another within contexts as diverse as linguistics and finance. While Rabelais uses the word "exchange" or "eschange" only twice, as a reference to the transition from life to death (*OC, TB*, Prol., 326; *FB*, Prol., 524), the structure itself permeates the entire Rabelaisian text.[8] The prologue of the *Pantagruel* catapults us into a wheeling-and-dealing marketplace where values fluctuate and goods change hands constantly, and while the peddler's caravan remains curtained thereafter, the first book's commercial framework provides a unifying backdrop to the Pantagrueline Tales. Coins and currency such as *ecuz* and *caroluz* flow almost as freely as linguistic tokens on the pages of Rabelais's text, which is liberally punctuated with references to money, profit, buying, selling, and financial transactions in general.[9] Inherently dialectic by virtue of their commerce with otherness, these monetary transactions are often the locus of paradox and ambiguity, which act to further destabilize the Renaissance epic's inherently shaky value system. Panurge's charitable contributions in chapter 17 of *Pantagruel* prove to be a screen for theft, and the same character's "Praise of Debt," which he justifies as a form of *caritas* and cooperation, is one of the most famous paradoxes of all literature. In a slightly different vein, Panurge's confusion of the golden bough, a spiritual token used by Aeneas to gain entrance to the underworld, and *caroluz* or "golden coins" (*TB*, XVII, 354), adds to the deterioration of an already eroded value system by suggesting that rewards in the new world of the Renaissance go not to the worthiest knight but rather to the highest bidder and craftiest bargainer.

Here and in the Frozen Words episode (*FB*, LVI, 650), where Panurge talks of "selling" language, it becomes clear that financial references are both a theme in their own right, reflective of the inflationary times, and a metonym of exchange in general, which in Rabelais comprises borrowing from the ancients, attempts at commerce with the supernatural, linguistic exchange, the economy of salvation, symbolic substitutions, and trade with other cultures. These processes are so prevalent in the Pantagrueline Tales that one may view the entire saga as an anatomy of exchange, an inquest into its laws and its limitations. In the *Gargantua*, the head-on encounter of two radically different systems of agricultural exchange precipitates the entire Picrocholine War, which itself finds resolution in the utopian Abbey of Thélème, a model of perfect reciprocity. The *Third Book*, which chronicles Panurge's quandary over whether or not to marry, combines a debate on the merits of commerce with alterity with an inquest on the limits of intellectual commerce, and the *Fourth Book*, which advances by means of a sea voyage, extends the first prologue theme of marketing to the level of intercultural commerce.

Not just the plot but microunits of the text as well form variations on the theme of exchange. Such episodes as Badebec's death, Gargantua's letter on learning, the court case of Kissarse and Bumfondle, Epistemon's hell, Gargantua's color symbolism, and "The Praise of the Pantagruelion" feed into the epic's vast network of exchange. Though many of these episodes contain no mention of money, they are articulated in terms and patterns consistent with the original financial metonym. Within the Pantagrueline Tales, both linguistic and financial exchange are marred by inflation, devaluation, two-sided tokens, middlemen, and the specter of profit.

The felicitous conjunction of economic theory and linguistic terminology, which refers to words as tokens, helps us appreciate the relationship between Rabelais's original financial metonym and other exchange networks within the saga. The analogy between words and money is far from anachronistic, for economics and monetary theory appear as subsets of semiotics and linguistic theory throughout the Middle Ages, and attempts to enrich the French language and literary style in the sixteenth century are often couched in monetary terms. In his *Deffence et illustration de la langue françoyse (1549)*, for example, Joachim du Bellay urges the French to pillage "without conscience" the wealth of ancient languages, and the correspondence between the two humanistic giants Guillaume Budé and Erasmus is dense with economic signifiers used as financial, stylistic, and epistemological referents.[10] To read and write, for the dean of French humanists and his illustrious Flemish counterpart, is both to "pillage libraries" (98) and to "spend" (56) one's intellect upon literary "treasures" (64, 67) that are "profitable" (74). Taken together, these and similar examples suggest that Rabelais fully intends his financial references, and even the market backdrop of his first prologue, to reflect on and function as signifiers within his epistemological and linguistic quest.

Because of its traditional prominence in the debate between nominalists and realists, and because of the gap between its absolute and relative value in the Renaissance, money is particularly well adapted to help figure the crisis of signification outlined in Rabelais. Coins themselves were viewed by economic realists in the early feudal era as verbal symbols whose face value corresponded perfectly to the quantity and quality of substance contained within them.[11] With the advent of economic nominalism in the later Middle Ages, however, "money came to constitute a mobile measure," and there occurred a "gradual loosening of the relation between the face value and the metallic value of coins."[12] As coins and paper notes proliferated in the sixteenth century, their value decreased, prompting Jean Bodin to speculate in 1568 that fluctuations in monetary value were a function of abundance versus rarity, and that the depreciation of French currency could be directly linked to its profusion.

Because of the similarity between the floating of monetary values and Rabelais's own floating of linguistic signifiers, both articulated in opposition to an immovable ideal, it seems likely that the author is consciously inscribing his financial subtext within a broader meditation on the problematics of signification in the absence of symbolic transparency. Structurally, moreover, the two-sided physical configuration of the verbal and monetary tokens in which the narrator-barker-alchemist traffics effectively emblematizes the binary configuration of the Rabelaisian text. And at the same time, on a thematic level, money's pejorative connotations as a fallen symbol and as an object of postlapsarian *cupiditas* provide a vehicle for the author's critique of greed, which he both contrasts with the unselfish prelapsarian ideal of caritas and links subversively with the economics of excess or hubris underlying the Renaissance voyages of discovery.

Changing Times and Patterns of Exchange

In addition to being consistent with preexisting literary and philosophical models and imbued with internal logic, the exchange-oriented cast of Rabelais's fiction has roots in his life and times. Like the

Pantagrueline Tales, Rabelais's biography is a string of enigmas, inconsistencies, migrations, and transmutations played out against a background of intellectual, social, and financial ferment, which was characteristic of the sixteenth century. While our knowledge of Rabelais's early years is sketchy, we do know that he was one of three surviving children born to the lawyer Antoine Rabelais toward the end of the fifteenth century in the region of Chinon in west central France.

His precise date of birth is uncertain, but two provisional time frames are in circulation. A manuscript of epitaphs, found in Saint Paul's Church in Paris and probably dating from the eighteenth century, indicates that Rabelais was 70 at the time of his death in 1553, which would place his date of birth in 1483. Yet in a letter dated 1521 to Guillaume Budé, Rabelais's own claim to be an *adulescens*, a Latin term designating the period between 14 and 28 years, has resulted in the wide acceptance of 1494 as an alternative birthdate. The major flaw in this appealing hypothesis, which would make Rabelais 38 instead of 49 when he penned his first novel, is the fact that *adulescens* is occasionally used figuratively by humanists, denoting a period of literary apprenticeship unrelated to biological age. Given Budé's fame as an intellectual in 1521, it is entirely plausible that an obscure Franciscan monk, newly enamored of classicizing studies, would consider himself an "adolescent" in comparison with the father of French humanism. Like the elusive "meaning" of his epic, then, Rabelais's birthdate has become a puzzle of textuality, contingent upon the accuracy of an unknown scribe and the value of a two-sided linguistic token.

While knowing the exact date of Rabelais's birth is appealing, it is less crucial to our understanding of his text than is our grasp of the century between 1453 and 1553, the year of Rabelais's death. Like our own era, the late fifteenth and early sixteenth centuries were a time of radical and widespread changes in such varied areas as art, politics, religion, geography, astronomy, jurisprudence, technology, and economics. On an international level, 1453 marks the fall of Constantinople to the Turks, effectively ending medieval Christendom's efforts to occupy the Holy Land. Not only the outcome but the nature of the conflict proved decisive, for the Turks' use of artillery and massive cannonballs broke radically with the one-on-one combat of chivalry and its emphasis upon personal honor.

On the domestic front, 1453 also marks the end of the Hundred Years War, which together with the plague and recurring famines decimated France's population and paralyzed its economy during the late Middle

Ages. The decades immediately following the decisive battle of Castillon were characterized by an intense rebuilding effort, which may well have inspired Rabelais's preoccupation with growth, procreation, productivity, and trade. Demographic data for the period are limited, but growth curves in a number of towns suggest that the population of France increased by at least half during the century following the war with England.[13] Forests that had grown up untended during the war, such as that in the sixteenth chapter of *Gargantua*, were razed to make way for new farmland, and agricultural productivity leapt forward to keep pace with the population explosion. This increased demand for produce also contributed to a general rise in agricultural prices and profits, allowing newly affluent landowners to purchase luxury items that in turn boosted trade and urban production. Though this upward economic spiral was to become inflationary as early as the 1530s, a phenomenon due in part to the excess bullion imported from central Europe and the Americas, it is fair to say that the initial economic surge brought a visible degree of prosperity to late fifteenth- and early sixteenth-century France.

By using this newfound wealth to promote scholarship, renovate castles, upgrade the arts, and amass books, King Francis I (1515–47) generally succeeded in wresting France out of the Middle Ages and into the Renaissance, but the route toward modernization and enlightenment was not without its underside. France ultimately failed in its military effort to annex Milan and Naples, and the decades of war, primarily against Emperor Charles V, badly depleted the French treasury, which was simultaneously being drained by the court's newly acquired taste for luxury. Despite the country's increased productivity, moreover, there is some indication that this surface prosperity was not fully shared by the peasantry, which was observed in 1517 to be "more oppressed than dogs or slaves."[14] For scholars and writers, moreover, the climate of religious tolerance and intellectual openness fostered by Francis I during the first decades of his reign was resisted at every step by the conservative Sorbonne and Parlement, which banned the study of Greek, condemned freethinkers as heretics, and ordered that a number of suspected Reformers be burned at the stake. Following the Affaire des Placards in 1534, a massive demonstration against the papal mass that was more or less contemporaneous with the publication of Rabelais's *Gargantua*, even the liberal Francis joined in the crackdown on dissidents, perhaps sensing that intellectual ferment was fast becoming religious schism. Despite the reinstitution of the inquisitional Chambre Ardente in 1547 by his son and successor Henry II, the tide of change could not be stemmed, and less than a decade after Rabelais's death, the nation was embroiled in a bloody and devastating civil war that in the end, 30 years later, would leave only the ashes of France's burgeoning golden age.

Many of the changes that helped define the Renaissance were fueled in part by exchange with Italy, a country that first captured the imagination of French soldiers during the peninsular campaigns of the late fifteenth and early sixteenth centuries. The gilded ceilings, bright sensual paintings, silken garments, bubbling fountains, and voluptuous sculptures of the Italian courts left an indelible impression upon the Frenchmen who accompanied Charles VIII and his successors in their assault upon Naples and Milan. Accustomed to more spartan fare, the northerners eagerly embraced the land of Petrarch and Botticelli, whose luminous esthetic achievements camouflaged a profound ethical and epistemological crisis.

Beginning in the fourteenth century, perhaps as a result of intellectual ferment at the court of Avignon, Italian artists and philosophers rediscovered pagan antiquity and began to break loose from the restrictive confines of ecclesiastical dogma, which for centuries had dominated medieval art and scholarship.[15] The result was a dynamic era of "rebirth" that informed the thought of Rabelais 150 years later. In the graphic arts, vitality and movement returned to representations of the human body. Freed from their Christian interpretations, classical texts also opened up a rich variety of behavioral and cognitive models that at once enriched and destabilized the decision-making processes and value systems of Renaissance humanists. Whereas the late-medieval Dante could still reconcile divine and terrestrial love in a single figure, the humanist Petrarch vacillated erratically between the two poles, and Boccaccio changed the short exemplum with its clear-cut moral into a complex tapestry of relative values and situational ethics. This legacy of moral and epistemological polyvalence, a problematic byproduct of cultural rebirth, permeates the Rabelaisian text even more radically than it does the texts of Rabelais's Italian ancestors.

In Italy as in France, this profoundly altered outlook on life was not entirely literary in origin. Instead, it was fueled by changing patterns of financial as well as intellectual exchange. As fiefs disintegrated, the increasing migration of peasants from rural farmlands to dense urban centers, the growth of an ever more powerful middle class, and the evolution from local to national and international markets contributed to the substitution of pragmatic values for medieval and feudal idealism. For scholars, renewed contact with antiquity represented an equally important form of commerce that served to cross-pollinate previously homogeneous values. While this grafting of pagan borrowings onto fundamentally Christian texts is generally labeled "syncretic," a term denoting the absence of discord between pluralistic credos, the polysemous system of borrowing that Rabelais inherited from Italy necessarily contributes to the ambiguity of his text. True, the syncretic potpourri of ideas placed in circulation by Italian and French humanists was in the main neither atheistic nor anti-Christian. Although they strayed from the narrow confines of Catholic dogma, philosophers such as Giovanni Pico della Mirandola and Marsilio Ficino were ultimately seeking to reconcile their own religion and pagan antiquity in a new synthesis. Inevitably, however, the antitheses inherent in this attempted synthesis attracted satirists such as Luigi Pulci, Teofilo Folengo, and Ludovico Ariosto, whose irreverent mock epics poking fun at chivalry elicited charges of impiety that paralleled and foreshadowed the Sorbonne's denunciation of Rabelais. Not coincidentally, all three Italian writers are cited by the Gallic doctor, who openly espouses their parodic legacy in the writing of his own burlesque epic.

Much more subversive to the long-range interests of the Church than these high-spirited spoofs of chivalry was the growing interest in philology, historical exegesis, and the resurrection of dead languages by humanists such as Lorenzo Valla, who in 1457 demonstrated that the "Donation of Constantine," a document supporting the papacy's claim to secular power, was in fact a forgery or linguistic counterfeit. While this discovery did not generate an immediate backlash at the Vatican, which prior to the Counter-Reformation patronized the new learning on an even grander scale than did Francis I, Nicola Beda and the Sorbonne in France were to take a much dimmer view of anything that even smacked of the new learning, going so far as to confiscate Greek books, censor humanist publications, and denounce scholars such as Jacques Lefèvre d'Etaples as heretics. It is against this polarized backdrop that Gargantua urges his son to learn Greek, Hebrew, and Arabic as well as the requisite Latin (P, VIII, 193), and much of Rabelais's own linguistic ambivalence stems from a familiarity with Greek and Hebrew etymologies that he uses to enrich and equivocize the meaning of French words. At the same time, the enhanced sensitivity to linguistic misrepresentation growing out of Vallas's work converges in Rabelais with the old quarrel between nominalists and realists over the existence in nature of universals figuring in discourse.

While it is common to talk of Renaissance France's debt to Italy,

French religious ferment in the sixteenth century was also shaped by events taking place in the North. Martin Luther's theses decrying Church abuses had been posted in 1517, and his ideology quickly spread to France, where religious dissenters were labeled *Lutheristes* by the Sorbonne at least as early as the 1520s. An even more important German contribution to French Renaissance culture was Johannes Gutenberg's invention in the 1440s and early 1450s of printing with movable type, which would become a powerful catalyst in both the Renaissance and the Reform. By the end of the century, presses had been set up all over Europe, including Paris and Lyon, and the writings of both ancient and modern classicists, as well as those of scientists and theologians, became available to would-be scholars as fast as the printers could produce them. Though the sudden deluge of printed material in the Renaissance, available only in rare manuscripts prior to the 1450s, may seem minor in comparison with the twentieth century's computer-aided information explosion, the analogy does give us a clearer perspective on Gargantua's wish for his son to become an "inexhaustible storehouse [*abysme*] of knowledge" (*P*, VIII, 194), a dream fueled in part by the vast quantities of information placed in circulation by the new technology.

The massive breadth of Rabelais's own erudition, evident in his easy references to Lucian, Pliny, Heraclitus, and dozens of other authors, is a clear product of the printing revolution, which allowed scholars to amass, cross-reference, and compare numerous texts from highly divergent sources instead of devoting years to a single rare manuscript.[16] At the same time, though, it is safe to say that the invention contributed to the epistemological crisis of Rabelais and other discerning contemporaries. First of all, the mass-production on paper of words that had been recited face to face in oral literature, and that later were transcribed by a hand-held quill, doubtless aggravates the sense of distance between signified and signifier informing the Rabelaisian text. Not coincidentally, the crisis of representation that accompanies the birth of printing is most evident in the proliferation of printed monetary notes worth far less than the gold standard they symbolize: these paper notes, arguably, are the "monkeymoney" exchanged at Medamothi, made not from precious metal but copied apishly onto leaves made from trees.

Second, the vast quantity of data from heterogeneous sources that was placed in circulation by the printing process tended on the whole to raise more questions than it answered, making scholars like Rabelais acutely aware of contradictions within canonical bodies of knowledge. In the years between 1534 and 1546, Gargantua's optimism about the wealth of learning available to his son had evolved into Panurge's *lacs de perplexité* or "gin of perplexity" (*TB*, XXXVII, 430), a state of total confusion before the mass of information confronting him. Clearly, accelerated change and exchange in the Renaissance had negative as well as positive ramifications.

Not just vehicles of intellectual commerce and catalysts of social change, printed books in the Renaissance were also significant objects of exchange, contributing to the prosperity of cities like Lyon and Paris. As a result, literacy itself became even more of a marketable commodity than it had been previously, a fact reflected by the sizable number of intellectuals who found work, often part-time, in and around the printing industry. Despite his evocation of the oral-aural tradition and the reservations about the longevity of printing he voices in the prologue to *Pantagruel*, Rabelais capitalized as fully as any intellectual of his time on the advantages afforded him by the new medium, churning out almanacs, prognostications, and popular novels in addition to medical and legal translations. True, royalties as we know them did not exist in the sixteenth century, and the margin of profit associated with printing was relatively low, suggesting to some scholars that authors received no financial remuneration. Given the nature and timing of Rabelais's output, however, which regularly appeared during periods of economic hardship for the doctor, it seems reasonable to accept, at least hypothetically, the author's own contention that he is serving Pantagruel *à gaiges* or "for wages" (*OC, P*, Prol., 169).

Not all the publishing ventures of the sixteenth century were as successful as the Pantagrueline Tales, to be sure. One of the industry's signal failures, at least in terms of sales and dissemination, was a small, unprepossessing volume, entitled *De Revolutionibus*, in which Copernicus upended the centuries-old premises of Ptolomeic cosmography. Published in 1543, the treatise further destabilized the cognitive and epistemological underpinnings of Western culture by proposing that the earth, far from being the stable center of the universe, is in fact mobile, revolving around the sun. Though there is no clear reference to *De Revolutionibus* in the Pantagrueline Tales, it is appealing to imagine that Rabelais had read or heard of the Copernican text prior to the composition of his vertiginous *Fourth Book* in the late 1540s. Even if this is not the case, the similarities between Rabelais's mobile world and that of Copernicus represent kindred manifestations of the intellectual ferment sweeping over Europe in the sixteenth century.

While Copernicus was turning the medieval laws of astrophysics upside down, Renaissance navigators were making some revolutionary discoveries of their own. In 1519 Ferdinand Magellan sailed around the world, demonstrating once and for all that the earth was spherical instead of flat, and between them, Christopher Columbus and Amerigo Vespucci discovered a new continent. It is generally agreed that these voyages of discovery, like *De Revolutionibus*, had little immediate impact upon the public consciousness. Nevertheless, Rabelais's clear allusion in his *Fourth Book* to Jacques Cartier's quest for a northwest passage, along with the entire ocean voyage sequence and his familiarity with shipbuilders' jargon, bears witness to a mind profoundly imprinted with the known world's sudden expansion.

Adapation and Variation: The Making of a Renaissance Man

On a biographical level, Rabelais's own turbulent life was a mirror of the changing times in which he lived. Though his first vocation was that of a Franciscan monk, which by its very nature implies stability and even a resistance to change, Rabelais not only switched monasteries and monastic orders over the years, becoming a Benedictine and eventually a secular monk, but also traveled extensively throughout France and Italy and wore a variety of different professional hats: philologist, physician, scholar, editor, novelist, poet, secretary, librarian, botanist, and diplomat. While today we often stigmatize such career fluctuations as "unstable," well-roundedness was a Renaissance ideal, evident not only in the characterization of Panurge as a jack-of-all-trades and in the broad liberal education of the giants, but also in the real-life versatility of men like Leonardo da Vinci, at once poet and painter, inventor and architect. This drive to know and do that we see in the prototypical *uomo universale* or "Renaissance man" reflects the radically expanding horizons of learned culture as a whole during the Renaissance, in fields as diverse as geography, cosmology, theology, and philology.

At the same time, the erratic track of Rabelais's biography cannot be wholly explained as a desire for intellectual fulfillment, for to do so ignores the economic realities that clearly affected some of his career changes. The social mobility that enabled Renaissance men such as Rabelais to break away from their farms, families, and traditional economic base to pursue their own individual talents and interests carried with it newfound monetary pressures that were largely absent within the protective womb of home and cloister. Though Rabelais's family was affluent, his share of their wealth very likely devolved to the Church when he took his vows. In any event, the financial references in Rabelais's fiction and his correspondence allow us to speculate that part of his evolution, including his shift from humanist physician to scatological novelist and his association with a parade of patrons, was financially as well as ideologically motivated.

Compounding the artist's financial worries was political pressure from the Sorbonne, Parlement, the Church, the Franciscans, and the Benedictines. Their repressive policies elicited from Rabelais a circuitous series of adaptive tactics that resemble the parrying and thrusting, dodging and darting of an experienced jouster. By using a pseudonym, veiling his discourse in ambiguity, applying to well-placed patrons, and generally living his life à tâtons (gropingly), he managed to deflect his opposition again and again. As a result, the biographical tracks he has left us mimic the constantly changing course of a navigator, who adjusts his speed and direction repeatedly to compensate for wind shifts, icebergs, and enemy vessels.

Rabelais's life is characterized not only by change but by exchange as well. Our first documented glimpse of him is his letter of 4 March 1521 to Guillaume Budé, the spiritual father of French humanism, in which Rabelais expresses admiration for Budé's scholarship and a desire to follow in his footsteps. We learn from the letter that Rabelais was at the time a Franciscan monk or novice at the monastery of Puy-Saint-Martin in Fontenay-le-Comte, a feudal town known for its flourishing market and for the plethora of lawyers attached to the royal courts based there.[17] Though the abbey would prove overly restrictive in the long term, Rabelais made the acquaintance there of another young humanist, Pierre Amy, and together they exchanged ideas about the new learning and Roman law with lawyers from the town.

One of the more notable advocates privy to these discussions was André Tiraqueau, who in 1513 had published two treatises on marriage portraying woman as an inferior creature subordinate to her husband. It is likely that the seed for Rabelais's Third Book, which revolves around the querelle des femmes or "woman question," was planted during this period, since his name figures in the foreword of a profeminist volume written by Amaury Bouchard and published by Josse Bade in 1522.

Shortly after the Sorbonne's confiscation of his Greek texts in 1523, Rabelais applied for and was granted a papal indult to leave the Franciscan convent at Puy-Saint-Martin and join the Benedictine Abbey of

Maillezais at Saint-Pierre-de-la-Fontaine-le-Comte, then under the bishopric of Geoffroy d'Estissac. Very soon after his arrival, Rabelais entered the bishop's service at the priory of Ligugé as a secretary and perhaps tutor to the bishop's nephew, Louis. Rabelais's duties involved accompanying his patron to supervise construction projects throughout Poitou, a region that crops up repeatedly in the Pantagrueline Tales. Rabelais apparently left Ligugé in or around 1527, the year in which the bishop's nephew was married. From that year until 1530, when Rabelais matriculated as a medical student at the University of Montpellier, we have no documents concerning his activities, but the wealth of information about Paris and France's provincial university towns suggests to some scholars that Rabelais undertook a peripatetic educational tour similar to that of Pantagruel, visiting the universities of Bordeaux, Toulouse, Bourges, Orleans, and Paris during the closing years of the decade. It is likely that Rabelais was engaging in commerce of a different kind on the side. Two of his natural children, Junie and François, were probably born to a Parisian widow during this period, the fruit of a type of liaison formally forbidden but widely practiced among clerics.

On 17 September 1530 Rabelais reappears in the historical record when he registered as a medical student at the University of Montpellier, long recognized throughout Europe for the distinction of its medical faculty. Like most humanists, Rabelais had already acquainted himself with the principal medical texts of antiquity, a fact that helps explain his acquisition of a bachelor's degree 15 days after the beginning of lectures. While Rabelais is famous for having participated in some of the first dissections and autopsies at Montpellier, it would be inaccurate to deduce that his course of studies was primarily clinical. On the contrary, ancient texts were the primary source of medical lore for budding physicians at Montpellier. We know that Rabelais himself obtained his medical credentials by expurgating the *Aphorisms* of Hippocrates and Galen's *Ars parva*, both in the original Greek.

If medicine was a natural extension of Rabelais's humanistic studies, there was one important distinction: the medical degree enabled him to exchange knowledge for money by working as a paid physician. Rabelais's first known appointment as a doctor took place on 1 November 1532 at the Hôtel-Dieu in Lyon, one of the most important financial and trade centers in Europe. Situated on a major waterway and at the intersection of trade routes linking Flanders, Germany, Switzerland, Italy, and Spain, Lyon was a natural hub of international commerce and hosted four major fairs annually, attracting buyers and sellers from all over the continent. One of Lyon's principal industries in 1532 was the printing trade, which inevitably attracted literati eager to discuss and participate in the production of humanistic texts. Because of the presses there, impoverished scholars had the opportunity to supplement their income by working as editors, proofreaders, and translators, an option that probably influenced Rabelais's decision to settle there in 1532. Shortly after his arrival in Lyon, and several months prior to his medical appointment, Rabelais provided an introduction to the medical writings of Jean Manardi, a Ferrarese doctor, which were published by Sebastien Gryphius in 1532 upon Rabelais's recommendation. During the summer of his relocation to Lyon, Rabelais also published with Gryphius the edition of Hippocrates' *Aphorisms* that he had prepared at Montpellier. Within the intellectual marketplace, these two learned editions helped establish Rabelais's reputation as a medical authority and enhanced his opportunities for more lucrative and stimulating employment.

Receiving an appointment at the Hôtel-Dieu, an old and prestigious hospital in Lyon, was a signal honor for Rabelais, who helped lower the mortality rate by 2–3 percent during his tenure there.[18] In exchange for his efforts, he received the rather modest sum of 40 *livres tournois* (pounds) per annum.[19] Given the currency's decreasing buying power during the inflationary 1530s, it seems likely that Rabelais's hospital stipend only partially alleviated the *faulte d'argent* (lack of money) about which he wrote repeatedly during this era. That he turned to fiction at precisely this point, after leaving the financial security of cloistered life and before entering the service of a wealthy patron, suggests that the rhetoric of buying and selling in the prologue of *Pantagruel*, the first book, has biographical as well as metaphorical resonances. Like a fair number of scholars today, Rabelais supplemented his income by writing fiction on the side under a pseudonym, beginning with a scatological mock epic entitled *Pantagruel*, published in the fall of 1532 by Claude Nourry.

The early 1530s were an extraordinarily eventful period in the life of Rabelais. In addition to taking his first medical degree, becoming a practicing physician, and publishing the three texts previously mentioned, Rabelais edited the *Will of Lucius Cupidus*, an apocryphal legal document that scholars in the Renaissance believed to be an ancient Roman codicil. In late 1532 or early 1533, he capitalized on the prevailing vogue for astrological and prophetic literature by publishing at least two parodies of the genre: the *Pantagrueline Prognostication* and the *Almanac for the Year 1533*, of which only brief fragments survive. Presumably the works met with considerable commercial success, for

Rabelais continued to produce almanacs well into the next decade, probably earning a small but significant income from their sale. Resourcefully fanning the flame of success, Rabelais followed his *Pantagruel* with a sequel entitled *Gargantua* in 1534, published before the public's enthusiasm for the first volume had had a chance to wane.

Rabelais first visited Italy earlier that same year when Jean du Bellay, Bishop of Paris, engaged the physician to treat his sciatica during negotiations with the pope regarding Henry VIII's divorce. Because of its rich history and distinguished writers, Rome was considered by Renaissance humanists to be the capital of the world (*OC*, 970), and well before arriving Rabelais had mapped out an itinerary for his pilgrimage, which he shared with Jean du Bellay in a letter dated 31 August 1534. First, he planned to engage in intellectual commerce, conferring with Italian humanists and studying the indigenous flora and fauna of the region. The dialogues that Rabelais opened with fellow scholars in Italy were apparently a source of satisfaction to him, but his botanical studies were considerably less successful, primarily because the "sameness" of Rome's flora and fauna rendered the acquisition of this knowledge unproductive. "Italy," Rabelais tells us in the letter, "has no plant, no animal, that I had not seen previously."[20] In the same letter, the doctor indicates that he had also intended to prepare a topography of Rome, but the Italian scholar Bartolomeo Marliani stole a march upon him, producing a map so ingenious that Rabelais abandoned his own project and arranged for Marliani's topography to be printed in France. Interestingly enough, Rabelais phrases the entire episode in economic terms. The topography was to have been the "fruit" (*OC*, 972) or profit reaped from time invested exploring the streets of Rome, yet far from being resentful at Marliani, Rabelais proclaims himself to be indebted (*je lui dois* [*OC*, 972]) to his colleague for bringing the dream to fruition. That Rabelais considered himself "indebted" further suggests that he ultimately viewed wealth as intellectual rather than financial, at least at this point in his career.

Rabelais's second visit to Rome coincided with the lavishly staged arrival of Charles V, who, having just defeated the pirate Barbarossa in Tunisia, was marching northward from Sicily in an effort to strengthen his power base in Italy and obtain funding from Italian princes, including the pope. The imperial visit set off a flurry of politicking and posturing that is chronicled by Rabelais in his correspondence with Geoffroy d'Estissac. Though these epistles are again laced with economic terminology, they differ radically in tone and subject matter from the

high-minded letters to Jean du Bellay following Rabelais's first visit to
Rome. Whereas the earlier letter focuses upon intellectual profit and
moral debts, Rabelais in his second series of Roman letters dwells almost
entirely upon the underside of the Eternal City's economy. In a style
curiously devoid of humor, Rabelais deplores the gratuities required in
Rome for simple services like mail delivery, the bribes necessary for
favorable legal and ecclesiastical decisions, the lack of compensation to
owners whose property is annexed by the papacy, and the unjust taxation
of even artisans and laborers to support the Vatican's extravagance.

Permeated with references to money, these epistles reveal the shaky
state of Rabelais's own finances, a problem exacerbated by living in
Rome. To help defray his unexpected expenses and ease the tightening of
his purse strings, Rabelais requested financial assistance from his mentor
over and above the loan he had already received and spent. "I am
constrained to appeal to you again for alms," writes Rabelais, "for the
thirty *ecuz* you graciously had delivered to me here are almost gone, and
I have not spent them on wickedness or food."[21] Not only was the cost of
living high in Rome, he explained, but his finances had been depleted by
efforts to regularize his standing with the Church. As a favor to du
Bellay, the pope eventually granted Rabelais an indult free of charge,
pardoning him for abandoning the cloister, but the costs of preparing the
appeal, obtaining the proper documentation, and expediting the review
process were substantial.

That Rabelais should request such an indult, risking personal bankruptcy in exchange for papal forgiveness, seems at first glance inconsistent with the satire of ecclesiastical favors that permeates the pages of his
fiction. Janotus de Bragamardo, who attempts to ransom the bells of
Notre Dame with the "pardons and indulgences" (*G*, XIX, 56) in which
prelates traditionally traffic, commands only scorn and pity from the
wayward Gargantua, whose decision to return the bells that he stole is a
moral one, undertaken in direct opposition to all the "deals" the Church
has to offer. Unlike the wealthy and self-sufficient Utopian prince,
however, who can thumb his nose at ecclesiastical favor with impunity,
Rabelais the man was subject to the same economic constraints that cause
the Papefigues (Popefiggers) of the *Fourth Book* to pay tribute to the
Church, despite their irreverence toward the papacy. By obtaining
the papal indult, Rabelais improved his shaky financial prospects, putting himself in line for revenues from ecclesiastical benefices for which he
would otherwise have been ineligible. Within the economy of salvation,
moreover, he was hedging his bets a century earlier than Pascal: for if

divine judgment does hinge on pardons and indulgences, a proposition that Rabelais the writer deemed unlikely, the cash he had spent to obtain the indult was clearly a blue-chip investment.

In the fall of 1539, Rabelais's career branched off in yet another direction. France at the time occupied the northern Italian province of Piemonte, which Francis I hoped to use as a stepping-stone to the duchy of Milan, and in 1539 Guillaume du Bellay, Sieur de Langey and brother of the recently elevated cardinal, was appointed governor of the territory. As his physician he chose Rabelais, who during his sojourn in Turin maintained the governor's library and pursued the botanical studies he had begun in Poitou many years earlier. Despite his admiration for Langey and the generally fulfilling nature of his duties, Rabelais's tenure as the governor's secretary and physician was fraught with trials that again tested his resiliency. In 1540 his epistolary candor caused a stir when a letter of his detailing the du Bellay family's tolerant attitude toward Reformers was made public, resulting in embarrassment to both Rabelais and his patron. Not long afterwards, during a brief return home the next year, Rabelais responded to the increasingly restrictive atmosphere in France by toning down the theological satire in revised editions of his first two novels. That the new volumes failed to pass muster with the Sorbonne's censors, despite changes designed specifically to placate the theology faculty, may be partially explained by Etienne Dolet's mischief. That very same year, without Rabelais's permission, he published pirated editions of the original *Gargantua* and *Pantagruel*, effectively nullifying Rabelais's painstaking efforts to maintain a low and politically correct profile. Openly derisive toward Sorbonne theologians, who are scornfully referred to as *sorbonagres* and *sorbonicoles*, these peppery texts from the early 1530s served to keep Rabelais's youthful outspokenness in the public eye during an era of increasing repression.

On a more personal level, the "exchange" from life to death that so fascinates the mature Rabelais, subtending the entire *Fourth Book*, struck close to home during the early 1540s. The loss of his third illegitimate child, a two-year-old son named Théodule, is documented in a Latin poem by Jean Boyssonné, who also poeticized the passing of Langey's wife in 1541, writing an elegy that he transmitted to the governor via Rabelais. Less than two years later, in January of 1543, Langey himself would also die after a long and painful illness, willing Rabelais a yearly income that ironically went to pay the governor's own creditors. Only a few months afterward, Rabelais lost his first and lifelong mentor, Geoffroy d'Estissac.

Between Langey's death in 1543 and the publication of the *Third Book* in 1546, Rabelais appears to have weathered the Sorbonne's disapproval by maintaining the good favor of Francis I. In his *Discours de la Court*, published in 1543, Claude Chappuys lists Rabelais among the Masters of the King's Requests, an honorary title accorded to scholars and poets in the monarch's entourage. Two years later, in 1545, Francis granted "my beloved and faithful François Rabelais" a ten-year privilege for publication of his Pantagrueline Tales. Based on the limited biographical traces to which we have access, however, it appears that the doctor's favored status with the monarchy changed radically in 1546, with publication of the controversial *Third Book*.

That Rabelais willingly jeopardized his standing with the king is unlikely. Given the death of his mentors, his lack of revenue from Langey's estate, and the purely titular nature of his position as Master of Requests, Rabelais was probably strapped for funds when he wrote his third novel, which opens with a three-chapter discourse on debt. Less overtly irreverent than its predecessors, the *Third Book* was nonetheless censored by the Sorbonne, ostensibly for a one-word printing error confusing "soul" (âme) with "ass" (âne). The king's apparent failure to protect his "beloved and faithful" writer this time, as he had on several previous occasions, reflects a growing tendency on the part of Francis I to give Parlement and the Sorbonne a free rein in their crackdown on dissidence. That same year, Etienne Dolet was burned at the stake for questioning the immortality of the soul.

Possibly to avoid a similar fate, Rabelais fled to Metz, a town outside French soil at that time that was known for its tolerance toward Reformers. City records indicate that during his brief stay there Rabelais earned 120 livres annually for unspecified services to the municipality, a modest sum that the doctor attempted to bolster by asking Jean du Bellay for assistance. While the cardinal's response to Rabelais's plea for help is unknown, a year later he summoned his former physician to accompany him to Italy on a mission for the new king, Henry II. On the way south, Rabelais presented to his publisher a partial edition of the *Fourth Book*, the uncharacteristic sloppiness of which suggests two possibilities: either Rabelais was low on cash or he was seeking a quick forum to refute the Sorbonne's charges of heresy.

The move to Rome marked an upturn in Rabelais's vacillating fortunes insofar as it returned him to the epicenter of intellectual ferment in Europe, enhancing his opportunities for philosophical commerce, and provided him access to the cardinal's powerful intimates, who could bend the king's ear in his favor. A particular admirer of Rabelais among this group was Cardinal Odet de Coligny, to whom the doctor dedicated his *Fourth Book*. Embittered by the diatribe of Gabriel du Puy Herbault, which appeared in 1549, Rabelais apparently was on the verge of laying down his pen altogether, threatening to "write no jot more" (*FB*, Dedicatory Epistle to Monseigneur Odet, 491). Fortunately for us, Odet de Coligny persuaded Rabelais to seek special permission to publish from King Henry II, who, like his father, turned out to be a fan of the Pantagrueline Tales.

Never averse to turning a profit, Rabelais did his best to exploit this happy coincidence, churning out a royal panegyric in 1549 that is markedly un-Rabelaisian. His *Sciomachie*, a mundane account of the festivities orchestrated by Cardinal du Bellay to celebrate the birth of Henry's son, represents more than anything else a foray into the economy of favors and influence. By eulogizing du Bellay's devotion to his king, Rabelais invites a reciprocal loyalty on the part of Henry, who had demoted the cardinal earlier that year. At the same time, Rabelais himself undoubtedly hoped to benefit from the *Sciomachie*, using it as a tribute to be traded for patronage and protection.[22]

The strategy almost succeeded: as late as 1551 Rabelais seemed to be secure in the favor of the king and untroubled by his eternal "lack of money." Thanks to his old patron, Jean du Bellay, Rabelais was during that year appointed curé of Saint-Martin-de-Meudon, a benefice that entitled him to at least 300 livres per annum. Concurrently, he was finishing up an expanded edition of his *Fourth Book*, where for the first time he laced his writing with potshots at the papacy, a ploy apparently calculated to garner favor with the French monarchy, which had been at loggerheads with the Vatican since 1547. As it turned out, however, Rabelais had hitched his political destiny to a falling star. The wind of international politics into which he cast his "plume" or feather pen (*OC, FB*, Dedicatory Epistle to Monseigneur Odet, 521) dramatically shifted prior to the *Fourth Book*'s publication early in 1552, as Julius III apologized to Henry II and the wheels of reconciliation were set in motion. Antipapal rhetoric fell out of fashion, and the *Fourth Book* of Rabelais was summarily censured by the Sorbonne and banned by the Parlement.

What happened to Rabelais thereafter, in the wake of his investment in a bandwagon that foundered, remains shrouded in mystery. Two epitaphs published the next year, one in May by Jacques Tahureau and the other in November by Pierre de Ronsard, suggest that Rabelais probably died in early 1553, transacting his ultimate "exchange." Following his death, unauthorized editions of his works continued to flood the market, and in 1562 the *Isle Sonante* (Ringing Island) appeared, the first installment of what now constitutes the *Fifth Book*. Though this posthumous novel continues the navigations of Pantagruel, the ecclesiastical satire is so transparent and the invective so virulent that most scholars dispute its authenticity, leaving us with yet another mystery.

Beginning and ending with a question mark, then, Rabelais's biographical and literary tracks continue to perplex readers even today. Instead of trying to reshape these ill-fitting puzzle parts into a monolithic whole, we propose to seek Rabelais's *sustantificque mouelle* in the ambiguities and bipolarities that he has left us, seeking the explanation for this polyvalence in the twin forces of change and exchange.

Chapter Two
Pantagruel

Like his rapscallion character Panurge, who suffers from chronic "impecunitis" (*faulte d'argent*) (P, XVI, 224), the physician Rabelais was probably short of funds in 1532 when he sat down to write his first novel. This hypothesis, along with Lyon's importance as a trade center, would help explain why so much of his *Pantagruel* is dominated by the rhetoric and processes of exchange.

An Economic Overview

The narrator who introduces and concludes the fiction doubles as a peddler who is selling his wares at the market. Like a basketful of produce, his "cornucopian text" is unveiled against the backdrop of an agrarian economy, which alternates between cycles of feast and famine. This rhythmic interplay of production and consumption results eventually in the birth of a hero named Pantagruel, whose own growth is described in economic terms such as acquisition and profit.

What complicates the expanding economy of the fiction, which in turn represents intellectual and economic growth in the Renaissance, is its clearly inflationary nature: the masses of things accumulated in the *Pantagruel* are devalued by their very quantity. A second complication is the narrator's propensity for trafficking in two-sided tokens. The obverse or face value of his discourse at once confirms and inflates the bright new world of Renaissance learning. The reverse is an "abyss" of lack and negativity that subtends the ideological discourse from start to finish, pointing us toward a series of alternative readings that effectively turn the novel upside down.[1]

Partly inspired by Rabelais's own financial struggle and by the inflationary budget of Renaissance France, the economic cast of the *Pantagruel* also has roots in the processes of humanistic scholarship, which set about to "enrich" both the vernacular and French literature with masses of borrowed linguistic and literary tokens. Representing the obverse of this process is the hero Pantagruel, whose father tells him to "model your

Greek style on Plato, your Latin on Cicero" (*P*, VIII, 193). By integrating this "acquired" or "gained" wealth into preexisting coffers and using it with "wisdom" and "conscience" (194), he approaches the model of a philosopher-prince, who devotes all his financial and intellectual resources to the common good. The other side of the coin is the antihero Panurge, whose 63 ways of acquiring money (*P*, XVI) not only refer to Rabelais's own creative financing but also directly parallel the sundry ways in which the rogue acquired his education and linguistic prowess, in which he traffics for personal advancement. Of his money-making techniques, which can also be applied to learning, the "most ordinary and honorable" (*P*, XVI, 224) is theft, a practice that is upgraded to borrowing in the *Third Book* as a concession to the rogue's gentrification. These debts are intellectual as well as monetary and refer in part to Rabelais's own literary practices.

Like Panurge, Rabelais pilfered, looted, and then marketed his booty in an effort to ease his lack of money. Despite his claim that the *Pantagruel* is "peerless" and "incomparable" (*P*, Prol., 162), a brief glance at the text shows that the ingredients he used were plundered from a plethora of intertexts. The *Pantagruel*, probably published in November 1532, owes its existence to the *Grandes et inestimables cronicques du grant et énorme géant Gargantua* (Great and Inestimable Chronicles of the Great and Enormous Giant Gargantua), an anonymous best-seller that, according to the narrator, sold more copies at the Lyon fair than "Bibles for nine years to come" (162). The protagonist of this rough-hewn chronicle, of which there are several versions, is Gargantua, a folkloric giant whom Rabelais appropriates to father his own Pantagruel. The young giant's name, which Rabelais defines as *tout altéré* or "all-athirst" (*P*, II, 172), is itself borrowed from a small demon in fifteenth-century mysteries who threw salt into the mouths of drunkards, causing them to imbibe again. Along with the name, Rabelais appropriates the demon's characterization as a thirst producer, but Pantagruel's borrowed thirst and giganticism have been recast as humanistic metaphors, accruing usurious new meanings that enhance their old values. Not only large in stature, Rabelais's Pantagruel has an even greater mental capacity, and his unending thirst symbolizes the appetite for knowledge that characterizes Renaissance man. Associated with both the oral and gastric cavities, this appetite will prove to be a paradoxical figure connoting vertiginous emptiness as well as intellectual plenitude.

Also borrowed is the nominal setting of the *Pantagruel*, a fantastic and idealized country named Utopia, which Rabelais has filched from the

Englishman Thomas More and changed from a democracy into an enlightened principality. Notwithstanding the material wealth and dense population of the country, where the "city is so overcrowded that a man has barely room to turn around in the streets" (*P*, XXXI, 280) and where the inhabitants "have always multiplied like rabbits" (*TB*, I, 300), Utopia itself is another example of a paradoxical abyss whose literal meaning is "nowhere." Appropriately enough, Pantagruel spends most of his time elsewhere, leaving Utopia in chapter 5, during his youth, and returning only in chapter 24, when he comes home to defend his country from the invading Dipsodians. In transit, he passes through Meden, Uti, and Udem (*P*, XXIV, 252), whose Greek names all mean "nothing."

Underneath his digressions, Rabelais also adheres loosely to the tripartite progression structuring many tales of chivalry, which detail the birth, education, and prowesses of their hero. All three sections unfold under the emblem of exchange, but it is in the third section that Rabelais effects the most subversive changes in his model by thrusting a rootless upstart on center stage who is the reversed image of Pantagruel. Panurge, whose name denotes his willingness to "do anything," is a cross between the uomo universale and a trickster in the tradition of Germany's Till Eulenspiegel. The void of his genealogy contrasts pointedly with Pantagruel's fully documented family tree, and his extratextual antecedents are almost as uncertain. Scholars have likened him to Folengo's Cingar, the comic companion in *Baldus* (1517–52); to the Greek Sophists, who used brilliant rhetoric to befuddle their adversaries; and to medieval devils, who according to Church tradition sought to divert good Christians from the straight and narrow. [2]

Whatever his antecedents, the rogue's feats depart radically from those of the traditional chivalric hero, who acquires glory and proves his mettle through a combination of arms and honor. By way of contrast, the "heroics" of Panurge bypass arms in favor of rhetoric and sleight of hand: he is conniving, scatological, sadistic, and downright mercenary—a far cry from the knightly models of old. Partly a throwback to the amoral and pragmatic schemers of French popular tradition, Panurge also reflects the new mercantile ethics already flourishing in Italy in which sheer economic survival outweighed traditional moral considerations. By giving this antihero equal time, and by making him the duplicitous other of Pantagruel, Rabelais has fragmented the medieval tale of chivalry to reflect the ethical and epistemological crisis of his own era. Far from being limited to Panurge, this counterdiscourse swells as the novel progresses, arguably becoming the dominant voice in such episodes as

Epistemon's hell and the journey inside Pantagruel's mouth, where the hero's medal or coin is reversed to reveal the underside of the Renaissance.

Structures of Exchange in the Prologue

From the opening pages of his prologue, Rabelais structures his narrative around a series of economic paradigms. Words such as "profit," "buy," "sold," "priceless," and "spent" (P, Prol., 161–63) permeate the discourse, and the hyperbolic style in which the narrator presents his wares smacks strongly of the marketplace. "Find me a book in any language," he challenges boastfully, "that possesses such virtues, properties and prerogatives. Find it, I say, and I will buy you a pint of tripes!" (162). While Rabelais does not refer specifically to the Lyon fair in his prologue, waiting until the book's end to promise a sequel "next spring at the time of the Frankfort Fair" (P, XXXIV, 288), his combination of financial terminology and vending rhetoric effectively establishes the fairground as a locus of literary exchange.

By the same token, the persona of the narrator, at least in parts of the discourse, is that of a carnival barker or patent-medicine peddler, who solicits customers through grossly exaggerated boasts, outrageous promises, dares, insults, and overplayed obsequiousness. Experienced hawker that he is, the narrator-seller caters to our vanity from the outset, drawing us into his net by referring to us hyperbolically as "most illustrious and most valorous champions" (P, Prol., 161). Equally superlative is the book he is marketing, which, in addition to being "nonpareil" and "unique," boasts a plethora of curative powers rivaling those of traditional patent medicines: in an attempt to maximize the appeal of his product, the narrator cagily hints that his potion will bring "manifest relief" to sufferers of depression, toothache, gout, and syphilis. Conversely, those who choose not to "buy" what the narrator is peddling are threatened with "epileptic jitters," "festers," and "erysipelatous fire" (163). Like any good huckster, the narrator also denigrates competing products such as Ariosto's *Orlando Furioso* and the anonymous *Robert the Devil*, which, despite their occult properties and "high timber," are not comparable to the medicine he is peddling (162).[3]

If the peddler's rhetoric seems incongruous in the mouth of the mainstream physician Rabelais, we must remember that he has traded in his respectable public persona for an anagrammatic alter ego named Alcofribas Nasier, who is not above quackery. This pseudonymous narrator's marketplace language serves as an antechamber to the text, which is not only graced by learned references but teems with alternative modes of discourse, including carnival elements, monetary allusions, and multilayered structures of exchange. The narrator's marketplace rhetoric, which mimics that of real-life hawkers, also reminds us that literary exchange, underneath its fine trappings, is fundamentally an economic transaction. The book in the Renaissance had become a commodity that the writer and his printer hoped to sell for profit. At the same time, the financial sales pitch is a metaphor for the rhetoric of persuasion used by all writers to "sell" their message.

The economic paradigm that Alcofribas outlines is a model of reciprocity and fair exchange. The reader's outlay of time, which was an integral part of economic equations in the Renaissance, is matched by that of the writer. The reader will not only buy the book but immerse himself in it indefinitely, setting aside his preexisting responsibilities until the text is permanently imprinted in his memory and in that of his children: "I intend each and every reader," says Alcofribas, "to lay aside his business, to abandon his trade, to relinquish his profession, and to concentrate wholly upon my work" (*P*, Prol., 161). Just as the reader is asked to devote his entire future to *Pantagruel*, the narrator has made a comparable investment in the past, claiming to have been in Pantagruel's hire "from infancy [*dès ce que je fuz hors de page*] until now" (163). If Alcofribas demands a slow and attentive reading from his buyer, it is because the book has been long in the making. This paradigm does not necessarily coincide with extratextual fact, since Rabelais probably wrote the bulk of the *Pantagruel* in 1532, but it does serve to establish an intratextual symmetry between the role of reader and writer in the literary process.

While Alcofribas at no time mentions the financial investment required of his reader, the exchange of money is an implicit component of the market setting he evokes: if the *Gargantuan Chronicles* "sold" (*P*, Prol., 162) well, their new and improved sequel should generate even higher revenues. In response to the reader's implicit outlay of money, Alcofribas counters with guarantees and pledges of his own. First, he will pay a "pint of tripes" (162) if we customers are dissatisfied with his product; second, he vouches for the book's quality, *jusques au feu exclusive* (*OC*, 168) or "in the teeth of hellfire" (162); and third, he wagers "body and soul, belly and bowels" (163) on its veracity. Primarily facetious, these pledges also remind readers that Alcofribas has more at stake than we do. Given the Sorbonne's censorship and the harsh punishments meted out to suspected Protestants, any writer who even touched on sensitive subjects was laying his reputation, his freedom, and his life itself on the line.

The equitability of the economic model outlined by Alcofribas extends to returns as well as investments. The narrator-seller's *gaiges* (*OC*, *P*, Prol. 169) (wages) he receives for serving Pantagruel are matched by the nonfinancial profit (*fruict*) (*OC*, 167) of the reader, which, in addition to improved health and emotional tranquillity, includes the hint of spiritual enlightenment: in addition to its entertainment value, which is detailed in the prologue's first paragraph, the *Pantagruel* is compared to "mystic religious lore" (*P*, Prol., 161) that should be passed down from generation to generation.

Even as he sketches out a model of equitable exchange in which buyer and seller benefit more or less equally, Rabelais plants the seeds of doubt in his discourse with allusions to imperfect exchange, in which a copious investment yields no return. "Others upon this planet . . . ," he admits, "being chronic sufferers from toothache, vainly spent all their worldly fortune upon physicians" (*P*, Prol., 161). This self-referential jab at doctors, a commonplace of Renaissance literature, alternates the true physician's face value as a healer with the reverse of the same coin: a quack who is marketing a counterfeit potion that is the mirror opposite of a bargain. Instead of getting something for nothing, his clients receive nothing in exchange for "all their fortune," a transaction that is colloquially called a "rip-off" in our own culture. On the face of it, this uneven ratio between investment and return, weighted entirely in favor of the seller, is the antithesis of the deal being offered by Alcofribas: like the *Gargantuan Chronicles*, a modest investment whose curative power far outstrips that of higher priced remedies, the *Pantagruel* promises to be a bargain whose true worth exceeds the face value assigned it by literary arbiters. "Is there not greater profit in them than a rabble of critics would have you believe?" demands Alcofribas indignantly. "And what critics! Scabby-faced windbags, who understand these droll anecdotes even less than Raclet, the silver-tongued Professor of Law at Dôle, understands the *Institutes* of Justinian" (161). Implicit here are two additional equations of inequality that shed light on the undervaluation of popular literature. The judgmental "windbags" with their empty rhetoric are, first of all, unequal to the task of judging "droll anecdotes," and their worth as critics is even "less" than that of Raclet, whose face value as a "silver-tongued" expert on the law camouflages his lack of understanding.

These rhetorical equations of disproportion in the prologue are reinforced by a vocabulary of inequality, which reflects the polarized social structure in Renaissance France. Alcofribas follows the "proud and powerful lords" (*P*, Prol., 161) mentioned early in his discourse with systematic references to the poor and disempowered: syphilitics ("those wretched devils plagued by pox"), women ("just as women in travail do"), and finally a slave ("your humble servant") (162). Insofar as it mirrors the various rungs in France's social ladder, listed in descending order, this progression from master to slave appears to confirm rather than contest the status quo. As in the feast of fools, however, where monarchs are deposed in favor of peasants and idiots, the slave Alcofribas ("your humble servant") verbally topples his noble reader, consigning the lord to failure ("they failed to track down the deer"), stripping him of his "prey," leaving him disappointed ("in their disappointment"), subjecting him to insults, and gradually eliminating him from the discourse (161). On an intratextual level, this process of inversion anticipates the full-blown upside-down world of Epistemon's hell (*P*, XXX), where lords are made menial laborers, the impoverished become rich, and syphilitics trade places with the uninfected.

The Opening Chapters: An Ambivalent Tribute to Growth, Profit, and Production

Rabelais's interest in the structures and processes of exchange does not abate but rather expands and flourishes in the body of the text. The opening chapters, which are centered on Pantagruel's birth, focus on natural cycles of production and consumption. Despite periodic downturns, the basic economic curve is positive. Chapter 1 chronicles the year of gross medlars—a bumper crop of extra-large and tasty crabapples that trigger localized swelling in those who taste their juice. Transmitted to subsequent generations, this genetic mutation results not only in potbellies, hunchbacks, and families with large ears and bulbous noses; it also produces a race of giants who "grew in length of body" (*P*, I, 167), culminating in Pantagruel. Already, however, this positive growth pattern is subverted by its fratricidal, lapsarian origins and by the traditionally negative connotations of giants: for the medlars are fertilized by the blood of Abel, and the titans generated by the tainted fruit double as heroes and a fallen race.[4]

Despite this connotative negativity, both the year of gross medlars and the birth of Pantagruel, which occurs in chapter 2, are described in terms of agricultural productivity and plenty. In the first instance, Rabelais tells us that the earth was "fertile in all fruits" and that medlars were "particularly plentiful and large, just three to the bushel" (*P*, I, 165). In the second episode, livestock is so abundant that the gluttonous baby giant "lapped up the milk of forty-six hundred cows" (*P*, IV, 175) at every repast. In cyclical fashion, both these periods of plenty are directly preceded by scourges. Just as the gross medlars are fertilized by death and decay, Pantagruel is born at the end of a drought in which trees stood barren even in summer: "No tree on earth bore leaf or flower. The grass had no verdure; rivers and springs ran dry; the luckless fishes, abandoned by their element, crawled on solid earth, crying and screaming most horribly. Birds fell from the air for want of moisture; wolves, foxes, harts, wild boars, fallow deer, hares, rabbits, weasels, martens, badgers, and other beasts were found dead in the fields, their mouths agape" (*P*, II, 170). In this paradoxically rich account of drought and famine, Rabelais uses the rhetorical process of accumulation, more often associated with growth and plentitude, to describe death and emptiness of an extraordinary magnitude. The vacuity underlying this rhetorical *copia* (plenty) finds expression in repeated references to absence, extending from the initial pair of negations ("no tree . . . no verdure") to the gaping mouths of the moisture-starved animals, which approximate the mathematical symbol zero, a signifier of nothingness.

Lack and plenty are again two sides of the same coin in the description of Pantagruel's birth, during which copious numbers of thirst-related foods and fauna precede the baby out of the womb: included in the caravan are "seventy-eight salt-vendors, each leading a salt-laden mule . . . nine dromedaries, bearing hams and smoked oxtongues; seven camels bearing chitterlings; twenty-five cartloads of leeks, garlic, onions and chives" (*P*, II, 172–73). Understandably, Pantagruel's mother, Badebec, does not survive the experience: for in the midst of the drought she has produced a child "so extraordinarily large and heavy that he could not possibly come to light without suffocating his mother" (170).

Productivity in these chapters is inextricably linked with death and decay, but Rabelais repeatedly emphasizes the regenerative side of this cycle. Given the option of crying "over the death of his wife" or laughing "over the birth of his son" (*P*, III, 173), Gargantua deliberates for all of two minutes before opting for the second alternative: "Must I cry myself blind? . . . My wife is dead; well then, by God—*da jurandi veniam*, excuse my language—my tears will not resurrect her. It is well with her . . . she is in Paradise at least, if no higher . . . God help the survivor, I must think of finding me another wife" (174). The scene's regenerative value is reinforced by the laughter it elicits from the reader, a laughter that stems in part from Gargantua's incongruous use of Scholastic arguments, "frame[d] . . . capitally *in modo et figura*" (173), to help cope with his grief. The giant's application of the syllogisms is so formulaic that upon occasion he neglects to fill in the blanks: "Shall I weep?" he cried. "Ay . . . And why? Because my dear wife is dead! She was the most *this* and *that* who ever lived!" (173).

On one level, what emerges from Gargantua's discourse on Badebec is not a person but a "generic" wife, who can be replaced like the favorite "pump" or "slipper" (*P*, III, 174) to which he compares her; this representation of woman as a commodity or object of exchange will inform the *Third Book* colloquium on marriage. On the other hand, the very ineptness of Gargantua's groping analogies, which function as verbal substitutes for the thing itself, draws attention to the shortcomings of linguistic tokens as substitutes for either objective or subjective reality. On a connotative level, to be sure, the slippers and codpiece to which Gargantua likens Badebec succeed admirably as signifiers of both sexuality and familiarity: both physically and psychologically, the queen is as comfortable as an old shoe that has been well broken in. The connotative value of each signifier is limited, however, and the very plethora of comparisons to which Gargantua resorts suggests that none can fully express either the complexity of the couple's relationship or the magnitude of the royal family's loss.

By articulating Pantagruel's birth as the other side of his mother's death, Rabelais has inscribed the hero's nativity within a cyclical pattern of (re)production and consumption in which the old is exchanged for the new. The generational newness that Pantagruel embodies, along with his later development as a uomo universale, inevitably causes readers to identify the baby giant's birth with the rebirth of learning now known as the Renaissance. By extension, his hyperbolic hunger and thirst, which lead him to chew up the cow he is suckling and swallow a bear "in one fine hot mouthful" (*P*, IV, 176), symbolize the intellectual appetite of humanists like his creator, who resemble "starving wolves" after a period of epistemological drought. Not surprisingly, it is the prospect of food that prompts the infant Pantagruel to break the "great cables" (176) that tie him to his cradle, in a rupture that symbolizes the shift from the Middle Ages to the Renaissance; and while, on the occasion of a state banquet, he fails to break the "great iron chains" that have replaced the smaller cables, the starving baby is so determined to eat with the grownups that he pushes his feet through one end of the cradle and stands upright, carrying the bed on his back to the banquet hall before "smashing it into more than five hundred thousand pieces" (177). In addition to its comic value, and its associations with sleep or stagnation, the cradle represents the inflexible shell ("like a tortoise") of an outgrown ideology that inevitably clings to the fledgling humanist and restricts his growth, even when it is upended ("advancing on end") (177). When he smashes the cradle, Pantagruel not only breaks symbolically with the past, substituting openness for its restrictive closure, but also causes the era's impoverished oneness to fragment into the copious multiplicity of "five hundred thousand pieces."

Given Pantagruel's association with the Renaissance, it is not surprising that his ancestors (*P*, I) were creative as well as procreative. The requisite family tree, which is a takeoff on both Renaissance and biblical genealogies, includes a fair number of inventors in its ranks; but in a typically Rabelaisian inversion, their inventions enhance the modes of consumption rather than production. In chronological order, the innovators include Eryx, who thought up "the game of Tippling" (*P*, I, 167); Gabbara, the originator of "the drinking of toasts"; Morgan, the first to play dice with his spectacles; Gemmagog, the inventor of pointed shoes; Happemouche, who developed the process for smoking oxtongues; and Galehault, who invented flagons (168). Contrasting comically with the hyperbolic stature of their inventors, these curiously trivial inventions at once parody and glorify Renaissance creativity, which inevitably fell short of the superlative models mapped out by philosophers like Pico. Though a far cry from Leonardo's flying machine, the smaller minded inventions of Pantagruel's ancestors accurately reflect the interests of most Renaissance aristocrats, who invested the bulk of their time and energy in food, wine, clothes, and games.

On an intratextual level, and in a more positive way, these inventions foreshadow the creativity of both young Gargantua (*G*, XIII), who perfects the arsewipe, and the mature Pantagruel, who in the *Third Book* finds dozens of uses for a single plant.[5] In chapter 27 of the *Pantagruel*, we learn that even his flatulence is so fertile that it begets "over fifty-three thousand little men" and "as many little stoop-shouldered women" (*P*, XXVII, 261). While the breath of life here is anal rather than oral, the metamorphosis clearly mimics biblical creation, which produced abundant life from a void.

Creativity and adaptability also figure prominently in the paragraphs immediately preceding the genealogy, which focus upon the deformities afflicting men and women who overindulge in the bumper crop of giant medlars. "One and all suffered a most terrible swelling in their bodies," Alcofribas tells us, "though not each in the same place" (*P*, I, 166). A fair number of the mutations, which are exaggerated enough to merit inclusion in a carnival sideshow, affect parts of the body associated with creativity, productivity, and procreation. The swollen ears and noses visited on some scourge victims arguably represent two of the five senses, which were widely associated with artistic productivity in the Renaissance. While Alcofribas does not tell us that hearing and smelling are enhanced in the afflicted, an omission so glaring that we tend to suspect the converse, he does mention that two mutant lines have produced artists: the fabler Aesop, descended from the hunchbacks, and the poet Ovidius Naso or Ovid, whose name suggests kinship with large-nosed medlar eaters.

Predictably, the mutation also affects the male genitalia, although in this instance there appears to be an inverse correlation between quantity and quality: instead of increasing in fertility, as one might expect, "the race is utterly spent and lost" (*P*, I, 166), either because of wasteful "spending" or for purely logistical reasons. Notwithstanding their lack of viability in the long term, those medlar eaters whose "appendage . . . grew amazingly long" succeed admirably at turning their affliction to profit in the short term, using the oversized genitalia as belts. Similarly, the scourge victims who sprout elephant ears learn to use their liability for gain, wrapping the pliant skin around them to form "a doublet, a pair of breeches and a jacket" (167).

Clearly there is a ludic element in this tribute to creativity, which lends itself to multiple readings: at times the narrator appears to mock the very myth of productivity he is promulgating, and at other times his humor merely seems high-spirited, alive with the same sharp wit, ebullience, and creative energy that caused Renaissance culture to thrive. His playfulness parallels his culture's ludic tendencies, which function on the one hand as the retrogressive antithesis of productivity. For example, the French monarchy's investment in lavish pageantry and ceremonial games was one of many factors that brought the treasury close to bankruptcy by midcentury. On the other hand, creative play in children, such as the young Pantagruel, serves as a training ground for future production. In recognition of this fact, and for parodical reasons as well, part of the giant's education is ludic: at the University of Orléans, he learns to play tennis like a champion without ever opening a book (*P*,

V, 180). This emphasis upon play, and the interrelationship between play and productivity, will become more pronounced in the *Gargantua*, where the young prince playfully experiments with more than 50 arse-wipes (*G*, XIII) and engages in at least 218 games (*G*, XXII) to alleviate the boredom of his Scholastic curriculum before systematically combining work and play under his humanistic preceptor (*G*, XXIII).

On a stylistic level, Rabelais's own language reflects the same ludic and creative tendencies we see manifested in his characters. His description of swelling noses itself swells, mutates, and reproduces joyfully, as sounds couple and engender new sounds, each one similar and yet different from the first. The nose "looked like the beak of an alembic," he tells us, "all bediapered and bespangled with pimples, pullulant and bepurpled with nobs, enamelled, buttoned and embroidered with gules and crimson" (*P*, I, 167). While a number of alliterative, assonant, and semantic nuances are necessarily displaced in this excellent translation, it nonetheless approximates the phonetic and semantic fertility of Rabelais's style. Dense with the letters *b*, *p*, *e*, and *u*, the words seem to reproduce on contact, yielding new meanings along with the sounds. Like the cask of the *Third Book* prologue, this passage constitutes a verbal horn of plenty overflowing with fruit for the discerning reader.

Besides being comical, the alembic, in which substances were refined and distilled in the Renaissance, connotes the act of poetic creation itself, a reference that is reinforced by the word "pullulant." Directly preceded by *bubeletes* or "little pustules" (*OC*, *P*, I, 173) in the French edition, the term "pullulant" at first glance appears triggered by purely phonetic exigencies, springing gratuitously from the *u*, *l*, and plosive *b* of the preceding word. In a striking example of onomatopoeia, however, this term that seems to sprout from contiguous phonemes literally denotes "sprouting" or "germination," a semantic content that is reinforced phonetically by the sounds that replicate inside the word itself (*ul-lu-l*), and that in turn reinforces the chapter's overall theme of generation.

Within the same passage, the word "buttoned" proves to be a reversible token that reflects positively and negatively on creativity. When juxtaposed with other dressmaking words such as "embroidered," "bediapered," and "bespangled," the term "buttoned" appears to celebrate the blossoming of fashion and the decorative arts in Renaissance France. In French a *bouton* is also a pimple, however, an alternative meaning that one might ignore were it not for the previous mention of pustules. Both the pimple and the pustule connote swelling that is consistent with the theme of growth and productivity; more like the baroque bubble than the inflated Renaissance cornucopia, however, both blisters are diseased and eventually burst to reveal nothingness and negativity.

From Inflation to Deflation

Following Pantagruel's genealogy and birth, the figure of copia thus far used to connote agricultural and biological growth reappears in an intellectual context. For the most part, the hero's education unfolds in France rather than Utopia, a move intended to expand his cognitive horizons in a manner proportional to his physical growth: having "profited" physically at home, he is sent to study in Poitiers, where he "profited greatly" (*P*, V, 178) before matriculating at La Rochelle, Toulouse, Montpellier, Avignon, Angers, Bourges, and Orléans. This geographical expansion is offset by a simultaneous contraction in the stature of the populace, the epistemological implications of which are exemplified by a young law graduate in Orléans whose "learning would have fit in a nutshell" (*P*, V, 180). By the end of chapter 5, moreover, copious book-learning is for the first time equated with cognitive loss rather than profit, when Pantagruel ceases to study for fear of losing his physical and intellectual sight (*OC*, *P*, V, 190).

Traditionally scholars have distinguished between the empty plenitude of Pantagruel's medieval book-learning, inflated by glosses, and the progressive fullness of the humanistic regimen with its emphasis upon original and "digested" texts, including "Plutarch's *Morals*, Plato's noble *Dialogues*" (*P*, VIII, 193), and the Old and New Testaments in Hebrew and Greek, respectively (193–94). Like its medieval forerunner, the new pedagogy expounded by Gargantua in his famous letter involves massive and time-consuming book-learning. In this much-quoted epistle, which many consider a manifesto of humanistic learning, Gargantua urges his son to become an *abysme de science* or "abyss of knowledge," taking advantage of the humanistic advances that have brought "light and dignity" (192) to learning in his lifetime. The curriculum that Gargantua proposes includes Greek, Latin, Hebrew, Chaldean, and Arabic; geometry, arithmetic, and music, from the liberal arts; civil law; "facts of nature" relating to fish, birds, trees, plants, and metals; medical theory, based on classical texts as well as dissection; and the Bible instead of biblical commentaries. In typical humanistic fashion, Gargantua further instructs his son not to dabble in the "vanity and imposture" (193) of astrology, and he closes the epistle with a sober but formulaic reminder that "science without conscience spells but destruction for the spirit" (194).

Breaking with medieval tradition in its emphasis upon original texts, Gargantua's humanistic curriculum expands into a plethora of areas that Scholastic pedagogy of the Middle Ages failed to address, including the study of Greek, which was expressly forbidden by the Sorbonne. An equally important difference between the two educational systems is methodological. Despite their "priceless" (P, V, 180) contents, the law books at Bourges are "edged with excrement" (180) and impossible for Pantagruel to stomach. By way of contrast, Gargantua tries to make his own curriculum as palatable as possible to his son by first savoring it himself ("I delight in reading" [P, VIII, 193]) and then giving his son "a taste" (193) at an early age. To increase Pantagruel's demand for knowledge, Gargantua further compares it to "heavenly manna," a precious commodity far superior to ordinary food.

This understated rhetoric of persuasion would be labeled a "sales pitch" in our own culture, an analogy reinforced by Gargantua's recurrent economic metaphors. On the one hand, he urges his son to "acquire" knowledge, to "profit" from his education, and to "spend [his] youth making the most of [his] studies" (P, VIII, 193). Through his use of economic terminology, Gargantua implicitly equates knowledge with monetary wealth, with one important distinction: in their official posture at least, the French noblesse d'épée and literary knights errant typically scorned monetary gain, as evidenced by Pantagruel's insistence in the Fourth Book that the crew is traveling "without thought of gain or profit" (FB, XXV, 577). Instead, they are motivated by the same higher minded avidity that informs Gargantua's letter: a desire "to know" and "to understand" (577) that posits knowledge as an alternative and ultimately superior form of wealth.

While the curriculum that Gargantua outlines is exceedingly time-intensive, he emphasizes the short-term nature of the investment. In return for "a few hours a day" during his "youth" (P, VIII, 193), Pantagruel will reap long-term benefits during an adulthood of "action" and "attacks" (194) that will require every ounce of wisdom he can muster. The transaction is by no means one-sided, however, for Pantagruel himself represents an investment for his father, who has "spared nothing" (191) in the upbringing of his child. As the repository of this copious outlay of resources, Pantagruel constitutes a living "treasure" (191) that, if properly managed, will acquérir or "acquire" (OC, P, VIII, 202) for Gargantua a kind of "immortality" (P, VIII, 190). This immor-

tality itself constitutes an exchange of sorts, in which the dying Gargantua will be replaced by his "visible image" (191) who also bears his name.
Twice stamped as an "other" Gargantua, Pantagruel will function as
both a biological and legal token for his father. Despite their identical
face value, however, Gargantua allows for a difference between referent
and representation. For ultimately it is Pantagruel's "soul" (191) or inner
worth that will determine his adequacy as an image of his father, and this
inner worth, unlike the name or face value, is susceptible to devaluation
and appreciation through time. As the guardian of this spiritual patrimony, Pantagruel is exhorted not just to avoid losses but to "go on doing
ever better" and to profit by "constant improvement" (191).

Strangely enough, Rabelais's choice to couch his pedagogical theories
in economic terms helps to generate some critical ambiguities in the
text. While the primary extratextual referent of his exchange metaphors
is humanistic learning, a secondary referent is the "boom" economy of
sixteenth-century France, in which increased spending and a proliferating money supply were accompanied by a progressive devaluation of the
currency and a shrinking treasury. By analogy, the rhetorical processes of
accumulation and hyperbole that Rabelais uses to plot the growth of
humanistic studies at times have an inflationary ring to them. With
more ambition than common sense, Gargantua exhorts his son to learn
languages "perfectly," to commit the entire legal code to memory, and to
study "all" the fauna, "all" the flora, "all" the metals, and "all" the
precious stones of the earth until "nothing" is unknown to him (*P*, VIII,
193). The king culminates his appeal with the curious expression that
scholars have traditionally interpreted positively: "Somme, que je voy un
abysme de science" (*OC*, *P*, VIII, 206) says Gargantua, urging his son to
become an "abyss of knowledge." LeClercq translates the word *abysme*
unequivocally as "storehouse," effectively closing an alternative interpretive route that would subvert Gargantua's panegyric of learning.
When reinstated, the term *abysme* functions as a hinge or two-sided
token, on one face connoting a "well-filled head" and on the other face a
cognitive void. This reversible hinge word allows us to glimpse in the
Renaissance man a shadow of the hollow-headed Songecreux.

At first glance, this two-sided interpretation of the word *abysme*
appears to confirm the controversial thesis, promulgated by a handful of
scholars in recent decades, that Gargantua's entire letter is a parody.[6] By
itself, however, this full-blown parodical reading goes too far in discred-
iting the very real panegyric of humanistic learning that shines through
in Gargantua's measured Ciceronian style. That Rabelais himself shared

this fervor for humane letters is abundantly demonstrated in a letter to André Tiraqueau dating from the same period, where the physician praises the new learning in terms strikingly similar to those of Gargantua. In the letter, dated 3 June 1532, Rabelais contrasts the immense "light" accompanying the restitution of "the best disciplines" with the "shadows" and "fog" of medieval scholarship (OC, 954).[7] The metaphor, which is a commonplace of humanistic writing, reappears in Gargantua's boast that "light" and "dignity" have revitalized learning within the short span of his own lifetime, banishing the "dark" or "shadow[y]" pedagogical practices of his youth (P, VIII, 192). Far from being pure parody, this fervent tribute to humanistic studies functions as the reverse of a two-sided coin: Rabelais's enthusiasm for the new learning leaves its imprint on one face of the "medal" or text, but the underside of the token constitutes a simultaneous interrogation of the very premises of humanistic scholarship.

This dual reading of Gargantua's letter is reinforced by surrounding episodes, where the inflated rhetoric and swollen glosses of medieval Scholasticism are satirized and ultimately deflated. The chapter preceding the giant's epistle contains a copious inventory of the Library of Saint-Victor, a list that Pantagruel peruses during his educational tour of Paris. Included in it are 139 tomes with fancy formulaic titles such as *Bragueta juris* (The Codpiece of the Law) and *La Cornemuse des prelatz* (The Prelates' Bagpipes). Despite the books' plenitude and pretentious titles, it is clear that they are full of hot air, much like the prelates' bagpipes or Songecreux's head. Broadly satirical of both the legal and ecclesiastical professions, whose pompous jargon is soundly debunked, the episode poses some important questions about books and book-learning in general, which can easily be overvalued. One such example in fact opens the chapter. For 214 years, Rabelais tells us, the citizens of Orléans have been trying to lift and transport a large bell intended for the church tower at Saint Aignan. To this end, they have read Vitruvius, Albertus, Euclid, Theon, Archimedes, and Hero of Alexandria, all "to no avail" (P, VII, 184): "Tout n'y servit à rien" (OC, P, VII, 194), says the French version, clearly implying that the plentiful *tout*, meaning "all" or "everything," is worth *rien* (nothing) when misapplied. Taking a much more pragmatic approach, Pantagruel ironically lifts the bell with his little finger.

The Library of Saint-Victor inventory is preceded by an equally trenchant satire of book-learning, which is misapplied and distorted by the Limousin schoolboy, a Parisian student whom Pantagruel encounters during a visit to the capital. Despite the fact that Pantagruel speaks standard French, the Limousin schoolboy persists in using a grossly Latinized jargon, apparently forgetting that the ultimate goal of any currency is not to shine but rather to facilitate exchange. Designed to increase his worth in the eyes of Pantagruel, his inflated rhetoric is devaluated not only by its minimal exchange value but also by the gap between real and face value: the schoolboy is in fact poor and of humble origins. Having ended the charade with a show of force, which elicits a comic stream of Latin from the frightened schoolboy, Pantagruel commends his fellow student for finally using a common linguistic currency: "Now you are speaking naturally" (*P*, VI, 184).

Pantagruel puts his own advice to good use in the episode of Baisecul (Kissarse) and Humevesne (Bumfondle [*P*, X–XIII]), a legal dispute involving such obscure points of law that after 46 weeks even the most illustrious jurists in Europe are incapable of reaching a decision or even comprehending the case. After being engaged as an outside consultant, Pantagruel's first order of business is to burn the piles of circuitous opinions, briefs, transcripts, and affidavits upon which the court was prepared to base its decision, declaring them worthless. Like paper money, the legal documents, or signifiers, function as a substitute for the original dispute, or signified. Somewhere in the process, though, the substitutes or signifiers have become inflated, both in quantity and importance, with the result that they now have little resemblance to the discourse they supposedly represent.

In an act of exegesis that resembles that of humanist philologists, Pantagruel opts to base his decision not on translations or glosses but rather on a reading—or, in this case, a *hearing*—of the original text or discourse. While it initially appears that the dispute hinges on money, the case is complicated by the fact that both men, as Pantagruel puts it, are fools. Likewise, their language—a rambling hodgepodge of misplaced metaphors, half-finished maxims, and non sequiturs—is the language of madness, a strange mirror of legalese. Pantagruel's genius is to respond in kind, using the disputants' own linguistic currency to settle the dispute. Neither we nor the jurists have a clue about what Pantagruel is saying, but by adopting the discourse of madness he has mediated a successful exchange, leaving both Baisecul and Humevesne pleased with the verdict.

The gap between signified and signifier, message and means of conveying it, is perhaps most pronounced in chapter 9, where we and Pantagruel first encounter the giant's future friend Panurge. From the outset there is a discrepancy between the stranger's appearance and his perceived character. Though Panurge looks like a hobo—all skin and bones, his clothes tattered and torn—Pantagruel assures his companions that the transient's form or outward value and his substance or inner worth are not consistent: "Upon my word, he is poor only in fortune; his face bespeaks a rich and noble family" (*P*, IX, 195). Similarly, the form of Panurge's discourse is diametrically at odds with its substance. Going the Limousin schoolboy one better, Panurge speaks to Pantagruel in not one but thirteen foreign languages, flaunting his linguistic prowess as if it were wealth. In contrast to the inflationary plenitude of his linguistic means, however, Panurge's message is one of lack, emptiness, and penury. Despite saying "I am hungry" in thirteen different languages, the exchange is not completed and Panurge is not fed until he offers an acceptable currency: his own native French.

Of all the currencies used in the *Pantagruel*, the most unusual and comic is that of Thaumaste (*P*, XVIII–XX), a famous English cleric whose name evokes both *thau*, the "sign of signs" in the Hebrew alphabet, and *thaumastos*, the Greek word for "magician."[8] Having learned of Pantagruel's intellectual prowesses, Thaumaste hopes to debate him in sign language, a set of signifiers that, according to Renaissance theory, often resembles the signified and hence circumvents the ambiguities and uncertainties of conventional language and graphemes. Feeling tired, uninspired, and skeptical about the entire affair, however, Pantagruel allows the irreverent Panurge to replace him, an event that results not in harmonious debate between like minds but rather in two independent discourses at cross-purposes.

Even though both men use sign language, the tokens offered do not belong to the same semantic currency: Thaumaste's gestures are esoteric, and Panurge's predictably obscene. Oblivious to the fact that he is being swindled, Thaumaste accepts the worthless gestures at face value and moreover thanks Panurge afterward for having opened to him an "abyss of . . . learning" (*P*, XX, 242). The term is apt, for despite Thaumaste's satisfaction with the exchange, it is difficult to shake the suspicion that his inflated rhetoric of silence, copious in its own way, is no less vacuous than the bookish jargon it seeks to bypass and transcend.

The Other Side of the Coin

Sexual and Textual Otherness: The Woman Question.   Though we usually associate the "woman question" with Rabelais's *Third Book*, exchange with women is already flawed in the *Pantagruel*. Panurge is the primary culprit, for he sees females not so much as persons to engage in commerce with as commodities to be used and traded. In chapter 15, as he and Pantagruel discuss the economics of wall building, Panurge observes that the cheapest building block available would be female genitalia.[9] Verbally dismembered and dehumanized, woman is depicted here by Panurge as one product among many, nothing more. Cheaper than rock and more resistant than metal, the "callibristrys," says Panurge, are available in three different sizes, can be stacked symmetrically, and, as an added bonus, have all been blessed by the Church. If they are a bargain, it is in part because they are plentiful, devalued through a process of rhetorical inflation.

In the same chapter, Panurge pursues his mockery of women with an even more scatological fable, in which a lion and a fox attempt to dress an old woman's "wound." On one level, the anecdote echoes the paradigm of reciprocity sketched out in the prologue. Since a human helped the lion when he incurred a similar injury, he feels obligated to return the favor. The exchange is perverted, however, by two complicating factors. First, the analogy the lion has made between his own wound and that of the woman is based upon the erroneous assumption that tokens have the same value in her economy and his, and that her need can be deduced from a knowledge of his. Second, the fact that the woman is rendered speechless when even the animals can talk eliminates the possibility of clearing up the miscommunication with an alternative set of signifiers.

The haughty lady of chapter 21 is not technically mute, but Panurge effectively neutralizes her voice by refusing to honor her linguistic currency at face value. Though she repeatedly says "no" to his advances, Panurge takes her refusal to mean "yes," reassigning new values to her words in the light of his own needs and wants. As a result, he assumes reciprocity where none exists. In return for the holy water he gives her, Panurge goads the young matron into giving him her gold rosary, a "gift" he interprets as a token of affection that he, in his turn, will reciprocate. "Would you like my knife?" (*P*, XXI, 245), he offers, referring both to the blade with which he severed her beads and to his own "virile member."

For the lady, on the other hand, the rosary beads are less a gift than a bribe: in essence, she pays Panurge to go away and leave her alone. When Panurge reneges on his side of the bargain, she responds by asking him to return the payment, thereby nullifying the verbal contract. Here he cannot oblige, for he has long since pawned the beads. Despite all his noble talk of gifts, moreover, it is clear from the conditions he attaches to

them that Panurge's motives are far from charitable; instead, he is
wrapping up a deal. Continuing to operate on the premise that women
are commodities, available to the highest bidder, Panurge makes his
offers with currencies of escalating values: flowery but empty rhetoric;
his own overinflated reputation for virility; precious metals and jewels he
cannot pay for; and beads far more valuable than those given to the lady
by her husband. To hear Panurge talk, the balance of profit is all on her
side. "What I want will cost you nothing [*rien*]" he insists (*P*, XXI, 246),
failing to recognize that *rien* and *bien* have reversed values for him and
her. The wealth (*biens*) that he offers is worth nothing (*rien*) to her, while
conversely the *rien* that he disparages turns out to be the *bien* or treasure
she values most: her honor.[10]

The theme of nothingness recurs during Pantagruel's commerce with
his own haughty lady (*P*, XXIV), a Parisian who sends him a cryptic
epistle lamenting the fact that he has abandoned her. None of this is
apparent at the outset. Not only is the woman absent, but her letter is
itself a blank, and the keepsake that accompanies it is a false diamond
ring with a hole in the center. The ensuing exegesis of nothingness, or
her-story, which is far removed from the copia of his-story, or history,
finally yields a coded message: "Why hast thou forsaken me?" (*P*, XXIV
252), written in Hebrew inside the band. Coupled with the false diamond (*diamant faux*), whose homonym is "Dis, amant faux" (Say, false
lover), the biblical quotation takes on new meaning: "Say, false lover,
why have you abandoned me?" Ironically, the message so elaborately
expurgated out of nothingness is itself a void: not a statement but a
question, not a presence but an absence, not commerce but a continued
lack of mutual understanding.

The above examples of imperfect, inflationary, and devalued exchange
find parallels in the narrator's own commerce with us, the readers. His
rich abyss of erudition, which he enthusiastically shares with us, is
almost as copious as that outlined in Gargantua's letter to his son, and yet
the manner in which he displays that learning is full of reservations,
irony, and doubt about its ultimate worth. Like the celebrated jurists of
the Baisecul-Humevesne episode, Alcofribas is prone to overuse legal
jargon, and he clearly shares the esoteric semiological interests of Thaumaste. Yet unlike these monomaniacal, myopic characters, Alcofribas
invariably bursts his own balloon with scatological interjections and
self-criticism. Similarly, his systematic deflation of the pretentious
books in the Library of Saint-Victor may be read as an interrogation of his
own book, which certainly contains a fair amount of hot air. These

inflated and deflated passages reflect an intuition, on Rabelais's part, that material and literary plenty do not necessarily constitute worth; that language, no matter how erudite or esoteric, does not necessarily reflect the truth; and that learning, no matter how copious, does not necessarily constitute a panacea for all the ills of society.

At the same time, the constant deciphering, dismembering, and misinterpretation that take place in the *Pantagruel* suggest an equal fascination with the way in which we, the readers, will view his work. An experienced reader himself, Rabelais foresees that we will dismember and dehumanize his text, deforming its message to suit our own particular critical prejudices: interpreting "no" as "yes," seeing wounds where they do not exist, violating and plundering the text time after time.

The author's decision to express his linguistic and epistemological concerns through economic paradigms may be explained by a brief look at France's economy during this period. Though outwardly prosperous, much like Rabelais's text, it was by and large an inflationary period: currency was ever more plentiful, but its buying power was decreasing rapidly, owing in part to the flooding of European markets with American bullion. To make matters worse, the French treasury borrowed periodically to finance its war efforts and printed large quantities of paper money, which further devalued the currency already in circulation. Given the Renaissance love of analogy, it is not surprising that Rabelais would make the connection, seeing a similarity between his own copious learning, the surface prosperity of France, and the plentiful supply of increasingly devaluated currency. His text reflects this profusion of money: words denoting coins, such as *écus* (crowns), *fleurins* (florins), and *ducatz* (ducats), circulate plentifully throughout his discourse, and yet Panurge, the primary handler of this wealth, remains suspiciously poor. Part of the problem, as we shall see in the *Third Book*, is a function of Panurge's own poor husbanding of his resources; but at the same time, we must remember that Panurge's copious coins are ultimately a fiction, worth no more than the paper they are printed on.

Of Paupers and Princes: Panurge and Pantagruel. In the prologue to *Pantagruel*, Alcofribas changes gear in midstream and turns his attention from "noble dames" (*P*, Prol., 161) and "powerful lords" (162) to syphilitics and the gouty. This radical shift in perspective is mirrored in the body of the text itself, as the philosopher-prince Pantagruel, aristocratic hero of the Christian epic, is pushed to one side to make way for his roguish companion, Panurge. Between Pantagruel's intellectual feats in the Baisecul-Humevesne episode (*P*, X–XIII) and his call to military duty in the Dipsodian War (*P*, XXIII), the rogue's antifeats supplement and effectively supplant the prince's prowesses. Stealing, persecuting, violating, and maiming, he leaves behind him a trail of antiheroics that constitute an abyss of negativity at the core of the epic.

The differences between Panurge and Pantagruel stem from an economic disproportion. While both are of noble birth, "fortune" has frowned upon Panurge, making him and the prince opposite sides of the same coin (*P*, IX, 195). One is a have and the other a have-not, one a prince and the other a pauper. This inequality is mirrored in their physiques. Unlike the young giant, who is described as "long in body," we learn that the newcomer is more modest in stature: "of medium height, neither too tall nor too short" (*P*, XVI, 224). In contrast to Pantagruel, who has both a father and a genealogy stretching back to biblical times, Panurge is the best son in the world (*le meilleur filz du monde* [*OC*, *P*, XVI, 237]) because he has no parents. As a result of his family background, Pantagruel is a man of considerable property, whereas Panurge has "no house or lands" (*P*, XVII, 231) and suffers perpetually from *faulte d'argent* (*OC*, 237) or "lack of money" (*P*, XVIII, 237), immediately dissipating any funds that come his way.[10] One dramatic illustration of the dissimilarity in their circumstances is found in chapters 3 and 19: as an infant, Pantagruel drank the milk of 146,000 cows at every meal, in direct contrast to Panurge, who is starving and begging for food when we first meet him.

Though he is almost the mirror opposite of Pantagruel, Panurge's intrusion into the giant's epic is not totally gratuitous. First, he is a Renaissance type no less authentic than his master. The roguish sidekick from a less privileged stratum of society had already replaced the traditional noble companion of medieval epic in Folengo's *Baldus*, and other incarnations of Panourgos, the trickster, had been part of the public consciousness at least since antiquity.[11] In the Renaissance, however, the rogue's literary and folkloric resourcefulness is grafted onto that of the middle-class *arriviste*, often unlanded and separated from family, who lives by his wits alone. Arguably there is an element of Panourgos in Rabelais himself, whose chronic *faulte d'argent* and ever-changing adaptive tactics mirror those of his wheeling-and-dealing character.

More important for our purposes, Panurge's chronic lack at once echoes and reinforces corollary voids and emptinesses in the text. His empty stomach and physical hunger, so at odds with the copia that dominates the discourse, constitute a synchronic reprise of a diachronic sequence that we thought had been resolved: the drought and famine preceding Pantagruel's birth. Panurge's *faulte d'argent* also foreshadows the world in Pantagruel's mouth, where peasants eke out a living planting cabbages and poverty is rampant. Much like this netherworld, Panurge's lack—be it monetary, familial, or gastric—is an abyss interconnected to all the other abysses that interrupt the prosperous landscape of the *Pantagruel*: the old woman, Pantagruel's overcharged brain, Panurge's gestures to Thaumaste, and the world inside Pantagruel's mouth are all rents in the fabric of the text. Along with the word "nothing," which also occurs repeatedly in the Rabelaisian text, these abysses are gaping holes through which a curious reader, much like Lewis Carroll's Alice, can stumble and fall, discovering the underside of Renaissance culture.

If Panurge is an abyss, Pantagruel is a mountain, and together hero and antihero constitute a synergistic duo. Economically, one is a surplus and the other a deficit; one is associated with caritas and the other with cupiditas. Despite the emphasis on Pantagruel's profit in the letter of chapter 8, his feats consist in the dispersion of the "wealth" he has acquired and inherited. In the Baisecul-Humevesne episode, he shares his wisdom with fools, and during the Dipsodian War, he makes a gift of his strength, cunning, and military training to defend the peaceful Amaurotes. Refusing to accept a judgeship in payment for his services in the first episode, he makes a point of asking for a "present" (*P*, XIV, 215), a request that inscribes his own prowesses within the moral economy of gifts rather than the market economy of loans and favors.

Prior to his *Third Book* investiture as Chastellain de Salmiguondin (Lord of Salmagundi), on the other hand, Panurge has so few monetary resources that he rarely aids the less fortunate. Unlike the prince, whose gifts help raise up the oppressed, Panurge tends to topple oppressors and bedevil the *more* fortunate: slipping excrement into the hoods of theologians, throwing vermin down the backs of noblewomen, and causing a cordelier to expose himself. In addition to being negative, these antiheroics are also "featlets," as small, base, and trivial as Pantagruel's heroics are massive, lofty, and memorable. Whereas the prince uses an enormous "mast" to fell the giant Loup Garou (Werewolf) in chapter 29, Panurge arms himself with fleas, lice, and dung.

Because of his monetary want, moreover, Panurge differs from his cohero by taking more frequently than he gives, adopting an economy of survival where "anything goes" that is far removed from the moral gift economy of his friend. In his vast repertory of money-making schemes, we may recall, larceny figures as the most honorable, as Panurge robs the Church (*P*, XVII, 229–30), practices quackery, swindles money changers (*P*, XVI, 228), traffics in learning (*P*, IX), and even murders to make ends meet. The killing, ironically, doubles as both a gift and a repayment of debt. For the suicidal landowner in Turkey whom Panurge puts out of his misery once saved Panurge's life, and Rabelais's rogue reciprocates the favor in his own upside-down way: "If you like, *I'll* kill you," he offers. "Outright, too: you'll not feel a thing. You can trust me: I've killed a heap of others and they were never the worse off" (*P*, XIV, 218). Turning even his past sins into a marketable commodity, Panurge nets a handsome profit from the mercy killing, for which the landowner gives him "six hundred seraphs . . . and some rubies, and some flawless diamonds" (218).

Almost always Panurge's altruism is suspect. When he puts his offering in the collection box at church, the gift is a subterfuge for theft: "When I gave them my first penny," he boasts, "I laid it down so neatly that it looked like three-pence. So with one hand, I took up three, six, ninepence, indeed, a shilling or even two; while with the other, I raked in as much again. So it went, in all the churches we visited" (*P*, XVII, 230). When in the same chapter he provides dowries, hires husbands, and throws wedding feasts for toothless hags, the largesse again benefits Panurge, who ironically *buys* the hereditary droit de seigneur that allowed noblemen to arrange marriages for their dependents. In his role as a reverser of conventional values, Panurge provides dowries not to beautiful young virgins who spurn male advances but rather to ugly old whores who are generous with their favors, rewarding the ugliest and most promiscuous with the largest dowries. As the episode unfolds, however, it becomes clear that Panurge's primary motivation is neither to right wrongs nor to afford women pleasure by "treat[ing] them to one more branglebump before they die" (231). Instead, the artificial micro-economy that he has created is a triumph of market over moral principles, revealing the price people will pay in human dignity in return for money and sex.

As if tutored by his roguish companion, whose pragmatic lessons in survival supplement the bookish curriculum of chapter 8, Pantagruel himself effectively couches chicanery in charity during the Dipsodian War, provisioning a freed prisoner with kind words, erroneous information, and a present of tainted jam that together lower the enemy's guard and allow the Utopians to triumph. That Pantagruel abandons pure caritas in favor of its self-serving twin, Panurgian cupiditas, bears witness to the altered circumstances in which he finds himself: the immoral economy of war demands the strategies of survival that Panurge has practiced all his life. It is from the clash of these two different value systems that the prince's situational ethics are born.

The World Upside Down: The Dipsodian War and the Netherworlds. Negative exchange reaches its apogee in battle, a requisite of the epic. The battle is occasioned in *Pantagruel* by the Dipsodes' invasion of Utopia. In economic terms, the invasion triggering the Dipsodian War is not a gift but its diametrical opposite: a theft that is precipitated by the perception in Dipsody that Gargantua's "translat[ion] to Fairyland by Morgan the Fay" (*P*, XXIII, 250) has weakened Utopian defenses. In an act of perfect but negative reciprocity, Pantagruel will, over the course of eight chapters, turn back the enemy, retake the city of the Amaurotes, and, finally, "attack the Dipsodes and occupy their kingdom" (*P*, XXXI, 280), just as the Dipsodes occupied Utopia and seized the prince's land. Like Panurge but in a different way, the Dipsodes figure as the negative other of Pantagruel and Utopia: their name itself means "thirsty people" (*P*, XXVI, 258), linking them semantically to the prince, and their ranks are reinforced with 300 giants rivaling Pantagruel in physical (though not moral and intellectual) stature.

To overcome the Dipsodian force, the Utopians plot their strategy in terms of negative intellectual exchange. Determined to "have" information about the enemy's "strength" and "organization" (*P*, XXIV, 253), Pantagruel's companions plan to infiltrate the Dipsodian camp and appropriate or steal this knowledge by means of subterfuge. If caught, both Panurge and Epistemon vow to misrepresent themselves. "I am of the lineage of Zopirus" (253), boasts Panurge in an unexpected gesture of altruism, alluding to the Persian hero who cut off his nose and ears in order to pass himself off among the Babylonians as a deserter mutilated by his master Darius. Similarly, Epistemon invokes the false gift of the Trojan horse and claims that he can "mak[e] them believe anything [he] like[s]," using "stratagems and ruses of the brave captains of old" (253) that consist in part of counterfeit verbal and sartorial tokens.

As it turns out, the Dipsodes launch an offensive before the Utopians have a chance to test these information-gathering strategies; but in keeping with classical tradition, Pantagruel's forces prevail through a mixture of brains and brawn. Standing within a circle of cables that has been lined with straw and gunpowder, the Utopians Eusthenes and Carpalim "offer" themselves to the enemy and "pretend to surrender."

This counterfeit gift enables Pantagruel's men to lure the enemy inside the circle and burn them "like damned souls in hell" (*P*, XXV, 255). Only one marauder survives, and from him Pantagruel elicits a flood of information by misrepresenting himself as an "eat[er] of little children" (*P*, XXVI, 257).

In a move of perfect reciprocity, the Utopians answer the assault against them with a counterattack on the enemy camp that partially mirrors the earlier confrontation: for again the Dipsodes, who have become drunk in an attempt to quench the thirst produced by Pantagruel's gift of syrup, find themselves in flames as Carpalim torches their tents and explodes all their gunpowder. In a final gesture of negative largesse, Pantagruel liberally salts the enemies' gaping mouths (*il leur en remplit tout le gouzier* [*OC*, *P*, XXVIII, 287]) and then quenches their thirst permanently by urinating on their camp "so freely and [copiously] as to drown them all" (*P*, XXVIII, 266). When they awaken, the Dipsodes find "their camp blazing on one hand and Pantagruel's urinal inundation on the other," in a double rite of purification that resembles "the end of the world" (266).

Before he establishes a new order, where positive reciprocity will reign, Pantagruel must dispose of the remaining giants, who escaped the inundation and conflagration with their king. The battle that ensues between Pantagruel and Loup Garou is articulated in the language of exchange. First Loup Garou "addressed himself" (*s'adressa* [*OC*, *P*, XXIX, 290]) to Pantagruel with a steel mast, and in return Pantagruel "gave" (*luy donna* [292]) him blows in the breast and genitals. Once Loup Garou falls, Pantagruel picks him up by his feet and swings the armor-clad giant like a scythe to mow down his comrades. In the process, we learn that Loup Garou "lost" (*perdit* [294]) his head, in a literal reprise of the figurative "lost head" that prompted him to thirst for territorial gain. The entire sequence of upending the giant, felling his head, and flattening his army reaches its nadir in chapter 31, where King Anarchus, the original transgressor of Utopia's moral economy, reaps the negative rewards of his greed: not only is his socioeconomic status reversed, but by becoming a lowly hawker of green sauce and marrying a prostitute, he is transformed into a permanent symbol of the amoral market values that first led him astray.

The Dipsodian War ends with three netherworld sequences: Epistemon's visit to hell (*P*, XXX), the narrator's tour of Pantagruel's mouth (*P*, XXXII), and a medical expedition into the prince's stomach and intestines (*P*, XXXIII). In the first episode, Pantagruel's wise friend

Epistemon loses his head in battle, just like Loup Garou, but is resuscitated by the fool and sometime quack Panurge, who reattaches the dead man's head nerve by nerve and vessel by vessel. When he revives, Epistemon recounts his otherworldly adventures in accordance with mythic and epic norms. Far from presenting a classical underworld where heroes are glorified, however, or a Dantean afterlife that rewrites history according to Christian values, Epistemon describes an upside-down world in which dead men exchange economic roles with their earthly opposites. This upside-down afterworld has its roots in the New Testament premise that "the first shall be last," but its specifics are profoundly satiric toward the Church and, even more markedly, toward classical antiquity and the entire heroic tradition that gave birth to Pantagruel. Perhaps because he appropriated "fat" from Church revenues in life, Pope Boniface VIII is condemned to skim old soup pots (*P*, XXX, 275) in Epistemon's hell, and Ulysses, who cut down his adversaries in life, is a mower of hay (273) in the afterworld. Despite its structural adherence to epic norms, then, the Rabelaisian underworld is profoundly antiheroic in its systematic leveling of heroes.[13]

On one level, Rabelais's upside-down afterlife is self-referential, for inscribed within the netherworld are unmistakable traces of the bard's financially strapped life as a poet. Undervalued by sixteenth-century France, Rabelais used his prerogative as creator to fashion a salvational economy consistent with his talents: in Epistemon's netherworld, poets are lords for eternity, or at least until fortune's wheel makes another half-revolution. A producer and seller on earth, Rabelais would join the ranks of consumers in the afterlife, leaving the peddling and street vending he invokes in the prologue to the likes of Pope Julius, Cleopatra, Dido, Penthesilea, Xerxes, Hannibal, Priam, and Geoffrey with the Great Tooth. Ascribing meaning to this particular "punishment" is admittedly risky, for in many instances Rabelais's new career choices for dead heroes correspond to stylistic rather than semantic exigencies. At the same time, however, it is difficult to avoid the similarities between Pope Julius II, who sells meat pies in the afterlife, and the poet Jean Lemaire de Belges, who hawks pardons in his new role as pope. Similarly, Cyrus's new identity as a beggar, who asks before receiving, reverses the dual economy of kingship and conquest that allowed the Persian ruler to take without asking during his lifetime. By the same leap of logic, the warriors Alexander and Darius spend eternity as thieves, unscrupulously picking the pockets of their predecessor. By implication, Rabelais assimilates the greed of heroic conquest to the acquisitiveness of petty marketing.

As if to reinforce the antimarket biases of his artificial economy, Rabelais assigns what is arguably the worst punishment to usurers or moneylenders who grow rich on the interest from their loans. Appropriately, it is Pantagruel, the figure of caritas and a proponent of moral gift economies, who inquires about the status of those who traffic in and profit from false gifts. "They were all scouring the gutters for rusty pins and old nails," replies Epistemon, "just like the beggars here. But a hundredweight of this ironware won't buy a crust of bread. . . . Yet day and night they toiled, waiting for a windfall" (P, XXX, 279). First of all, the usurers' relegation to gutters places them in a lower *bolgia* (realm of hell) than either the kings who pick pockets or the pope who skims pots: all three infernal loci are abysses. Second, the corroded ironware that the moneylenders collect contrasts negatively with the gold and silver that they accrued on earth, suggesting that the market economy in which they operate—and which sets gold as its standard—belongs not to the prelapsarian golden age but rather to the corrupt Age of Iron. And third, the moneylenders' hard work in hell for "one scurvy penny [a] year" (279) constitutes a mirror reversal of the massive profit they made from minimal work on earth.

Equally intriguing within the novel's self-reversing economy are the implications of this alternative system of exchange for the intrafictional characters. Not coincidentally, Epistemon either discovers or, like Rabelais, invents an afterlife that will reverse his dependent status in life by empowering him as part of an intellectual aristocracy: "Philosophers and such as had been needy on this planet became puissant lords in the inferno" (P, XXX, 277). For Epistemon, this rosy future is only slightly dimmed by the specter of syphilis, obligatory for all those who escaped the scourge in life (276). In part a condemnation of chastity and the refusal of sexual commerce that it implies, this counterdiscourse rewarding sexual incontinence provides the normally sober scholar a perfect excuse for indulging in Panurgian dalliances. The threat of syphilis has negative ramifications for Pantagruel as well. Not only is he at risk for the pox in Epistemon's hell, but his heroic feats and princely status on earth—offset only by his philosophizing tendencies—make him a prime candidate for menial labor in the afterlife. Given this fact, it is small wonder that the Utopian prince, the nominal hero of Rabelais's epic, interrupts Epistemon's narrative and urges his resuscitated friend to "keep the rest of these fine tales for a rainy afternoon" (279). Like the original introduction of Panurge into the narrative, Epistemon's nether-world upends the culturally ordained values represented by Pantagruel's princely status. Not surprisingly, it is Panurge—the engineer of Episte-mon's new mindset—who can look forward to the brightest future in this upside-down afterworld. As a survivor of the pox, he will be syphilis-free, and his poverty on earth will garner him wealth and power, a reward solidified by his status on earth as a poet.

Following directly on the heels of Epistemon's hell is a second neth-erworld episode: a journey into Pantagruel's mouth by the narrator Alcofribas, who seeks shelter under his master's tongue during a rain-storm and emerges more than six months later with a story to tell. What he finds is an "other world" of which the Utopians are ignorant; ironically, it is far more consistent with extratextual reality and the economics of sixteenth-century France than Utopia itself.[13] At first, the wondrous mountains and forests of this oral civilization convince Alco-fribas that he has discovered a New World, an intrafictional corollary of the Americas. On closer inspection, however, Alcofribas discovers that the oral substratum he has entered is far older than the rarefied spheres of civilization he has left behind. Like Epistemon's hell, then, the trip that begins under Pantagruel's tongue is a journey back in time that eluci-dates, on one level, the prince's personal past: for his mouth contains not just the literal foodstuff, produced by anonymous "cabbage growers" (*P*, XXXII, 284), that he has consumed during his lifetime, but also, in allegorical form, the work, sleep, and play that have contributed to his physical and intellectual development. Insofar as Pantagruel symbolizes learned culture in the Renaissance, we may further interpret the contents of his mouth as the diachronic underpinnings of the Renaissance, not its intellectual ancestors but its economic foundations. Not coincidentally, the agrarian atmosphere and the emphasis upon production and distri-bution inside the giant's oral netherworld take us back to the world prior to Pantagruel's birth in chapter 2, bringing the novel full circle.

On a synchronic level, the civilization within Pantagruel's mouth represents the underbelly or "abyss" of the humanists' bright new world: the other side of the coin. In contrast to Epistemon's hell, with its parade of famous names such as Jean Lemaire de Belges and Cyrus, the giant's oral netherworld is peopled by small, nameless, forgotten people like Panurge, including a cabbage grower, a pigeon keeper, plague victims, and brigands. Not just agrarian, it also consists of rich merchants and manufacturers, of the type who provide the books Pantagruel reads and the luxuries that surround him. In return, a small portion of Pantagruel's wealth—his pigeons, for example, who enter his mouth when he yawns (*P*, XXXII, 284)—trickles down to these "small" people as if by accident, without his ever being aware of their existence. Conversely, Pantagruel is equally oblivious to the negative effects his everyday actions have on this gasterworld, where the plague results directly from the giant's indigestion (285).

This indigestion gives way to full-fledged abdominal distress, which results in a third netherworld episode: a purgative expedition into Pantagruel's stomach and intestines by miners encased in giant-sized capsules or "globes" with "trap-doors" (*P*, XXXIII). After navigating a "gulf of corruption . . . more fetid than the marshes of Camerina, mentioned by Virgil," the miners with their lanterns, pickaxes, and shovels remove layer after layer of excrement from the "pit" (287–88). Functioning on one level as a parody of underworld scenes and on another level as sheer verbal fantasy, this third netherworld voyage again diverts the epic descent into hell from the noble hero to economic inferiors in a clear reversal of hierarchies: first Epistemon, then Alcofribas, and finally a team of peasants complete this trope in descending sociological order. In purely logistical terms, up becomes down and down becomes up for these servants, whose dirty work results in the giant's healing and purification. Like its predecessors, the final descent allegorizes social difference and interdependency and hypothesizes a fanciful "cure." For after the peasant archeologists chip away at misinformation and difference itself, the giant himself vomits them upward, restoring them symbolically to his own level before healing war-torn Dipsody. The entire episode doubles, finally, as an allegory of the book, which hammers away therapeutically at our ethical, epistemological, and sociological premises as we are engulfed in, and in turn consume, otherness.

This first essay in exchange concludes, appropriately enough, with a return of the huckster, who promises a sequel at the next Frankfurt fair. In another sense, however, it is clear that the hawker of the prologue never entirely disappears from the novel, even in the most erudite passages. Instead, we have seen that he leaves his imprint on the body of the text, which is permeated with variations on the structures of exchange that he first introduces in the prologue. Because the learned narrator remains part huckster, the myth of humanistic profit and growth that he peddles doubles as a hollow sales pitch, and the words in which he traffics are as unstable, inflationary, and two-sided as coins. Far from being a semantically indifferent posture, the marketing stance that frames the novel invites us to draw analogies between words and money, linguistic and monetary tokens, and to see the inflationary nature of literary as well as material copia in the Renaissance.

The sociological difference of the huckster is also mirrored in the text, which is subverted from the bottom by the roguish upstart Panurge, who is a literary cousin of the huckster. By taking over center stage from the aristocratic hero and accomplishing antifeats of his own, this small, poor, impious, and *un*courtly man interrogates the ethical premises, socioeconomic biases, heroic models, and salvational strategies of both epic and romance. Far from representing a new and superior behavioral ideal, this alternative sociological type and the netherworlds that follow add real-world complexity to the epic, completing Pantagruel's and our own education with vertiginous role reversals and upside-down perspectives conducive to self-criticism, reevaluation, and the bridging of difference.

Chapter Three
Gargantua

At first glance, the *Gargantua*, written in or around 1534, seems far removed from the wheeling-and-dealing world of exchange that leaves its mark so indelibly on the *Pantagruel*. Like its predecessor, the new volume was in all likelihood offered for sale at the Lyon fair, but few traces of this carnival atmosphere find their way into the text. Gone for the most part is the sideshow barker of the prologue to *Pantagruel*, who attempts to dredge up buyers for his text with outrageous boasts, scatology, and invective. In his place, or at least grafted onto his selling persona, is a patently humanistic narrator whose discourse is dense with learned references. Also absent from the new volume are the prince-and-pauper team of Pantagruel and Panurge, whose contrasting financial status polarizes the first novel along socioeconomic lines. Set in a time prior to their birth, the *Gargantua* instead chronicles the nativity, education, and prowesses of Pantagruel's father, who shares center stage not with a cowardly rogue but with a courageous monk called Friar John.

Appearances notwithstanding, the *Gargantua* is arguably more charged than its predecessor with economic allusions and structures of exchange. Though devoid of the peddler's rhetoric that would situate it squarely in the marketplace, the new prologue addresses an integral part of economic decision-making, the dialectics of assessment and evaluation. In this antechamber to the text, which is permeated with a vocabulary of pricing and estimation, Alcofribas explores the gap between outer appearance and inner worth that makes the reader-buyer's task a difficult one. By teasing and testing us with discrepancies between seeming and being, or representation and referent, Alcofribas generates a critical audience of savvy buyers who, unlike the gullible customer of the *Pantagruel*, are skeptical of face value or the "outward and visible sign" (*G*, Prol., 4). The reader-buyer's education under the tutelage of Alcofribas parallels that of the hero, who, in contrast to Pantagruel, develops *à tâtons* (gropingly) through a process similar to comparison shopping. As Gargantua progresses from Scholastic to humanistic teachers, from sloth to productivity, and from self-absorption to social awareness, he learns to test commodities—not just the famous arsewipe, but ethics and pedagogical philosophies as well—before "buying" or discarding them on the basis of their use value to him and their worth to the community as a whole.

Far from being limited to the handful of chapters that specifically address book-learning, Gargantua's education and maturation process extend over the entire course of the novel, whose trajectory marks the hero's evolution from a monologic to a dialogic consciousness, capable of engaging in commerce with otherness. In our discussion, we will see that the epic's central conflict, a war with King Picrochole that parallels the first novel's Dipsodian War, tests the young hero's commitment to the common good by pitting him against the self-absorbed antihero, who is a caricature of his own selfish ego. Supporting this paradigm is the fact that the war, ignited by a squabble over salable merchandise, is fundamentally an economic dispute, revolving around the Renaissance's historic shift from local to regional markets. The conflicting nature of this backdrop, finally, helps us understand the utopian Abbey of Thélème, which marks both the end of the war and the conclusion of Gargantua's education in a state of perfect reciprocity.

The Prologue: Learning to Judge the Product

The prologue to *Gargantua* opens with a sober display of erudition that distinguishes it from the ebullient *Pantagruel*. True, Rabelais's bawdy dedication of his second novel to "illustrious drinkers" and "pox-ridden comrades" (*G*, Prol., 3) seems initially to be a throwback to the *Pantagruel*'s marketplace banter, but the narrator's subsequent allusion to Plato's dialogue *The Banquet* causes us to redefine the tipplers' thirst and the syphilitics' love as figures of humankind's yearning for the truth. Where to find that precious commodity forms the core of the ensuing discussion, which revolves around the metaphor of Plato's *sileni*, grotesquely decorated boxes that Alcibiades likened to Socrates: "Sileni, in the days of yore, were small boxes such as you may see nowadays at your apothecary's. . . . The outside of these boxes bore gay, fantastically painted figures. . . . But inside these sileni, people kept priceless drugs . . . and other invaluable possessions"(3).

While the context of this extended metaphor is epistemological rather than carnivalesque, its locus is nonetheless a market of sorts: an apothecary or drugstore where "priceless drugs" are sold. This comparison of the *Gargantua* to medication builds upon the first novel's claim to curative powers (*P*, Prol., *162*), and the image of an apothecary echoes both the original narrator's stance as a patent-medicine peddler and the author's real-life role as a physician. Despite these similarities to the *Pantagruel*, however, Rabelais alters his original hard-sell techniques in a manner consistent with the quest for knowledge. Instead of demanding that we invest in his product, as he did in the *Pantagruel*, a more cerebral Alcofribas now urges us to examine the package and its contents before buying them at face value: "You should look beyond my title," he advises; "open my book and seriously weigh its subject matter" (*G*, Prol., 4). The word "weigh" belongs to a vocabulary of assessment interspersed throughout the prologue. Terms such as "priceless," "precious," "invaluable," "judging," "poor" (3), and "prize" (5) all relate to evaluation, an economic metaphor for judgment. More than a simple sales pitch, the prologue to *Gargantua* constitutes an essay in judgment, a problematic and dialogic faculty that fascinated Renaissance humanists. Within the corpus of the *Gargantua*, the development of judgment is an integral part of the young giant's maturation process, insofar as it enables him to use the massive erudition he has acquired.

In the prologue, however, the problem of judgment or of assessing value is complicated by the narrator's association of exchange and reversibility in the sileni metaphor. On a very basic level, the boxes represent the text that Alcofribas is selling: frivolous and apparently worthless on the outside, but filled with "priceless drugs" (*G*, Prol., 3) on the inside. In case we fail to grasp the analogy, Rabelais provides us a second one of the same ilk, based on Plato's original metaphor. Viewed from the outside and judged solely on appearance, Socrates would be worth less than an "onion skin" (3). Upon opening the "box" of his mind, however, discerning buyers would again find "priceless, celestial drugs," including "divine knowledge," "immortal understanding," and "perfect assurance" (3).

On a textual level, Alcofribas seems to be directing readers to interpret his *Gargantua* hermeneutically, a theory supported by his suggestion that we crack the "bone" of the text and suck out the "marrow" (*G*, Prol., 4). According to the narrator, this marrow consists of an "abstruse doctrine" (5)—reminiscent of the first novel's "occult properties" (*P*, Prol., 162)—that will teach us to become "valiant and wise" like Socrates and will reveal the "deepest mysteries" about "our economic life" (*G*, Prol., 5). The term "economic" usually referred to domestic order in the sixteenth century, but given the exchange-oriented context of the prologue, it is appealing to hypothesize that Rabelais was already alluding to the word's modern financial connotations.[1] Whatever his intention, readers certainly derive an economic lesson from the prologue that hinges upon the narrator's repeated about-faces. For the wisdom that Alcofribas is peddling consists paradoxically in a mistrust of the salesman, a skepticism he himself fosters by interrogating both "the visible sign" (4) and the hidden value of his product. Consistently inconsistent, Alcofribas touts the importance of marrow only to dispute its very existence, denigrating the allegorists who found hidden meaning in the *Iliad* and *Odyssey*. "Do you honestly believe that Homer . . . ever dreamed of the allegorical patchwork inflicted upon him by Plutarch . . . or by Politian?" demands Alcofribas. "If you do, you are miles away from my opinion" (5). Teasing us with meaning and then mocking us for taking the bait, Alcofribas illustrates in at least four different ways that outer as well as inner appearances can deceive readers or perspective buyers.[2]

Far from being merely ambiguous, the narrator's sileni evolve over the course of the prologue into figures of infinite reversibility, similar to Russian dolls that stack one inside the other, but also similar to the multilayered onion the narrator earlier uses to describe Socrates: each level of "skin" (*G*, Prol., 3) we peel back reveals a new surface, whose occasional transparency is a frustrating illusion.[3] Even the narrator's concluding contention that he wrote only while drinking, at first glance a disavowal of his earlier claim not to have written "in the exuberance of humor" (4), lends itself to alternative interpretations. For according to the philosophy of Bacchic inspiration, the stupor that accompanies drunkenness actually doubles as divine frenzy, a semiconscious state in which the poet, freed of his rational inhibitions, becomes a vehicle for the transmission of "sublime themes" and "profound wisdom" (5).

The epistemological implications of the narrator's claim to have written while drinking are thus double: his work may be worthless, pure drunken nonsense, or it may contain precious drugs. On an economic level, the claim also argues for the cost-effectiveness of the *Gargantua*. By completing two activities—writing and drinking—in the time allotted for one, Alcofribas has at once saved time and increased his potential margin of profit: "I gave the matter no more thought than you," he scoffs. "In composing this masterpiece I have not spent or wasted more leisure than is required for my bodily refection" (*G*, Prol., 5). This new time-intensive economic paradigm differs radically from the time-extensive equation of the *Pantagruel*, which is advertised as long in the making and requiring an exorbitant investment of time from readers. By way of contrast, Rabelais implies that his audience of "drinkers" (3) will follow the narrator's lead and read while imbibing, much like the young Gargantua, who studies and discusses literature at mealtime (*G*, XXIII).[4] This emphasis upon saving time is reinforced by the narrator's description of the readers as "fleet" in the pursuit of their text, and by his advice not to "tarry" (*demourer*) over frivolous passages (*G*, Prol., 5). The reader-buyer's major investment of time, such as it is, consists in the "prolonged meditation" (*méditation fréquente*) that follows "diligent reading" (5), as we "lend a loftier sense to what [we] first believed written in the exuberance of humor" (4).

While the second prologue contains a few traces of the rhetoric of persuasion we associate with selling, audience-pleasing considerations akin to our modern marketing strategies nonetheless help shape the text. In addition to offering readers a favorable profit-to-loss ratio, in which a small outlay of time yields long-term food for thought, the narrator plies us with paradoxes that hold us enthralled far more effectively than a conventional preview or introduction does. Taken in combination, such figures as the sileni and tippling poet constitute an intricately woven mind teaser, which stimulates our curiosity and critical faculties in much the same way a bone attracts dogs. In hunting for the elusive marrow, we ourselves become hooked by the puzzle of the text, in a mental addiction paralleling the physical dependency produced by "precious drugs." As frustrating as Rabelais's circuitous enigmas are for modern readers, whose impatience for answers often blinds them to the joys of the interrogative process, his erudite conundra are tailor-made for Renaissance humanists, who delighted in mental as well as physical labyrinths that honed and tested their judgment.

The Opening Chapters:
An Essay in Judgment and Worth

Much like the prologue, the opening pages of *Gargantua* are an essay in judgment and worth. Chapter 1, nominally devoted to the giant's "genealogy and antiquity," bypasses Gargantua's family tree altogether with a suggestion that noble readers ("your lordships" [*G*, I, 6]) who never tire of twice-told tales about bloodlines should consult the *Pantagruel*. In case we miss the hint that most pedigrees are fiction, "improve[d] by repetition" (6), Alcofribas concludes the chapter by admitting that Gargantua's genealogy, the best preserved of any "save the Messiah's" (7), was inscribed "on the bark of an elm tree . . . so worn by age that barely three consecutive letters were discernible" (8). If the "best preserved" and most "certain" genealogy is fiction, reconstructed from invisible letters or nothingness, it stands to reason that lesser pedigrees spring from even more spurious documentation. In an echo of Epistemon's hell, where princes are paupers and vice versa, Alcofribas speculates that some emperors, kings, dukes, princes, and popes of his own times are actually descended from "relic-peddlers and journeymen-carriers" (7). Conversely, he believes that he himself is the progeny of some "opulent monarch of olden days" (7). One goal of this discourse is to reassociate the prologue's reversibility with the *Pantagruel*'s cyclical wheel of fortune, reminding us that "everything that goes around comes around." According to this logic, the impoverished Alcofribas, who is himself a "relic-peddler and journeyman-carrier" in this life, will again be a king in the afterworld.

Equally important in chapter 1 is the interrogation of human worth inherent in the narrator's musings, which find intertextual corollaries in Renaissance debates over the nature of true nobility, a quality that does not always coincide with socioeconomic rank. The reason for this discontinuity is twofold. First, nobility of birth is contingent upon unreliable bloodlines that are a function of pure chance or fortune rather than merit. Second, nobility of character or inner quality is neither limited to nor omnipresent among the aristocracy. Despite their impressive titles and trappings, symbols or tokens that constitute the currency of social exchange and the primary criteria used in judgment, some high and mighty lords are base and worthless individuals when judged on their character alone. Alcofribas, on the other hand, hints broadly that his own worth far exceeds his estate. That he "crave[s] kingship and wealth" (*G*, I, 7), without acquiring them, on one level constitutes a discontinuity between signified and signifier that will be resolved, according to Alcofribas, in an afterlife where inner and outer coincide: "Yet I am consoled as I reflect that I shall be all this in the next world, to a vaster extent even than I dare wish today" (7). Rather than lock us into this Platonizing interpretation of reality, however, in which elevated desires represent thwarted virtualities stemming from memories of prenatal grandeur, Rabelais mocks his own claims to inner worth by basing them on ignoble cravings to "live sumptuously," "do nothing," and "avoid worry" (7).

The second chapter of *Gargantua* is an enigma that reinforces the narrator's contention that judgment is problematic. According to Alcofribas, the enigma was found with Gargantua's genealogy and life history at the end of a book found inside a goblet lying within a tomb buried underneath a meadow. These four layers of "insideness" make the enigma quadruply difficult to decipher, as do the oxymoronic qualities of the text, which is at once big and little, moldy and fragrant. To complicate matters, rats and weasels ate the beginning of the enigma, and Alcofribas, apparently intent on making the first last and the last first, has characteristically reversed the document's relationship to the chronicle, placing the enigma before instead of after the giant's "antiquities." Filled with holes, non sequiturs, and unidentified allusions, the enigma has yet to be solved, partly because the narrator, who might well have included an explanation or gloss of his own, has chosen to respect antiquity and leave the text unedited: "The rest I append below," he tells us, "for the reverence I bear antiquity" (*G*, I, 8). Here the derogatory implications about how scholars orient our judgment by deciphering signs for us is unmistakable.

While Alcofribas does not repeat Gargantua's genealogy in his sequel, he does add a twist in chapter 3 that again challenges the family tree's ultimate worth: Gargantua, possibly because he is a giant, has an 11-month gestation period. The incident is not necessarily ironic, for it reflects the ongoing discussions among medical authorities, legists, and scholars of the period about the minimum and maximum lengths of pregnancies. The question had important legal ramifications, for it affected rights of succession and the disposition of property in cases where birth occurred either soon after a marriage or more than a few months after the husband's death. Generally, medical authorities in the Renaissance agreed that the normal gestation period was nine months, but Alcofribas accurately points out that pregnancies of ten and eleven months had been judged legitimate by the legists.[5] Alcofribas does not, then, imply that his hero is illegitimate; but by raising the issue of legitimacy and illegitimacy, he underlines the crucial "if" upon which the entire patrilineal system and name of the father hinges. If her-story coincides with his-story, the genealogy is valid, but a single infidelity can turn the name of the father into a legal fiction.

Gargantua's birth occurs after a copious tripe feast (*G*, IV) and drunken revel (*G*, V) in which Utopians and their neighbors consume the lower stomachs of 367,014 cows, guzzling them "all down to the last scrap" (*G*, IV, 15). In this curious variation on carpe diem, in which one participant at least drinks "for fear of dying" (G, V, 17), the revelers' immoderation is justified in economic terms: they eat unsparingly to fortify themselves for leaner times, symbolized by the approach of Lent, and to avoid wasting the tripe, which "could not be kept on hand long" (G, IV, 15) without spoiling. Despite Grandgousier's warning to "eat sparingly" (15) in view of her condition, the pregnant Gargamelle alone eats "sixteen quarters, two bushels, and six pecks" (16), with predictable results. Her effort to prevent external waste paradoxically generates internal waste, as the tripe, an organ of digestion, proves indigestible in such vast quantities. Not surprisingly, the stomach cramps that beset Gargamelle shortly thereafter, while she is dancing and cavorting, are a combination of labor, indigestion, food poisoning, and sheer gluttony. To treat the diarrhea, one of the midwives gives Gargamelle an astringent so powerful that it constricts both the sphincter and birth canal, forcing the already resourceful Gargantua to exit via his mother's ear, shouting "Drink, drink, drink!" (G, VI, 23).

Rabelais's decision to place Gargantua's birth under the emblem of drinking not only recalls the *Pantagruel*, in which physical appetite was a figure of Renaissance curiosity, but also echoes the ambiguous prologue, where the narrator claims to have written while drinking. According to this analogy, the birth of the novel, written in the throes of Bacchic furor, parallels that of the child, who sees the light of day after a night of drunken revelry. The philosophical resonances of Grandgousier's banquet find expression in the puzzling fifth chapter, entitled "Les Propos des bien yvres" (Palaver of the Potulent). This disjointed dialogue recording the revelers' drunken conversation consists of puns, deductive reasoning, casuistry, and banter—all on the subject of drink. In this representative passage, a tippler's emphasis upon the liquidity of wine effectively liquifies the libation's connotative value: "If the parchment of my writs drank as avidly as I do," he prattles, "no trace of writing would remain upon them. Then sirs, what bitter wine my creditors would taste when called upon to produce the evidence of my debts" (G, V, 18). Implicit in this reference to wine and ink that "run," thereby effacing ledger entries in which debts are recorded, is an irreverent echo of sacramental wine, which, once transubstantiated into the blood of Christ, "washes away" the sins or moral "debts" of the communicant. On a much larger scale, the entire chapter preceding Gargantua's birth serves to fragment the connotations of the token *boyre* or "drink," plunging us into an interpretive abyss similar to that of the tippler's creditor, who is left with a metamorphic text.

The birth scene that follows chapter 5 is a comic masterpiece, but instead of allowing us to enjoy it unthinkingly, Alcofribas prods our critical faculties awake by addressing the issue of credibility. "Now I suspect that you do not thoroughly believe this strange nativity," he breaks in (*G*, VI, 23), suddenly shattering the illusion of reality that held our judgment suspended during the narrative, and reminding us by his insistence on its veracity that the story is what we knew it to be all along: sheer fiction. The convoluted logic of this narrative intervention becomes clear when we realize its reference is not really *Gargantua* but the printed word in general, even works of nonfiction, which seriously purport to be true. Particularly when it is attributed to an authority, we tend to take what we hear and read at face value. By suggesting that this lack of critical thinking is a virtue, however, Alcofribas manages to elicit a negative reaction from even the most credulous reader. "An honest and sensible man always believes what he is told and what he finds written," argues Alcofribas glibly (23), taking a stance so ludicrous that we effectively reverse it in our minds, rereading the sentence according to the Silenus principle of *antiphrasis*: "A man of good sense always doubts." Later in the chapter, Alcofribas himself justifies this alternative reading by calling Pliny, the source of many strange nativities, a liar (*G*, VI, 24). Far from being a substantive indictment of the natural historian, to whom Rabelais is heavily indebted, this comic about-face constitutes a reminder that all texts, no matter how sacred, must be judged on their individual merits. By indicting one of his favorite authors so summarily, Alcofribas discredits credulity more than Pliny and simultaneously revalues doubt, the mirror opposite of the "faith" and "law" that underlie belief in the absence of rational evidence. Having taught rather than told us to be discerning consumers who look past the cover when judging any text, Alcofribas proceeds to give us a practical examination. In typical Renaissance fashion, Alcofribas gives his hero a meaningful name, based on the adjective *grand* or "big" (24), and decks him out in abundant and luxurious clothing, including a white velvet hat, linen shirt, white satin doublet, white broadcloth breeches and codpiece, leather points, white wool stockings, blue velvet shoes, a blue velvet coat, blue and white belt, and a blue velvet gown with gold flowers. Altogether these garments comprise almost 23,000 yards of fabric and more than 1,500 ells or points. At once a tribute to and a parody of Renaissance materialism, the inflated passage is sufficiently mercantile in orientation to elicit a sustained interrogation of the values represented by this sartorial cornucopia. That the livery costs a fortune goes without saying: Gargantua's ring alone has been valued at 69,894,018 French crowns (*G*, VIII, 29), a number so inflationary that it rings hollow. Similarly, Alcofribas's contention that the ring's price is inestimable leaves us wavering between two alternative readings of the inexpressibility topos: precious and worthless.

Whatever their numerical value, the fine trappings are posited as indicators of inner worth: Gargantua's huge hat is purported to represent the size of his head; his rings, his noble lineage; and his gigantic codpiece, the strength and amplitude of its contents. As in Gargantua's letter of 1532 to Pantagruel, however, where the encomium unravels if we explore the reversible "abyss of knowledge," Gargantua's livery hinges upon our reading of a central metaphor: the *longue braguette* or "long codpiece".[6] Because Gargantua is a giant whose virility we have no reason to doubt, we initially accept in good faith the premise that the inside of the codpiece is as "fully stocked and inexhaustible" (*G*, VIII, 27) as the outside. It is only when Alcofribas proposes the copious paradigm's antithesis, the possibility of a discontinuity between signifier and signified, or a hollow codpiece—"the hypocritical codpieces of a heap of noodles . . . crammed with only wind" (27)—that we begin to question the substance or value of Gargantua's livery along with the entire inflated discourse. Further inspection reveals that the encomium of Gargantua's codpiece is in fact constructed upon a lie that, if corrected, would turn the entire sense of the passage upside down. For despite the narrator's assertions, Pliny does not hold that emeralds such as those adorning Gargantua's codpiece are a sign of virility. On the contrary, the gem is more often associated with impotence.[7]

These tiny rents in the fabric of chapter 8 do not seriously discredit the virility of Gargantua, whose success at siring children has been documented in the *Pantagruel*, and whose virile member is much admired by the governesses in his retinue (*G*, XI, 38). What we do begin to question is the premise, expounded by Federico Fregoso in book 2 of Baldassare Castiglione's *Il Cortegiano* (The Courtier), that clothes, wealth, and appearance are basically accurate indicators of an individual's character or inner worth. Rabelais does not exclude the possibility that emblems may influence a person's character: indeed, the medallion of the half-male, half-female androgyne (*G*, VIII, 28), given to Gargantua as a child, foreshadows the perfect reciprocity of the Abbey of Thélème, which he helps to establish at the end of the novel. Similarly, Rabelais does not deny the utility of these signifiers in the process or formation of judgment. Instead, the doubt he instills in us is two-way: face value may or may not be an accurate indicator of inner value.

Alcofribas further clouds the issue of judgment by demonstrating that the signifiers we use to evaluate people, and that they use to represent themselves, may have two or more signifieds. According to the narrator, readers familiar with traditional color symbolism, as codified by the fifteenth-century Aragonese heraldist Sicile in his *Blason des couleurs* (In Praise of Colors), will see in Gargantua's blue and white livery a representation of faith and steadfastness. While these qualities, on one level, seem entirely unremarkable in a Christian prince, Alcofribas has already established "faith" as the antipode of critical thinking, and steadfastness connotes an inflexibility at odds with Renaissance pedagogical precepts. Instead of questioning the validity of traditional signifieds on experiential grounds, however, Alcofribas disputes the value of Sicile's symbolic currency by interrogating both the authority upon which it is founded and our own reasons for giving it credence: "What moves, impels, and induces you to believe what you do? Who told you that white means faith, and blue [steadfastness]?" (*G*, IX, 29). In the alternative symbolic currency chosen by Grandgousier for his son's livery, "white expresses joy, pleasure, delight, and rejoicing," and "blue denotes things celestial" (29). At first glance, this new symbolism seems no less arbitrary than the one it replaces, but upon further examination it has the advantage of being neither imposed nor instituted by one man, but "admitted by general consent of all men, in accordance with . . . universal law" (*G*, X, 32).[8] To be sure, the coexistence of multiple symbolic currencies makes the "text" of Gargantua's livery subject to misreading. To circumvent this miscommunication, Alcofribas is proposing a kind of international symbolic currency, based on universally understood analogies rather than on arbitrary conventions or narrow linguistic similarities.

Chapter 12, or the episode of the wooden horses, contains a further variation on the semantic polyvalence of signifiers used in exchange. Arriving at Utopia with a massive retinue of servants on a day when two other lords are visiting, the pretentious Seigneur de Painensac has difficulty fitting all his horses into the stable Grandgousier has provided. Suspecting that there is an additional stable elsewhere, two of the seigneur's attendants ask the pre-school-age prince where the "big horses" are kept. In response, Gargantua takes them on a circuitous journey that is a metaphor for textual exegesis. Climbing great stairways, traversing the hallway and gallery, and finally mounting another stairway leading to the "stable," the majordomo and master-of-the-horse figuratively enact the journey of reading itself, in which we gradually peel back layer after layer of meaning before honing in on the *sustantificque mouelle*. In this instance, the marrow they have gullibly "bought" is not a stable at all but another level of representation: for Gargantua has led them on a "wild horse chase," luring them upstairs to view a herd of toy steeds that are "stabled" in his own bedroom.

On one level, this lighthearted anecdote sympathetically captures the process of language acquisition in children, for whom the primary meaning of "horse" is often their own hobbyhorse. At the same time, this confusion dramatizes the more general fact that words, even among adults, have different connotations for different people. Upon hearing the word "horse," some of us visualize a black stallion and others imagine a roan mare. The linguistic token "horse" imperfectly represents the "thing itself" in much the same way that coins differ from the commodity they substitute, serving paradoxically to facilitate and complicate exchange. On a philosophical level, this confusion over the word "horse" also recalls the traditional debate between nominalists and realists over the existence of universals outside the mind, or in reality. Despite Alcofribas's mocking allusion to the nominalist William of Ockham (*G*, VIII, 26), his repeated interrogation of the relationship between reference and referent places him tentatively if not squarely within the Scottish philosopher's camp. At the very least, the Gallic physician reminds us that linguistic values fluctuate like those of any currency, and that, as a result, words must be "weighed" very carefully, as Alcofribas suggests in the prologue.[9] Interestingly enough, Painensac's majordomo and master-of-the-horse do weigh the face value of what Gargantua is saying against the reality of their own experience with stables: "This child is deceiving us," says the master-of-horse; "stables are never at the top of a house" (*G*, XII, 39). As it turns out, however, the geographical locus of "horses" proves no less polyvalent than their semantic locus: as the majordomo points out, some dwellings built "on the side of a hill" during Rabelais's time did have stables "at the top of the house" (39).

The education we receive from the narrator parallels that of the young giant himself, who develops by trial and error from a solipsistic child into a discerning and responsible prince, capable of interacting productively with his environment. Between the ages of three and five, prior to beginning his formal education, Gargantua "spends his time like other small children; namely, in drinking, eating and sleeping; in eating, sleeping and drinking; and in sleeping, drinking and eating" (*G*, XI, 36). Primarily consumptive in nature, this alimentary and digestive routine simultaneously helps produce a healthy body, recognized in the Renaissance as both a valuable commodity in its own right and a necessary corollary of intellectual development. At this stage, however,

the circularity and closure of Gargantua's activities permit little commerce with otherness or alterity, another sine qua non of the maturation
process. Instead, the child is largely self-absorbed, engaging in reflexive
actions directed toward his own body, such as urinating on his shoe,
defecating on his shirt, and wiping his nose on his sleeve. Even when he
interacts with external objects, attempting to appropriate them to meet
his needs, the young prince fails to comprehend their use value to him.
As a result, he appropriates *in*appropriately, using soup to wash his
hands, seeking shelter in water when it rains, combing his hair with a
drinking cup, and putting the cart before the horse.

It is in chapter 13, the *torchecul* or "arsewipe" episode, that Gargantua
begins to discern and assay the use value of objects around him. At once
a tribute to and a gentle parody of Renaissance ingenuity, this paradoxical encomium takes up the theme of invention first introduced in
Pantagruel's genealogy and resituates it in the regenerative lower bodily
strata of carnival. The result is a fresh view of invention, which Rabelais
associates with the intellectual development of both civilization as a
whole and the human child. Adopting a trial-and-error method similar
to that of contemporary empiricists, the young Gargantua cleans himself
successively with more than 20 swabs before deciding that the best
arsewipe is the neck of a plump downy goose (*G*, XIII, 44). The key to
Gargantua's success resides in the modification of exchange structures
used previously. Instead of using every object he encounters for a
different purpose, substituting both terms of the proposition "*a* facilitates *b*" in every activity, Gargantua learns to test the proposition by
substituting a single term at a time, then culling and ranking the
alternatives according to their value to him. Unlike the "adolescent" or
preschool-age Gargantua of chapter 11, who does nothing but eat, sleep,
and drink in no particular order, the maturing giant is a fully transitive
being who acts upon his environment for a specific purpose, identifying
his needs and systematically appropriating objects to fulfill them. The
new system is moreover economical, not in the sense of producing the
cheapest possible arsewipe, but because the time and energy required to
solve the problem have been pared. Like the arsewipe itself, this time-
cutting methodology cleans up waste in the system.

Just as the arsewipe is invented by trial and error, Gargantua's overall
development proceeds *à tâtons*: progressing, regressing, and progressing
once more. The most notable setback in Gargantua's intellectual growth
occurs under the tutelage of Thubal Holoferne and his successor, Jobelin
Bridé, Gargantua's Sorbonne tutors in chapter 14 who indoctrinate the

young giant in Scholastic argumentation, Christian dogma, and the offices of the Church. The result is a regressive state remarkably similar in structure to that of the prearsewipe Gargantua, whose nonproductive activities, such as his reversible "eating, drinking, and sleeping," are echoed by the rote memorization required by the sophist preceptors. After 5 years and 3 months under the tutelage of Thubal, for example, Gargantua can say his alphabet "by heart backwards" (*G*, XIV, 46), and at the end of an additional 18 years and 11 months, he can perform the same feat with *De modis significandi* and all of its glosses. Not only unproductive, Gargantua's studies under the Sorbonniqueurs constitute a regression to the prearsewipe days of corporal filth and squandered time. Ironically contending that "to brush one's hair, wash one's face and make oneself clean" is a "pure waste of time" (*G*, XXI, 61), the sophists instead commit 53 years and 10 months of Gargantua's young life to the alphabet, handwriting, and five stultifying books.

If the formation of judgment in *Gargantua* involves assessing the use value of objects, it also requires a similar evaluation of people. Having spared no time or expense in educating his son, Grandgousier "at last . . . realize[d] that though Gargantua was studying most industriously and spending all his time at it, he was profiting not at all" (*rien ne proffittoit*) (*OC*, 49). In addition to seeing no return on his investment, Grandgousier actually incurs a loss, for the once promising child has become "foolish" (*fou*) and "dull" (*niais* [49]), and the sophist pedagogy of Thubal and Jobelin is adjudged worse than nothing by a neighboring monarch: according to Don Philippe des Marais, "Gargantua would be better off learning nothing than studying books of that sort" (47). When compared with another youth his age, Gargantua proves to be inferior in virtually every category: his contemporary Eudemon, who has been tutored by the progressive Ponocrates, is described as having "better judgment, speech, bearing, and personality" (48) than the prince, despite a lesser investment of time ("but two years" [48]) in his studies.

Having given the sophist preceptors ample time to prove themselves, Grandgousier determines from the deterioration of their "product" that they are worthless as tutors. Consequently, the king discharges Jobelin and reinvests in Ponocrates, Eudemon's humanistic preceptor. Under the new regime, Gargantua once again cleans his body fastidiously, going so far as to "purge" from it the metaphoric waste that characterizes the Scholastic system. To avoid squandering time, the prince rises at four o'clock instead of his habitual nine o'clock each morning and combines mental and physical activities so effectively that not a single minute is lost. He hears lessons while in the bathroom, discusses them while dressing and eating meals, studies botany while returning from his physical workout, learns math while playing cards, and makes musical instruments while digesting. By discussing as well as memorizing his lessons, Gargantua assimilates and appropriates the material in a manner totally at odds with the Scholastic system, for after reciting his lessons by heart, he "argues certain practical, human, and utilitarian uses based upon the principles enumerated" (*G*, XXIV, 72). In addition to learning the use value of abstract lessons, Gargantua also comes to harness and manage his material environment productively, learning to play six instruments, protect himself with any weapon, swim under the most adverse circumstances, and scale trees as well as mountains.

The Bells of Notre Dame and the Picrocholine War: Perverted Structures of Exchange

Between Gargantua's Scholastic and humanistic training, he visits Paris and steals the bells of Notre Dame in a fascinating variation on the process of appropriation. While the theft may surprise modern readers in its deviation from social norms, more reminiscent of Panurge than a philosopher-prince, it is an integral part of the Gargantua legend. At the time of his transgression, the prince is in the charge of Ponocrates but is still a poorly educated and self-absorbed youth who has yet to begin his humanistic education. Coming almost directly on the heels of his sophistic education, the theft represents a payment in kind to the city of Paris, which, in addition to having "fools, dolts and gulls" (*G*, XVII, 51) for residents, also gave Gargantua his stultifying preceptors. That Gargantua himself views this episode in economic terms is suggested by his tit-for-tat explanation of a related transgression, in which he drowns countless Parisians in a stream of urine: "I think these boobies want me to pay my welcome here and give the bishop an offertory," he explains (51), offering his hosts death or nothingness in return for their inhospitality. His subsequent filching of the tower bells, which tolled at regular intervals to punctuate offices of the church, specifically "repays" the Sorbonne for the canonical hours he was forced to observe as a schoolboy.

Among all the theories attempting to justify the hero's aberrant crime, the most compelling by far is the simple fact that Gargantua wants the bells; unlike the pork-hunting friar who later attempts to steal the bells, "honestly" desisting because they are too heavy to carry,

Gargantua has the physical and political strength to appropriate virtually anything he covets. Oblivious to the moral and rational concerns that eventually make him a just and compassionate monarch, the prince acts out his selfish impulse like the child that he is, appropriating the bells to put around his mare's neck without pausing to consider their use value to others. To be sure, neither the friar nor Janotus de Bragamardo, the sophist charged with ransoming the bells, acts altruistically. As a member of the order of St. Anthony, which routinely collects ham and bacon from townspeople, the cleric hopes to use the bells to expedite his pork hunt, in an unwritten assimilation of *cloche* (bell) and *cochon* (pig). Similarly, Janotus stands to be rewarded with a pair of breeches and a yard and a half of sausage if the bells are returned to Notre Dame, in a second exchange of *cloche* for *cochon*.

More compellingly, though, Janotus points out that the bells are "for the good of the city" insofar as "everyone . . . uses them" (*G*, XIX, 56). While they may not protect the vineyards in quite the magical way Janotus suggests, the bells are indirectly linked to the economy of the entire area, helping residents organize their days and establishing the rhythm for grape harvests, which in turn supply the wine used in and after liturgical ceremonies by Janotus and his colleagues. By fragmenting the singular reference "bell," the narrator thus allows us—and the hero—to see that the microeconomic function of the bells for Gargantua is ultimately inferior to their macroeconomic function within the community as a whole.[10]

The harangue in which Janotus appeals for the return of the bells is at once a parody of Scholastic argumentation and a quid pro quo economic offer ultimately based less on the common good than on the same self-interest that prompted Gargantua to steal the bells in the first place. They are in fact profitable to the greedy Janotus, whose desire for the trousers promised as a reward for his services motivates him to work 18 days on his speech. Conversely, the bargaining chip that Janotus offers the Utopians is equally venial: if they return the bells, he promises them a roast pig—or still another exchange of *cloche* for *cochon*—as well as pardons and indulgences "without paying a penny" (*G*, XIX, 56). That the monks are willing to trade indulgences for stolen property suggests that the divine paradigm of salvation in return for good works has been perverted by the Church: as depicted by Rabelais, Janotus and his cohorts are in fact peddlers of eternal life, which they sell to the highest bidder regardless of moral qualifications.

True, there is a certain comic parity in the deal Janotus tries to strike with Gargantua. If we accept Janotus's contention that the bells are priceless, and that the Church has repeatedly refused "good money" from wishful buyers, then it makes perfect sense that Gargantua should be offered an equally precious ransom for their return, such as the forgiveness of his sins. The sublimity of this divine economy is eroded, however, by two extenuating factors. First, we know that the Church commonly sells indulgences for money, and second, the bells themselves are valued less as a transcendent link with God than for their salutary effect on the grape harvest, which in the short term provides the tippling monks a commodity more important than salvation. The fact that this commodity is wine, both a degrading substance and a transcendent symbol— linked with truth in the dictum *in vino veritas*—further interrogates this ecclesiastical economy by vacillating between celestial and terrestrial values.[11] This vertical vacillation helps explain Rabelais's contamination of the noun *cloche* (bell) with the verb *clocher*, "to limp," for if the Church and its symbols are not entirely crippled in this episode, it is fair to say that they emerge with a pronounced limp. This linguistic ambiguity first comes into play when the inebriated Janotus, waxing poetic about the bells in butchered Latin, speaks of "every bell . . . belling" ["*Omnis clocha . . . clochando, clochans*"] (*G*, XIX, 56). In Renaissance French, however, the gerund *clochant* means "limping," a pun that Janotus develops in a subsequent denunciation of his colleagues, urging them not to "limp [*clochez*] before cripples" (*G*, XX, 60).

After dismantling and reevaluating the metaphor "bells," Rabelais returns them to the *clocher* or "bell tower," a gesture decided upon by Gargantua prior to Janotus's harangue. The manner in which this decision is undertaken differs radically from the circumstances of the theft itself, when Gargantua acts alone and spontaneously. In the second sequence, when the sophists arrive to negotiate the bells' return, the humanist tutor Ponocrates pointedly gives his charge time to reflect on the situation, urging him to "have an answer and a plan ready" (*G*, XVIII, 54) prior to the interview. No longer acting alone, Gargantua reaches his decision through intellectual exchange with his friends, in a miniature Socratic banquet or colloquium. The restitution itself is a foregone conclusion, dictated by right reason, a sense of fair play, and Gargantua's growing awareness that the common good supersedes his own narrowly defined interests. In this sense, the return of the bells establishes the commerce with otherness that makes Thélème possible.

By returning the bells prior to Janotus's harangue, Gargantua turns the restitution of the bells into an act of conscience. Far from being totally altruistic, however, this premature surrender of the stolen goods is calculated to render Janotus's entire discourse worthless by depriving the signifiers or verbal tokens of their signifieds or underlying value. Like many a Scholastic philosopher before him, Janotus has constructed his entire *ratio* around a premise with no truth value. If his discourse is a fiction, then Janotus himself is a comedian similar to the famous Songecreux (*G*, XX, 58). For his time and the sheer comic brilliance of his plea, however, the Utopians shower him with the sausage and breeches that his colleagues had promised him for the return of the bells, along with firewood, wine, and, despite the austerity of his calling, a soft downy bed. Failing to grasp the quid pro quo nature of the transaction, in which his value as an entertainer is rewarded, Janotus interprets the Utopians' award as a gift freely given and proceeds to demand a second sausage and pair of breeches from the Sorbonne in payment for his role as an arbitrator. The university, however, refuses his request, not on the defensible grounds that Janotus provided no service, but rather on the more spurious grounds that their debt has been acquitted by Gargantua.

The episode of the purloined bells thus ends much as it began, in the realm of disputed exchange, but the locus has shifted from outside to inside the cloister, as Rabelais provides another satirical look at the Sorbonne theologians. The university's failure to recognize Gargantua's award to Janotus as a gift, first of all, reflects ironically upon the economic principles of the Church. Despite the nominal importance of giving in Christian theology, the concept of a gift with no strings attached, and motivated by "pure liberality" (*G*, XX, 59), rings false to Janotus's colleagues for rationalistic as well as financial reasons. For one thing, the term "gratis" or "free" that Janotus invokes as an explanation of the award carries connotations of gratuitousness, a concept diametrically opposed to Scholastic reason, its logical syllogisms, and its emphasis upon causality. The link between "gratis" and "grace" also echoes the extratextual dispute between Catholics and Reformers over the nature of salvation, viewed by the former as a commodity to be earned or bought, and by the latter as a gratuitous gift from God.

That the university reneges on its promised payment to Janotus further drains the theologians' rhetoric, like his own harangue, of all truth value. "You are not worth [anything]" (*G*, XX, 59), Janotus complains bitterly, moreover accusing his former colleagues of heresy, a misappropriation of divine theology that far exceeds Gargantua's original crime. It is not the giant, ironically, who winds up in court but the theologians themselves, as the litigation we expect between the Sorbonne and Utopians is displaced and trivialized. Instead of suing Gargantua for the return of the massive bells, Janotus draws up an indictment of his colleagues calling for the restitution of his sausage and breeches, symbolic of the manhood they have stripped from him. Far from resolving or clarifying the dispute, this transfer of the exchange process to a purely linguistic level merely results in waste: for the bodily waste accumulated by both camps during the lawsuit is a figure of time wasted by the litigation process, which is ludicrously disproportionate to the minimal quantity of goods being disputed.

The perverted structure of exchange outlined in the episode of the purloined bells finds fuller development in the Picrocholine War, whose arena is not religion but government and the marketplace. Like the previous episode, it too culminates in a gift: the Abbey of Thélème. Briefly stated, the *fouaciers* or "bakers" of Lerné, ruled by Picrochole, refuse to sell their *fouaces* or "cakes" to the shepherds of Seuilly, who, after pleading their case and receiving *fouets* or a "whipping" instead of *fouaces*, forcibly seize the merchandise and fling payment at their adversaries' feet. Even though Grandgousier apologizes and makes general reparation, Picrochole is so enraged that he rebuffs all efforts at conciliation, instead launching a full-scale war against the Utopians that he escalates into dreams of world conquest. In setting the stage for this dispute, the narrator goes out of his way to emphasize the state of perfect, albeit primitive, exchange that existed previously between the *bons voisins* or "good neighbors." The mere mention of shepherds conjures up visions of a golden-age economy in which goods are communally shared. While numerous references to money make it clear that the system at Lerné and Seuilly is not based on barter, the financial transactions described by the shepherd Frogier virtually exclude any profit motive, functioning instead for the fulfillment of mutual needs that is characteristic of moral rather than market economies: "Didn't you always sell us your cakes? And now you refuse to! It isn't neighborly of you. Do we do the same when you come here to purchase our fine corn that *makes* your cakes and your buns? What's more, we could have given you some of our grapes into the bargain" (*G*, XXV, 82).

By refusing to trade with their neighbors, the bakers disrupt the moral economy that previously prevailed and attempt to replace it with a market economy in which profit replaces sharing. Their decision to cart "ten or twelve horseloads" (*G*, XXV, 81) of cakes to Tours rather than exchange the goods locally reflects the real-life trend away from village markets and toward regional markets in the Renaissance. As they espouse a market economy over a moral one, the Lernéans implicitly devalue the old social ties that once bound them to the Utopians. Calling the Utopian peasants *riennevaulx* or "worthless" (*OC*, *G*, XXV, 79), the bakers denigrate their neighbors because they work outside with *étrons* or "excrement" instead of inside the kitchen. Labeling their former friends "turd herders" and "dung shepherds," the bakers claim that the socially inferior herdsmen are "unfit to taste dainty pastry" (81). Instead, say their neighbors, they should "be satisfied with coarse bread or hard-loaf" (81).

At once a parable on the origin of class and a satire of upward mobility in the Renaissance, this denigration of the older cultivator-producers by johnny-come-lately manufacturers ignores the dependency of the latter on the former. As the Utopian Frogier points out, it is the shepherds or cultivators who provide both the corn that goes into the cakes and the grapes for the wine with which they wash down the crumbs. To deny the debt is to forget that reciprocity is a two-way street, and that offenses as well as favors are usually returned: "Smother me in shit," says Frogier, "if you'll not be repenting of it, likely, when some fine day you have to call upon us. Then we'll do the like to you and don't forget it" (*G*, XXV, 82).

The bakers react to this warning with a gift, apparently seeking to restore friendly relations with the shepherds: "Step up, my lad," says the baker Marquet, "and I'll give you all the cake you can handle" (*G*, XXV, 82). The gift, however, turns out to be not a *fouace* but a *fouet*, which is also "given" (*bailla* [*OC*, *G*, XXV, 80]). The bakers' transition from a moral to a market economy is concomitant with a supplanting of reason by force, a documented state in the development of communal organizations that Rabelais structurally equates with folly. Blinded by greed, rage, and self-aggrandizement, the bellicose bakers fail to recognize that the rugged shepherds whom they are goading so foolhardily far outstrip them in sheer physical strength and courage: while the cooks ply their trade indoors with their lily-white hands, sheltered from the elements, the peace-loving shepherds battle wind, sun, rain, and carnivorous animals on a daily basis, in addition to tending the vineyards. To invoke jungle law against such a vastly superior opponent represents not just a breach of ethics but a breach of judgment as well, a misunderstanding of the basic economic principles that govern human behavior. Once attacked with a "gift" of blows, the shepherds have little choice but to return the favor in a show of reciprocity, physically overwhelming the weaker bakers and forcibly appropriating the disputed *fouaces/fouets*. Having triumphed according to the rules instituted by their opponents, the shepherds attempt to activate their own moral economy by paying for the booty at the "customary price" (82), offering the bakers a conciliatory gift of nuts and grapes in an attempt to restore harmony.

Instead of nursing their bruises and accepting the conciliatory gift, however, the defeated bakers return home in a funk and cry "foul play" to their king, who assembles an army on the spot "without stopping to consider the circumstances" (*G*, XXVI, 83). The conflict that ensues and the contrasts between the two opposing camps are couched largely in economic terms. While the Utopians are engaged in preparing grapes for harvest, the short-sighted Lernéans lay waste to the fields, "spoiling and ravaging" everywhere they pass and "sparing neither rich nor poor" (84). Like the Scholastic preceptors, they are wasteful. Further, the Lernéan infantry invades the Utopian cloister of Seuilly to *guaster* (*OC*, 83) or "lay waste" (*G*, XXVII, 85) to all the grape crop, in an ironic assimilation of *vengeance* and its near-homonym *vendange* or "harvest." Facing little initial resistance from the reclusive monks, who initially choose to pray rather than fight, the Lernéans lay down their arms to gather the grapes when they are attacked by a burlesque version of the Grim Reaper. Using his cross as both sword and scythe, the iconoclastic Friar John, who is described as "a true monk, if ever there was one" (86), at once harvests souls for God by mowing the enemy down like blades of wheat and saves the monastery's crop of grapes for wine from being harvested before their time and carted away. If Friar John's knightly demeanor is reinforced by the expressions "staff of the cross" (87), "clerk to the teeth" (86), "prowess" (89), and "heroically" (89) or "vaillamment" (*OC*, 87), his simultaneous role as harvester is evoked by our intratextual memory of Pantagruel, who in the preceding book swings Loup Garou like a *fauscheur* or "harvester" (*OC*, *P*, XXIX, 294). The analogy is reinforced by Friar John's back-and-forth style of fencing—"Thwack to the right, thwack to the left" (*G*, XXVII, 87)—and by the scythelike trajectory of his enemies' souls, which "go to Paradise on a road straight as a sickle" (88).

Just as the bakers run to their king in chapter 26, a shepherd informs Grandgousier of the Lernéans' wasteful assault on Utopia in a scene that deliberately mirrors its earlier counterpart. In diametrical contrast to Picrochole, however, who "bought" the bakers' jaundiced account of the proceedings "without asking any questions" (*sans plus oultre se interroguer*

[*OC*, *G*, XXVI, 81]), the astounded Grandgousier weighs and interrogates the information he has received, attempting to assimilate, understand, and react appropriately to the aberrant turn of events: "God . . . inspire me and counsel me for I know not what to do . . . all my life the one thing I worked for was peace, but now . . . I must . . . protect my unhappy people. . . . Nevertheless, I shall go to war only after I have exhausted every attempt at peace" (*G*, XXVIII, 90).

Throughout the novel's midsection, Rabelais systematically compares and contrasts the patterns of exchange espoused by the two kings and their communities. At the root of Picrochole's shortsighted politics of aggression lies greed and unbridled self-interest, at once a negative echo of the constructive hunger that heralds the advent of humanism in *Pantagruel* and a harbinger of Panurge's blinding *philautia* (selfish ego) of the *Third Book*. Grandgousier, on the other hand, is the diametrical opposite of his Lernéan rival, bending over backwards to placate and conciliate his neighbors. In addition to asking questions about the other side of events before buying the shepherd's story at face value, the Utopian monarch weighs the two kingdoms' past friendship against the current misunderstanding, attempts doggedly to fathom the logic and motivation behind Picrochole's aggression, showers the enemy camp with reparations and gifts of goodwill, and upon winning the eventual war, treats his prisoners humanely and grants them a stipend to facilitate their return home ("you shall each receive three months' wages" [*G*, L, 141]).

It is tempting to view Grandgousier's largesse as a function of Christian charity and noblesse oblige, two inherently moral stances that value giving over taking and that therefore are diametrically opposed to Picrochole's unholy greed and ignoble opportunism. The lines of demarcation are too blurred, however, to classify Picrochole along either religious or social lines. If on the one hand he is described as "abandoned" by God (*G*, XXXII, 96), he nonetheless views himself as a soldier of Christ bent on wiping out the "dogs, Turks, Mahomedans" (*G*, XXXIII, 101). Similarly, his parvenu tendencies, such as unabashed greed and a disregard for old familial bonds, are offset by allegations of similar class origins in Grandgousier, whose vast wealth paradoxically argues against his nobility: "For what *noble* prince ever had a farthing?" scoff Picrochole's advisers. "To hoard money is the act of a churl [*villain*]" (98).

Instead of following an inflexible moral code in which insults as well as favors are reciprocated in kind, Grandgousier exercises liberality based not only upon Christian teachings but upon rigorous cost-benefit analyses as well. Reparations are given to offending Lernéans not because they are due, but because they are of small cost in comparison to war: "Grandgousier announced that since it was only a question of a few cakes, he would attempt to conciliate Picrochole rather than go to war" (G, XXXII, 96). The Utopian king's willingness to make "a few" sacrifices to stave off massive losses contrasts dramatically with the economic mindset of Picrochole, who risks all his wealth, his kingdom, and his life to avenge the loss of "a few cakes."

Similarly, Grandgousier's generous treatment of prisoners and defeated enemies represents an investment that promises to pay high dividends. While Friar John chides the king for giving the prisoner Toucquedillon (Tickledingus) a fortune in gifts (G, XLVI, 132–33), the Lernéan is so moved by the gesture that he sacrifices his own life in an effort to restore peace. At the war's end, Grandgousier also "had each man given twelve hundred thousand crowns in cash" and "the castle and lands he preferred" (G, LI, 143). The rationale for this charity is based not upon biblical teachings but rather upon classical examples of "profitable" liberality and upon Grandgousier's own experience as a ruler. "By a ransom," points out Gargantua, referring to his father's generous treatment of an enemy named Alpharbal years earlier, "we might have extorted about twenty times one hundred thousand crowns. . . . Instead, they made themselves perpetual tributaries and undertook of their own accord to pay us yearly two million in gold at twenty-four carats fine. The first year they paid the entire sum; the second, of their own free will, twenty-three hundred thousand crowns; the third, twenty-six hundred thousand; the fourth, three millions" (G, L, 140–41). Even more than a loan, which must be repaid according to a predetermined schedule of interest, a gift generates dividends that far exceed the original investment, taking root and multiplying within the "hearts" (139) of recipients in the form of gratitude: "Their tribute increases in such proportions that soon we shall have to forbid them to bring us any more," continues Gargantua. "Such is the nature of gratitude. Time which mines and corrupts all other things on earth unfailingly increases and augments men's benefactions" (141). This advocacy of liberality, which is based upon the un-Picrocholian assumption that happy and prosperous subjects are less likely to revolt and more likely to be productive than their impoverished and discontented counterparts, will find further expression in the Utopians' colonization of Dipsody in the Third Book.[12]

If Grandgousier's approach to government coincides almost perfectly with the Socratic or Silenian principles of judgment outlined in the prologue, which are based on weighing and estimating situations and signifiers, the opposite holds true for Picrochole: the faculty for seeing both sides of the coin has failed the Lernéan king, whose unidimensional judgment propels him unchecked along the path of excess, greed, inflation, waste, and error. In addition to accepting the bakers' account of events at face value, the mentally crippled Lernéan king misjudges the worth of a subsequent token, the Utopians' peace offering. "Grandgousier is beshitting himself with terror," concludes Picrochole (*G*, XXXII, 97) upon seeing the cartloads of gold and coins from his old friend. By reading the reparations as an unambiguous sign of cowardice, however, Picrochole ignores the gift's alternative value as a gesture of goodwill, a misreading that causes him to overestimate his own military readiness relative to that of Utopia.

That the Lernéans are not prepared for war is clear. The troops are "rather poorly supplied with victuals," points out Captain Toucquedillon (*G*, XXXII, 97), referring to a state of famine in Lerné that arguably stems from Picrochole's oppressive political economy, which exploits and fails to nurture the downtrodden workers who provide his food. "Anoint a serf and he will whip you; whip a serf, he will anoint you," philosophizes Picrochole (*G*, XXXII, 97), in direct opposition to the liberality of Grandgousier.

In addition to overestimating their own resources, the Lernéans clearly undervalue the enemy's resistance, imagining that Grandgousier can be defeated "at the very outset" with a mere "half" (*G*, XXXIII, 98) of Picrochole's troops. Like military strategists thirsting to ply their craft, Picrochole's knights-in-waiting further fuel his greed and delusions by extending the projected locus of his aggression to France, Iberia, Italy, Africa, and the Holy Land. Like the aging Lear, who unwisely values empty flattery and empty promises over the unadorned truth, Picrochole accepts his advisers' flattery at face value, unable because of his mental dysfunction to weigh the value of their schemes against his own reality quotient or to recognize the signs of sycophancy and self-interest in their ambitious and fatuous prattle.

The inflationary prose of chapter 33, where the Lernéan military advisers generate a rhetorical copia on the theme of world conquest, is consubstantial with both the swelling of Picrochole's ego and the distended geographical contours of his imaginary empire. Representing the underbelly of Renaissance expansion and acquisition, Picrochole mentally gorges on plundered land and conquered peoples with a speed that precludes digestion. In contrast to Dipsody, onto which the Utopians painstakingly graft their own values in such a way that both cultures can thrive, the countries of Picrochole's imagined empire are quickly traversed and amassed much like coins or onomastic tokens—in an act of political as well as rhetorical *accumulatio*—rather than patiently assimilated and appropriated. Clearly Picrochole covets the countries to be annexed not for their projected use value, as part of a moral or material economy, but for their sheer impressiveness. In a reversal of Gargantua's belief that true wealth is knowledge—an underlying premise of the letter to Pantagruel (*P*, VIII)—Picrochole divorces *savoir* (knowing) from *avoir* (having) and envisions conquest without comprehension.

The Picrochole episode's intratextual echoes are inescapable; in its vacuity, the hyperbolic list of military objectives—which include "Carmania, Syria and all Palestine" (*G*, XXXIII, 101)—is reminiscent of the Limousin schoolboy's nonfunctional Latinisms, the Library of Saint-Victor's pompous titles, and Gargantua's massive but unproductive education under the sophists. At the same time, the scene's extratextual resonance should not be neglected. Often read as a caricature of Emperor Charles V, Picrochole reflects a rather widespread tendency on the part of Renaissance monarchs to engage in military, political, and geographical expansionism, often to the detriment of domestic stability and prosperity.

Within the parameters of Rabelais's fiction, the economic unbalance generated by Lerné's sudden shift from cooperation to competition and then conquest is paralleled by Picrochole's mental unbalance. If Grandgousier's approach to decision-making is measured and rational, the opposite holds true for Picrochole. Rabelais repeatedly describes the Lernéan king in terms of excess, disequilibrium, and unreason. "Picrochole is insane," says the Utopian chancellor Gallet, "our God has abandoned him" (*G*, XXXII, 96). The coupling of these epithets of insanity with godlessness further lends a metaphysical cast to Picrochole's excesses by excluding him from the divine economy that is the prototype and guarantor of equilibrated terrestrial exchange. When Gallet compares Picrochole to those who "break away from God and Reason to woo their own depraved inclinations (*G*, XXXI, 95), he attributes the renegade king's aberration to a fall from divine grace and guidance. At the same time, though, the divine economy itself is placed in question during the Picrocholine War by plague-related deaths, which seem to punish the just and reward the unjust in direct contra-

vention of fair rules of exchange. "Though the plague was raging in town
at the time," recounts the narrator, "[the Lernéans] broke in everywhere
spreading ruin and destruction as they went. Curiously enough, not one
of them fell ill; whereas the curates, vicars, preachers, physicians, sur-
geons and apothecaries who went to visit, dress, heal, preach and admin-
ister to the sick, had all died of infection. . . . Why was that,
gentlemen, I ask, and urge you to give the matter thought!" (*G*, XXVII,
85). Though both marauders and do-gooders enter plague-infected
households, none of the thieving Lernéans are tricked by the disease, but
doctors and priests contract it in droves in an apparent act of divine
injustice. In an alternative reading, however, the harsh judgment that
Rabelais metes out to priests and doctors, two professions he himself
practiced, satirically suggests that these professional do-gooders, far
from being universally beneficent, are on occasion far more greedy than
avowed thieves.

The writer's satire of monks, like his dissection of monarchs, is
couched primarily in economic terms. Just as he contrasts Picrochole's
greed and Grandgousier's largesse. Rabelais systematically compares the
wastefulness and sloth of most monks with the social involvement, work
ethic, and productivity of Friar John, an atypically thin monk who
deviates from all the medieval and Renaissance stereotypes of his profession. Thin and handsome, Friar John abjures the repetitive rituals that
fill the waking hours of his fellow monks at the monastery. Rabelais tells
us he "could polish off a mass or get through a vigil in record time" (*G*,
XXVII, 85–86) before moving on to more productive endeavors: "He
works hard, defends the oppressed, comforts the afflicted, succors the
ailing and guards the abbey's close" (*G*, XL, 117), in addition to catching
rabbits.

His colleagues, on the other hand, not just those in the monastery but
those who tutor Gargantua as well, use their time uneconomically by
sleeping late (*G*, XXI, 61) and avoiding productive activity in the fields
and vineyard. The typical monk, says Gargantua, "does not plow like the
peasant, defend his country like the soldier, heal the sick like the doctor"
(*G*, XL, 117). Perhaps because waste is an integral part of their daily
routine, the other monks at Seuilly initially do no more than pray when
the Lernéans pillage their vines, threatening to waste the entire harvest.
And while these prayers, according to Grandgousier, are said "to God on
our behalf" (117) in an effort to influence the divine economy, Gargantua
disputes even this contention: "If they pray for us, do you know why?
Because they're terrified of losing their white bread and savory stews"

(117). Far from altruistic, the prayerful "work" of monks, according to the prince, is ultimately selfish, for they use the heavenly economy to maintain their parasitic status within the earthly economy. Rabelais's clerics also play a disruptive role within the generational economy of (re)production. Their vows of celibacy, dating only from the eleventh century and a target of reform theology, officially relegated monks to the role of nonproducers: by officially refusing sexual commerce and opting instead for the *vita contemplativa* or nondialogic lifestyle, they became nonproductive cogs in the generational economy.

Thélème: The Ideal of Perfect Reciprocity

The imperfect structures of exchange that unfold in the *Gargantua*'s midsection find resolution in the Abbey of Thélème, which comprises chapters 52 through 58. Founded through the generosity of Gargantua, who makes a gift of the abbey to Friar John for services rendered during the war, Thélème constitutes a utopian solution to the theft, greed, war, and monastic abuses that have both interrupted and contributed to Gargantua's education. At once court and cloister, monastic and antimonastic, Thélème has a twofold structural function. With its emphasis on sharing, first of all, it provides a utopian resolution to the greed and self-interest of the Picrocholine War. Second, Thélème's admission of women as well as men, all of whom use their time productively, counterbalances the otherworldly nonproductivity of Friar John's first monastery. Just as the good king Grandgousier is contrasted with the bad king Picrochole in the *Gargantua*, and the good monk John with his bad colleagues at Seuilly, so the idealized Thélème is systematically compared with bad monasteries. Not only are women admitted, but this abbey has no walls, and activities are determined not by fixed canonical hours but by the dictates of reason: "Because all monasteries and convents on earth are compassed, limited and regulated by hours, at Thélème no clock or dial of any sort should be tolerated. On the contrary, their time here would be governed by what occasions and opportunities might arise" (*G*, LII, 144).

This emphasis on reason at Thélème both responds to and counters the unreason and excess of Picrochole and the rigid, unreasoning canons of religious orders. Other antimonastic characteristics of Thélème include its physical beauty and that of its residents, who are far removed from the "wall-eyed, lame, hunchbacked, ill-favored, misshapen, half-witted, [and] unreasonable" misfits who traditionally "took the veil" or "entered monasteries" (*G*, LII, 144). The clerics' traditional vows of poverty are moreover replaced at Thélème by luxury and wealth, and far from taking vows of celibacy for life, the inhabitants of Thélème are free to marry once they leave the monastery: "Since the religious usually made the triple vow of chastity, poverty and obedience, at Thélème all had full leave to marry honestly, to enjoy wealth and to live in perfect freedom" (145).

Just as Thélème corrects the unproductive and unnatural strictures of monasteries, figured by Seuilly, it also rectifies the Lernéans' greed and self-interest by proposing a system of exchange and government based upon concern for the interest of others. From the abbey's inception, males defer to the judgment of women in matters of fashion, and instead of arguing over activities, the inhabitants take turns indulging their respective special interests. The harmonious social organization and interpersonal relationships at the abbey owe their success at least in part to the flexible system of change and exchange that prevails. Instead of being locked into unidimensional codes of behavior and their own personal interests, the inhabitants of Thélème vary their behavior according to the exigencies of each moment and the will of others within the group. Each item of clothing is chosen "according to their taste and pleasure" (*G*, LVI, 151) as inhabitants vary the texture and color of items to suit the season, time of day, their sex, mood, and numerous other variables. Likewise, their schedules are governed not by "law, statute, or rule" but by "free will" (*G*, LVII, 154), respect for others, and common sense, all of which adapt to the exigencies of circumstance.

By providing a solution to the exchange-related problems dominating Rabelais's second novel, Thélème lends the *Gargantua* a structural and thematic "neatness" that is missing from the Gallic monk's other books. At first glance, Thélème appears uncharacteristic of Rabelais in that he has consolidated major themes, tied up loose ends, and resolved the exchange-related tensions in a single harmonious statement about human reciprocity. Gargantua's heuristic education, our own quest for judgment, the Picrocholine War, and Rabelais's monachal satire all find at least partial resolution in the dialogic give-and-take of the abbey, whose educated inhabitants base their decisions upon a concordant combination of personal inclination and consideration of others.

Despite the abbey's structural openness, however, it becomes evident upon closer analysis that the system succeeds largely by virtue of its nondialogic closure. The illusion of heterogeneity produced by admitting both sexes to the abbey is offset by the inhabitants' homogeneous background: all are "free, of gentle birth, [and] well-bred" (*G*, LVII,

154). Given this similar predisposition, it is not surprising that the inhabitants "all wished to do what they saw pleased one of their number" (154). Arguably these clonelike paragons are all of one will from the outset, and if this absence of difference fosters concord, it also precludes the possibility of true dialogue. While the men and ladies are active, moreover, the ones "so adroit on horseback and on foot, so athletic, so lively" (154) and the others "deft at handwork and needlework, so skilful in feminine arts" (155), it is clear from the diversionary nature of their pastimes that they are leisured consumers rather than working producers, living not of their own labor but off the labor of silent lower classes living in the shadow of the cloister.

   That Rabelais recognizes the limitations of his abbey, and its failure to constitute anything more than a dream, is indicated by several loose ends, typically Rabelaisian, that undermine the apparent neatness and uncharacteristic closure of the *Gargantua*.[13] Chapter 57, the last describing Thélème, ends with three paragraphs that effectively "deconstruct" the abbey. The first characterizes the inhabitants in terms of inexpressibility topoi—beginning with *jamais* (never)—that effectively relegate Thélème to the never-never land of fantasy: "Never had earth known knights so proud, so gallant. . . . Never were ladies seen so dainty, so comely . . . so frank and so free as these" (*G*, LVII, 154–55). Foreshadowing Panurge's quest for a wife, the next paragraph chronicles the exodus of certain inhabitants from the abbey for the purpose of marriage: "When the time came for a man to leave the abbey . . . he took with him one of the ladies . . . and they were married" (155). The last paragraph completes the abbey's deconstruction by introducing an enigma found in its foundation, possibly during its construction but just as probably after its destruction, when only ruins remain.

   By terminating his *Gargantua* with an enigma and the contradictory readings given it, Rabelais reaffirms the dialogic principles that are his trademark. Far from being Rabelais's definitive statement on human relations, Thélème is upstaged by the enigma and transformed into a utopian hypothesis engaging in eternal dialogue with a different sort of prophecy, its polar opposite: in opposition to the consonant and stable harmony of Thélème, the *Enigme en prophétie* (Prophetical Riddle) predicts a return to the same conflict and dissension characterizing the Picrocholine War. Now ascribed to Mellin de Saint-Gellais, the enigma counters the harmony of Thélème with discord and *débatz* in which "friend shall contend with friend" (*G*, LVIII, 156), "arrogant sons shall" rise up against their fathers, and subjects shall rebel against their masters

(156). The Thélèmites' common sense and good judgment are further replaced in the enigma by a return to blind authority and error: "Ay, one and all shall bow to doctrines and to rules / Set by a herd of ignoramuses and fools" (156).

Friar John's ludic reading of the discordant enigma, which he claims is the allegory of a tennis match (*G*, LVIII, 158), is consistent with the rhetorical games and badinage we associate with Mellin de Saint-Gellais. At first glance, it lessens the apocalyptic enigma's force as a response to the utopian abbey. Upon closer inspection, however, we note that Friar John's reading is preceded by Gargantua's more sobering interpretation of the allegory as a reference to the strife and dissension brewing in France over evangelical reforms. In more general terms, the enigma may be viewed as an allegory of reading itself, a dialogic process fraught with dissension and resembling the back-and-forth movement of a tennis ball being exchanged between two or more players. If that textual polyvalence frustrates our positivistic tendencies, we must remember that medieval allegories operated at not one but four levels: even before Rabelais, allegories commonly had more than one "meaning." As a figure of textuality, the enigma brings the *Gargantua* full circle by rearticulating the problems of reading and judgment posed in the prologue. Like the reversible Silenus box, and the medullar *os* or "bone," the tennis match is a reference to the dialogic nature of textuality. Together with the Thélèmites' marriage in chapter 57 and the theme of prophecy posed by the enigma, this inquiry into reading serves as a bridge to the *Third Book*, in which Panurge attempts to determine his future wife's fidelity through intellectual exchange, prophecy, and the reading of ambivalent texts.

As a view of history, moreover, the back-and-forth structure of the Prophetic Riddle echoes the first chapter of *Gargantua*, in which Alcofribas discourses on the inevitable fall of nobles and ascent of paupers through time: all subject to the wheel of fortune's vagaries, princes and paupers alike trade places with each half-revolution of the circle. Coming directly on the heels of Thélème, this cyclical view of history further erodes the abbey's value as a permanent solution to human conflict, disorder, and unreason by suggesting that just as peace follows war, conflict follows peace. For the harmony of Thélème is sandwiched between past and future discords: the Picrocholine War and the Prophetic Riddle. Thélème thus emerges as a transitory respite between past and future dissonances.

Despite the structural coherence and polished prose that have garnered the *Gargantua* accolades as his technical masterpiece, Rabelais ultimately eschews the temptation to give the book a harmonious resolution, opting instead to end it as he began: with a reversible dialogue between opposite readings that recalls the *Pantagruel*. To be sure, there are changes: Rabelais's earthiness has abated, his comedy is less broad, his satire less caustic, and his prose more overtly cerebral than visceral. Like the *Pantagruel*, however, the *Gargantua* is inextricably bound up in the world of exchange, and it is this dialogue between self and the other, between oneness and alterity, that more than any other element lends the work its conceptual unity.

Chapter Four
The *Third Book*

Rabelais apprehensively compares his *Third Book* to the two-toned slave, black on one side and white on the other, that Ptolemy I ceremoniously presented to the Egyptians following a campaign abroad. Instead of being awestruck by the slave's rare pigmentation as their leader had intended, the public "inveighed against what they considered a detestable monster spawned by a freak of nature" (*TB*, Prol., 297–98), failing to recognize the man's intrinsic humanness. By analogy, the Gallic monk's second sequel to the *Pantagruel*, published in 1546, departs so radically in appearance from the mock epic format and marketplace allure of its predecessors that some readers may view it as a literary monster that is un-Rabelaisian. Already on the wane in *Gargantua*, the carnivalesque elements so prevalent in Rabelais's first novel have been retired to the back burner in the *Third Book*. Also gone are the burlesque battle scenes, trumped-up genealogies, and far-fetched nativities of the mock epic tradition, along with the shifty voice of Alcofribas, who at once commands and undermines our credulity. Taking over his narrative duties is one of the learned doctors he mocks: not the patent-medicine peddler of the prologue to *Pantagruel* but his respectable alter ego, a noted physician named François Rabelais whose eminent reputation as a humanist is reflected in the classicizing bent of his discourse. Consisting of a colloquium on marriage flanked by two paradoxical encomia, both classically inspired forms in their broad outlines, the *Third Book* seems far removed from the literary sideshow that first opened its doors, and covers, to paying fair-goers in 1532.

Like an inside-out Silenus box, however, the seemingly staid *Third Book* proves "lively at the source and of perpetural flow" (Prol., 299), surprising us with the familiar flavor of its marrow. The new volume's story line is consistent with that of its predecessors, beginning where the *Pantagruel* leaves off, at the end of the Dipsodian War. After a 14-year hiatus, the sequel fails to conform in every detail to the advance billing given it by Alcofribas, who promises that Panurge will marry and be cuckolded within a week and that Pantagruel will marry the daughter of

Prester John, King of India. Instead of marrying off the protagonists as promised, the *Third Book* captures them on the uneasy brink of matrimony, debating its pros and cons with a parade of wise and foolish fools. For the Utopian prince, Gargantua's only direct heir, the question of whether or not to marry is moot: for reasons of state, lineage, and patrimony, his father will choose him a bride sight unseen. Far more complicated and hence richer in novelistic possibilities is the case of Panurge, whose footloose and fancy-free status leaves him such a plethora of options, matrimonial and otherwise, that he stands paralyzed before them like a child in a candy store, unable to decide on a single "purchase" for fear that another might prove tastier.

The exchange-related analogy is appropriate, for despite its learned trappings, the *Third Book* revolves around the same economic principles that govern transactions in the marketplace. The novel's central problem—Panurge's decision over whether to get married, and if so, to whom—is fundamentally a metaphor about investment that projects the *Gargantua*'s relatively simple cost-benefit analyses into a future filled with risks and contingencies. Suspended between his desire for "profit" (heirs) and his fear of risk (cuckoldry), Panurge proceeds to amass information about his "investment" (marriage) like any cautious investor today: analyzing his own needs, talking to friends, reading about the "product," and consulting investment counselors before committing himself to the venture. In sequence, he consults classical literature, his own dreams, a sibyl, a deaf-mute, a dying poet, his friend Epistemon, an astrologer, Friar John, a theologian, a physician, a philosopher, a judge, and a fool, hoping not so much for mere pros and cons as for risk-free, guaranteed "inside knowledge" about the future losses and/or earnings of his investment.

The erudition displayed in this *Third Book* colloquium is so massive that we often view it exclusively in terms of intellectual exchange, using it as a barometer of Rabelais's shift from popular to learned discourse. Certainly Panurge's consultations expand and enlarge upon the educational itinerary mapped out for Pantagruel in the letter from his father: by becoming an "abyss" of knowledge in his turn, Panurge hopes to resolve his matrimonial quandary. At the same time, however, the door-to-door "unveiling" of most discussants and the anomalous presence of a witch, a fool, and astrologer among them give the learned proceedings an unmistakable sideshow quality reminiscent of the early Rabelais. Far from rejecting the carnivalesque entirely, Rabelais has in fact grafted it onto his learned discourse, turning wise men and fools alike into freaks.

The same principle holds true for the mock-epic format of the first two books, which is transformed rather than eliminated from the new volume. Clearly the colloquium on marriage enables Rabelais to air his own thoughts on the popular "woman question," a debate on the merits and humanness of females that has roots in both medieval and classical literature. Overemphasizing the "woman question" has, however, led scholars to neglect the syntactical logic of marriage within the mock-epic format of the Pantagrueline Tales. Not a requisite step in the epic, which may or may not include a subplot involving the hero's marriage, matrimony is nonetheless a form of commerce with otherness that completes the protagonist's journey to adulthood, helping him sublimate his own greed and self-interest within the moral economy and (re)productive cycles of his culture.

Between Barker and Bard: The Selling of Skepticism in the Prologue

In confirmation of this thesis, we find echoes of both the epic bard and the carnival barker in the *Third Book* prologue, which underneath its learned patina is no less sales-oriented than its 1532 counterpart. By addressing himself to *buveurs* (*OC, TB*, Prol., 319) or "drinkers" and the "gouty" (*TB*, Prol., 293), the prologue's narrator refers figuratively to fellow humanists who thirst and hunger after truth. At the same time, though, the exact coincidence of his new narratees with the "gout[y]" (*P*, Prol., 162) and "drinkers" (*G*, Prol., 3) of the first two prologues leaves him with one foot planted on the sideshow caravan, suspending us between learned and popular readings of the text. The narrator's queries as to whether we have "seen" (*TB*, Prol., 293) the philosopher Diogenes explore the difference between physical sight and intellectual insight, without a doubt, but the repeated emphasis upon "seeing" reinforces the prologue's carnival overtones by transforming the barrel-rolling Diogenes, admittedly eccentric, into a sideshow attraction to be "viewed." Though he receives top billing, Diogenes is not the only idiosyncratic specimen of humanity on display on the proscenium of the prologue, which is an inherently theatrical form. Joining the cynical philosopher in this lineup of living oddities are a man blind from birth (293), King Midas of the monstrous ears (293), a two-humped camel from Asia (297), and the two-toned man who is black on one side and white on the other (297).

Lending further continuity to this alternative reading are the narrator's two mentions of *escuz* or "money" within the first three paragraphs. While the second of these is a commonplace allusion to the wealth of Midas—"you have not as many golden crowns as Midas" (*TB*, Prol., 293)—the first is a subversive analogy between sunlight or clarity and the glint of money: "It is beautiful to see the clarity of (wine and coins) the sun [*la clairté du (vin et escuz) soleil*]" (our translation; *OC*, 319). Both references give a mercenary flavor to what otherwise passes for pure literary exchange, reminding us that underneath his fancy rhetoric the huckster is making a sales pitch. Instead of "hyping" the new book's quality, as Alcofribas does in the prologue to *Pantagruel*, the *Third Book* narrator invites each reader to pass judgment on the contents, which may not be pleasing to all palates: "If it does not seem good to you, then by all means leave it," he advises (298). The new focus of his advertising campaign is not so much quality as quantity or copia: the appealing promise of more pleasure for less money in a something-for-nothing transaction. Inviting readers to "imbibe freely . . . without paying" (298), the narrator insists that his cask is "inexhaustible" (299).

This transformation of Rabelais's "wine" into a gift rather than a purchase automatically recalls evangelical theology, according to which salvation is freely given to the elect, a restricted group coinciding with Rabelais's selectively "invited" readership. While this theological reading is sustained by the biblical connotations of Rabelais's cask, whose lively source and perpetual flow echo the "everlasting fountain" of Christian teaching in the New Testament, the metaphor of (s)election also functions as an advertising ploy, designed to increase demand, and hence the book's selling value, by reducing its availability and distributing it "by invitation only."[1]

The barker's salesmanship is complemented by that of the bard, who uses Diogenes' barrel rolling during the siege of Corinth as a prelude to his own patriotic discourse on behalf of France, long beleaguered by Charles V. Since the narrator considers himself unfit for military duties, he tells us that he has opted to roll his textual "cask" or "tub" in service of his "most noble kingdom" (*TB*, Prol., 295), at once calling his comrades to action and applauding their return: "Since I may not be the fellow-soldier of our brave warriors, I shall be their excellent butler, ready to comfort them to the best of my poor ability and with the best of my rich wine, when they return from the alarms of war. I shall also be the tireless singer of their praises and prowesses" (297). These references to his countrymen's "prowesses" and "glorious feats [*glorieux faits d'armes*]" (our translation; *OC*, 326) recall the high style of classical epics and the medieval *chanson de geste*. By concluding the passage with a denigrating reference to the war god Mars, however, the shifty narrator deflates his epic alter ego in a move worthy of Alcofribas: "Nor shall I fail unless March [Mars] fails to fall in Lent, which the cunning lecher will take care not to do" (297).

Rabelais's juxtaposition of bard and barker within a single prologue also demonstrates that both narrative voices are engaged in selling, one overtly and the other covertly. When he praises both France and the war effort in general, the Rabelaisian bard is applying the barker's sales tactics to a new product: France's ongoing military effort in the sixteenth century, and more specifically, the king's attempt to raise financial support for that effort, which was beginning to deplete the treasury. Denigrating those "spectators" who watch the "performance" (*TB*, Prol., 296) without paying for it, the Rabelaisian bard-barker combines a call to arms with an implicit call for money: "Disgraceful, I repeat, not to contribute to the great cause this nothing which is my all. Tell me what honor falls to such as merely look on, liberal with their eyes but niggardly with their efforts, hoarding their money" (296).

Despite this show of patriotism, which was intended to increase his own wealth along with the royal coffers, Rabelais does not fully develop either the bard's voice or that of the barker. On the contrary, he deviates from the barker's style even more often than he adheres to it: his invitation to drink "without paying" (*TB*, Prol., 298), his "gift" of salable wine, and his fear that his latest venture may be a commercial failure are all out of character for the brash, greedy huckster.

Similarly, there is much in the *Third Book* that belies the prowar sales pitch of the Rabelaisian bard. For one thing, the presence of Diogenes, a cynic and doubter, within or at least alongside a discourse advocating blind allegiance to king and country results in two messages, one credulous and the other incredulous. While Rabelais claims to "almost agree" (*TB*, Prol., 295) with Heraclitus in thinking war (*bellum*) is beautiful (*belle*), his subsequent reference to the "tragic comedy [*tragicque comédie*]" (our translation; *OC*, 324) of France's military efforts makes us look critically at warmongers as well as detractors. The body itself of the *Third Book* bears out this ambivalent attitude toward the military ethos so glorified by the epic bards. The first chapter is devoted not to the Dipsodian War, described purely in negative terms, but rather to peace settlements, reconciliation, and the (re)production that follows conflict. Panurge's reluctance in chapter 7 to join the army, along with the entire discussion of marriage and reproduction that ensues, are diametrically opposed to the bard's prowar sales pitch in the prologue. For while it is true that marriage frequently follows war in the epic, the author's devotion of 40 chapters to matrimony and reproduction encourages us to reassess the bard's introductory advocacy of militarism.

Far from selling his country's war effort or blind patriotism, a reading that simply does not hold up under scrutiny, the bard-barker is marketing something entirely different. As the reference to Diogenes and the emphasis on "seeing" suggest, the real product being offered for consumption is not propaganda but judgment, an insight based upon systematic doubt rather than blind credulity. By virtue of its Christian connotations, the Rabelaisian "cask" symbolizing this commodity carries with it the promise of revelation inherent in the dictum *in vino veritas*. Because of the keg's simultaneous association with Diogenes, however, "truth" within the container proves to be uncertainty itself. Posited as both source and product of the Rabelaisian narrator's inspiration, the barrel with its mysterious contents joins a host of other receptacle or container images in Rabelais, such as the Silenus box and the marrow bone, that paradoxically hold and hide their contents.[2] Together they symbolize the dichotomous nature of textuality, analogous to the book's form or "cover."

By virtue of its connotative plurality, the *Third Book* cask constitutes a strong test of the "buying" skills of readers honed by the Silenus box. To invest in the cask is an act of faith. To facilitate our investment, the narrator offers us a free sample: the prologue itself. But the nature of this promised insight varies according to the traditions being invoked: alternately light and burdensome, heavy and light, the connotations of the cask range from skepticism to blind faith in revealed truth. Like the neon lights of modern advertising, which flash and then disappear, the cask tantalizes us with glimmers of skepticism, forbidden knowledge, Christian revelation and its blind faith, Bacchic illumination, hope and despair. All find their way into the epistemological kaleidoscope of Rabelais's cask. Because of its polyvalence, the cask challenges the buyer's judgment far more rigorously than does the ambivalent Silenus box.

Indeed, the entire *Third Book* prologue functions much like a modern billboard or preview, with one major difference: instead of "hyping" salient elements in the plot, the Rabelaisian prologue mirrors principal themes of the text to come. The narrator's quandary over what to do during the fortification of Paris, like the reader's choice about whether to invest in the textual sideshow, raises the question of commitment or investment that later informs Panurge's matrimonial dilemma. Likewise, the back-and-forth movement of the barrel foreshadows the reluctant bridegroom's vacillations on the subject of marriage, which stem in part from an innate skepticism foreshadowed by Diogenes' presence in the prologue. The curious application of this systematic doubt to the question of marriage, an anomaly that has long puzzled critics, is also linked by antiphrasis to the discourse on war dominating the prologue. By virtue of its procreational potential, matrimony represents the direct opposite of fighting, which is destructive. Viewed in this light, Panurge's colloquium may be seen as an extension of the war-related dilemma faced by Diogenes and the Rabelaisian narrator in the prologue.

Despite the dearth of women in both the prologue and text, the woman question itself is foreshadowed in the antechamber. In the body of the text, the depiction of females by Doctor Rondibilis as an aberration of nature (*TB*, XXXII) fits in with the sideshow atmosphere of the prologue: by virtue of her otherness or difference from man, woman logically fits into the parade of anomalies placed on display by the carnival barker. In addition to preparing the way thematically for the "woman question," the prologue also contains two mentions of women: the first, which foreshadows Panurge's fear of being beaten, is a sly tribute to the courage in combat of ancient Corinthian courtesans (*TB*, Prol, 294–95); the second is a comparison of the narrative "cask" to Pandora's forbidden jug (299), which upon being opened unleashes both hope and evil into the world. While the narrator mentions only the positive contents of the jar, which is the Greek equivalent of Eve's apple and the tree of knowledge, most humanists familiar with Hesiod's writings would have recognized that the bottle also contains despair. Because of its duality, the symbol constitutes not just an enticement to "buy" but a warning to prospective reader-buyers like Panurge who seek to unlock the secrets of women and, more generally, to mortals like Sisyphus, Prometheus, and Panurge who aspire to steal knowledge from the gods. Signaling both "come hither" and "go away," like women in androcentric mythology, the symbol exercises a double attraction by virtue of its very negativity.

Perhaps in recognition of this analogy, Rabelais dedicates his *Third Book* to a female, the king's sister Marguerite de Navarre, whose role as *destinataire* serves a textual as well as political function. Both female and humanist, therefore doubly curious, she symbolizes the inquisitive reader who will take up the narrator's challenge and open up the covers of Rabelais's half-forbidden text.

Reciprocity Revisited: From the Praise of Debts to the Project of Matrimony

If by virtue of its plot the *Third Book* is a sequel to *Pantagruel*, its thematic content more nearly resembles that of the *Gargantua*, whose concluding chapters are devoted to the ideal of positive reciprocity and moral economics. The same ideal governs the peace settlements implemented by Pantagruel and Gargantua after the Dipsodian War in chapter 1 of the *Third Book*, when Utopian rulers choose to nurse, support, and assist conquered nations instead of "pillaging, harrying, vexing, oppressing, and tyrannizing them" (*TB*, I, 301). To this end, they send a colony of Utopian intellectuals and craftsmen to improve the annexed territory, to share their talents with the newly subjugated people, and to educate the Dipsodian citizens as they do their own children, not only by precept but, more important, by example. In this way, the Utopians teach their neighbors justice by dealing with them fairly and earn their love and loyalty by treating them with caritas. Not wholly altruistic, this kid-gloved handling of the Dipsodians stems from a rigorous cost-benefit analysis on the part of Pantagruel: the least expensive way to win over the Dipsodians' loyalty, obedience, and affection is to treat them kindly, in such a way that "they will be convinced that never a . . . prince in Christendom seeks fewer enemies and more friends" (301). The narrator further suggests that this reciprocal pattern of exchange, in which the rulers "[give] suck" (301) to their subjects instead of feeding upon them (*les peuples mangeant* [*OC*, 331]), fosters a more productive economy than harsher political systems. The "well-fed" Utopians, who "imbibed the sweetness and light of [Pantagruel's] government" (301), multiply like locusts, while the less gently treated Dipsodians live in a land "sparsely inhabited and partly wilderness" (301).

A similar but far more egalitarian paradigm of reciprocity informs chapters 2 through 5 of the *Third Book*, as Panurge, the new Lord of Salmagundi, squanders the fortune Pantagruel has given him and proceeds to wax poetic about debt. This satirical episode, improbably entitled "Eloge des Debtes" (The Praise of Debts), is an example of paradoxical encomium, a genre in which objects of dubious merit are celebrated. If the form recalls Lucian and his panegyric of such lowly creatures as the fly and parasites, the content is a volatile and syncretic mixture of intertexts, including Plato, Aristotle, Saint Paul, and Erasmus, in which financial debt serves not only as a measure of the debtor's virtue but also serves as a metaphor for the following: cosmic cooperation or the harmony of the spheres; generational sharing or procreation; mutual assistance or caritas; and the interdependence of different organs in the human body.[3]

Like most paradoxical discourses, the encomium is so multifunctional that it is difficult to get a handle on it. On one level, Panurge's tribute to the golden age and his denigration of wealth for its own sake perpetuate many of the ideals of sharing and respect for others outlined in Thélème and in the postwar peace settlements of *Gargantua* and *Pantagruel*. Like many hypocrites, however, Panurge is espousing altruistic values for self-serving reasons, to justify his lack of fiscal responsibility. Because these altruistic and community-oriented principles of exchange are restated time after time in the Pantagrueline Tales, usually by virtuous figures such as Grandgousier, Gargantua, and Pantagruel, we have every reason to believe that Rabelais himself holds the ideals in high regard. By making his rogue the mouthpiece of these noble principles in defense of his own fiscal irresponsibility, however, the author destabilizes his discourse, inviting us to scrutinize both the values and the character paying lip service to them. Ever the sophist, Panurge has built an inflationary mountain of rich and swollen rhetoric to represent the abyss of his finances, half-humorously and half-seriously attempting to justify his improvidence by arguing that imprudence is prudence, hedonism temperance, cupiditas caritas, weakness a sign of strength, and borrowing a form of sharing. By incurring debts, he not only keeps creditors in business but also makes them solicitous of his health.

Alternately base and high-minded, ludicrous and lyrical, the discourse is not devoid of ethical merit and poetic appeal. His contention that humans are born for "mutual help and succor" (*TB*, III, 311) is a cornerstone of Christian charity and classical ethics with which few humanists would take issue. What rings false is not the principle but the analogy underlying its application to Panurge's bankruptcy. Far from being incurred for humanitarian reasons, as he would lead us to believe, Panurge's debts are in effect the result of gross overconsumption and self-indulgence. Instead of funding projects inspired by love for his neighbor, Panurge's borrowings help pay the prostitutes who satisfy his lust.

To discourage readers from "buying" Panurge's rationalization at face value, Rabelais draws our attention to the faulty analogies and specious reasoning upon which it is founded. "[For all your fine talk] you'll *not* find me contracting debts," asserts Pantagruel (*TB*, V, 315), cutting through his friend's rhetoric to point out its fundamental mendacity: "I agree with the Persians who hold that lying, as a vice, comes second only to owing. [For debts and lies are ordinarily linked together]" (316). Without rejecting either the concept of caritas or the occasional necessity of borrowing and lending, Pantagruel condemns chronic debt on the grounds that no reciprocity is involved: for despite Panurge's pretty talk of sharing, the borrowing he envisions is all one-sided. For all his talk of reciprocity, not only does Panurge fail to pay back his debts, or become a creditor in his own right, but he also uses the loans selfishly to sate his own appetite instead of reinvesting them in a socially responsible way that would profit both him and his compatriots. This inability to give or even to recognize the needs of others will play a major role in Panurge's matrimonial deliberations.

More than providing insight into Panurge's psychology, and perpetuating the theme of reciprocal exchange, "The Praise of Debts" reflects ironically upon fiscal and philosophical practices of the sixteenth century. Panurge's invocation of Platonic idealism as a metaphor for fiscal debt reflects satirically on Platonizing tendencies in Renaissance literature in the 1540s. The parodical overtones of Platonic cosmology are sustained by Panurge's application of its lofty principles to the material realm of physiology and generation more properly associated with Aristotle and by irreverent lapses into vulgarity ludicrously at odds with his idealistic rhetoric.

Not just a parody of literary excesses, "The Praise of Debts" reflects the very real fiscal crisis in France in the sixteenth century. On the one hand, debt was not a wholly negative phenomenon. Letters of credit had come increasingly into vogue in the late fifteenth and early sixteenth centuries, and their system of deferred payments enabled navigators, merchants, and investors to undertake investments they might otherwise have been forced to forgo. One early result of borrowing was increased international trade, a higher standard of living, industrial expansion, and a generally booming economy. On the negative side, however, the French monarchy's growing taste for opulence and borrowing to finance a series of disastrous wars had practically bankrupted the treasury by midcentury, rendering its royal bonds and banknotes virtually worthless; in conjunction with the increasing supplies of bullion pouring into

Europe, this debt-induced devaluation of currency helped generate an inflationary crisis affecting the buying power of even private citizens like Rabelais. Joining the parade of debtors was the old *noblesse d'epée* in France, whose penchant for luxury and lack of revenue led to wide-scale borrowing, for-profit deforestation of timberlands, and, in some cases, eventual sale of the manor to rich merchants and manufacturers.

If Panurge is a parody of Platonizing intertexts, then, he is also a parody of extratextual debtors, who are no less numerous than their literary counterparts. Less a debtor than a thief in the *Pantagruel*, the *Third Book* Panurge is only living up to his new status when he squanders his fortune and embarks on a borrowing spree. Rabelais uses the occasion to satirize ecclesiastical overspending, but in the main he is poking fun at the aristocracy, whose "lack of money" had become proverbial in the sixteenth century. The ground for Panurge's parody has already been laid, moreover, in chapter 9 of the *Pantagruel*, where the vagabond's portrayal is consistent with that of a nobleman who has fallen upon hard times. The theme of aristocratic poverty is further reinforced in the *Gargantua*, when Picrochole remarks that Grandgousier's wealth contradicts his noble status.

Like a good nobleman, then, Panurge depletes his newly acquired wealth not by "erecting colleges" or "establishing hospitals," but rather "in a thousand gay banquets" and by "fell[ing] whole forests of trees" (*TB*, II, 304). In keeping with his new rank, he buys "at a high price" and sells "cheap" (304), ostentatiously demonstrating the lack of financial acumen for which the nobility was notorious. Their financial ineptitude goes hand in hand with an "aristocratic" disdain for money shared even by Pantagruel, who rejustifies the posture in terms of Stoic philosophy: for Panurge's dilapidation of his fortune "neither offended [nor] grieved" the prince, who "knew well that everything heaven covers and earth bears . . . does not warrant our troubling our equanimity" (304–305).

Panurge's stance as a financial debtor is paralleled by his status as an intellectual debtor: just as the nobleman incurs flashy debt to maintain "appearances," humanists and writers likewise borrow from the ancients to embellish their own discourse, which beneath the rhetoric is often intellectually bankrupt. "The Praise of Debts," then, also functions as a metaphor for writing, which in the Renaissance was unabashedly derivative. Much like entrepreneurs who are encouraged to "borrow, borrow, borrow," the typical sixteenth-century humanist prided himself—and was judged by others—on both the quantity and quality of his borrowings. On the negative side, literary borrowings that are displayed superficially without being replanted, fertilized by new ideas, worked assiduously, and watered by inspiration, are hollow "abysses" of knowledge with no potential capacity for growth and real "profit." On the positive side, intellectual debt fosters the generational continuity and literary immortality eulogized by Pantagruel in chapter 4 of the *Third Book*, when he alludes to the process in which humans perpetuate themselves by "loan" (*TB*, IV, 315). Not only profitable to the lender, who sees a return, literary loans are also potentially profitable to the borrower, who through the process of deferred and differing payment generates new wealth—or meaning—over and beyond the sense-cents originally borrowed.

While we often draw analogies between "The Praise of Debts" and the later panegyric, "The Praise of the Pantagruelion," treating both as digressions, critics have a tendency to underestimate the threads that connect this satirical opening act of the *Third Book* to the main attraction, Panurge's debate on whether to marry. When viewed from an economic perspective, however, it becomes clear that Panurge's approach to the marriage question touches upon many of the same issues set forth in "The Praise of Debts."[4] An ideal marriage also carries with it the potential for mutual aid and comfort that Panurge finds in the institution of debt. Moreover, both debt and marriage function as metaphors of harmony and reciprocity, but the analogy between the successive episodes extends far beyond this single resemblance. For the nonreciprocated nature of Panurge's debts foreshadows his one-sided concept of marriage, an institution in which he proposes to be the "taker," and his deferred loan payments are mirrored by the deferral of his marriage. Finally, the financial nature of debt helps us to see the marriage question as an economic phenomenon.

Although it is the end of *Pantagruel* that lays the groundwork for Panurge's eventual marriage, the theme finds its conceptual roots as an exchange model in Gargantua's emblem, the androgyne. Symbolizing the division of humankind into two sexes at its inception, this (re)unified figure with its two heads and two bottoms (*G*, VIII, 28) has a grotesque quality that is well suited to the sideshow overtones maintained by Rabelais throughout his novel. As a model of reciprocity, moreover, the androgyne sets the stage for both the marriage of ex-Thélèmites and Panurge's marriage quandary in the *Third Book*. Pantagruel seconds this ideal by admitting that good marriages resemble "paradisial joys" (*TB*, X, 328), a transcendent state in which selfishness, differences, and misunderstandings no longer exist. This androgynous ideal is reinforced by the fact that Panurge contemplates marriage when he does, at the end of the Dipsodian War, during an era of reconciliation with the other and during a merger of two previously separate and hostile economies. Lest we miss the connection, Rabelais makes the point again in chapter 7, where Panurge casts off his magnificent codpiece, the "first piece of military armor" (*TB*, VIII, 322), to don an outfit signifying his readiness to marry.[5] First he puts on a single earring set with a flea; then, "taking four ells of coarse brown cloth, he draped the material about him like a long closed coat, threw away his breeches and tied a pair of spectacles to his cap" (*TB*, VII, 320). This freakish costume, which prepares Panurge for the offbeat sideshow consultations, is as rich and ambiguous in its connotations as the Rabelaisian cask. As an advertisement of marriageability, however, the strange disguise falls short of the mark. Despite Panurge's contention that the toga is a symbol of peace, the long dark shirt hanging past his knees more nearly resembles the robe of an eccentric monk. "To see me from afar, you would say I was Jan Bourgeoys," admits Panurge (our translation; *OC*, 353), alluding to a well-known Franciscan of the late fifteenth century. Not only associated with war instead of reconciliation, the monk's garb connotes an aversion to marriage rather than a readiness for the institution. More important, the "flouting of current usage" (320), or Panurge's choice of a symbol meaningful only to himself, is at cross-purposes with the dialogic nature of marriage, which necessarily entails concessions to and communication with the otherness of her-story.

While (re)productive physical exchange does take place between male and female characters, at least in the interstices of the Pantagrueline tales, intellectual and philosophical commerce between the two sexes is rare and largely limited to the cloister of Thélème, which contains an anomalously egalitarian portrait of women. Not just an ideal, Thélème reflects the high social and intellectual respect accorded women in Italianate courts of the Renaissance, where aristocratic males and females received similar educations and interacted almost as equals. For the most part, however, Rabelais appropriates his material about women from intertextual traditions that emphasize the otherness of women, who are posited alternately as inferior and superior to men. The old lady described by the narrator in the fifteenth chapter of *Pantagruel* is even lower than the animals who come to her assistance, while Panurge's Parisian lady is described as *haulte* or "high" (*XXI, 243*) and Pantagruel's abandoned lover is physically distant from the men who attempt to decipher her message. Even in the relatively egalitarian *Gargantua*,

Gargantua's *sages femmes* or "old wives" (*G*, XI) revere the very locus of
difference between the two sexes, while males at Thélème defer to female
judgment in the matter of dress. Dating back to the very origins of
androcentric discourse, this tendency to define female difference in either
positive or negative terms was refueled by sixteenth-century France's
information explosion, which provided new and contradictory documentation from antiquity and Renaissance Italy for detractors and supporters
of femininity. Already, in the 1520s, the debate sketched out by Guillaume de Lorris and Jean de Meung during the thirteenth and fourteenth
centuries was in full swing among Rabelais's Benedictine cronies at the
Maillezais abbey, and by the 1540s the dialogue had been enriched by
Petrarchist idealism, which virtually invited a negative response.[6] This
idealized Petrarchist-Platonist woman is a distant cousin of the "rose,"
first adored by Guillaume de Lorris and later vilified by Jean de Meung,
that had polarized debate on the woman question centuries earlier. By
placing woman on a pedestal replete with Platonic overtones, moreover,
both Guillaume de Lorris and his Petrarchist counterparts in the sixteenth century virtually invited a response from realists, misogynists,
and polemicists of no particular persuasion who were spoiling for a good
fight.[7]

Given woman's otherness, and the popularity of the controversial
"woman question" in the 1540s, it is not surprising that Rabelais
extends his investigation of structures of exchange and reciprocity to the
arena of marriage. Not just a social and philosophical ideal, it also comes
preequipped with negative possibilities that are inherent in commerce
with otherness. Ironically, though, Panurge's reluctance to marry seems
based less on a fear of alterity than on a nagging suspicion that women are
actually much like men. Obsessed with a fear of being cuckolded,
robbed, and beaten by his future bride, Panurge fails to realize that the
domineering wife he fears is a mirror image of himself: adulterous,
thieving, and physically abusive. Unlike idealized female characters in
Rabelais, this emasculating shrew is a type taken straight from the annals
of farce, a popular genre we more commonly associate with Rabelais's
first two books. Wielding a club or stick with obvious phallic connotations, the domineering wife of medieval farce typically turns the tables
and peppers her spouse with verbal and physical abuse, running circles
around him with her mental and physical superiority. Given Panurge's
previously defined role as a prankster, his fear of being tricked by his wife
evokes memories of standard role reversals on the popular stage such as
the "robbed robber" and "tricked trickster." More than merely farcical,

Panurge's hypothetical cuckoldry constitutes a rent in the fabric of both sexual and textual structures of exchange, an analogy justified by Panurge's repeated characterization as a storyteller and would-be writer. The character's fear that his wife will be unfaithful and give birth to illegitimate children bearing his name parallels the author's own concern that the reader-wife will be unfaithful, producing unauthorized readings or "children" that are both temporally and contextually different from the author's original conception. That Rabelais, unlike his character, actually solicits such "other" readings is suggested by two facts: by his dedication of the text to a female reader, a woman whose otherness will enrich and expand the text, and by his comparison of the text to Pandora's bottle, which must be opened by a curious and disobedient woman.

Panurge's fear of marriage in the *Third Book*, which becomes a fear of death in the *Fourth Book*, fits into the economic paradigm set forth by the author in the prologue. Just as readers may be apprehensive about investing their time and money in the cask without sampling its contents, Panurge by the same token is fearful of wagering his estate, his physical well-being, and his self-esteem on an unknown quantity. Not entirely pejorative, Panurge's tendency to view his wife as an investment reflects what was almost a businesslike approach to marriage in many parts of sixteenth-century France, where couples often married to unite farms, secure dowries, and join families. In chapter 48, Pantagruel himself gives voice to this sentiment, referring to marriage (*les noces*) as a *négoce* or "business arrangement" (495) that should be contracted between heads of households rather than between the possible bride and groom, who may not have the best interests—or "possessions, wealth and inheritance" (467)—of the entire family at heart. The king's insistence upon familial participation in the marriage contract directly attacks the ecclesiastical practice of marrying couples without parental sanction. He contends that the practice enables brigands to "steal" young women, pay priests to legalize their crimes via matrimony, and subsequently use their brides as bargaining chips in extortion. His contention that fathers might rightfully kill such a son-in-law and daughter, and moreover cast the remains to wild animals to prevent church burial, at first glance seems discordant with Gargantua's earlier record of liberality. When viewed as an economic transaction, however, the hypothetical execution takes on a peculiar logic. For once the daughter's use value to the family as a breeder, sociopolitical pawn, object of affection, and confirmation of their own value system has ended and she has become a liability, her father feels justified in eliminating her eternally from the (re)productive economy of the family.

Gargantua's transformation of woman into a commodity in the *Third Book* has roots in the opening pages of *Pantagruel*, where the grieving king proposes to shop for another wife. That woman constitutes a commodity in Panurge's eyes as well is suggested by his efforts to "buy" the haughty Parisian lady in *Pantagruel* and by the way he finds dowries in the *Fourth Book* for syphilitic old hags, whom he subsequently trades to fortune hunters.

Intellectual Exchange and the Question of Futures

At once a quest for truth, a test of human knowledge, and a voyage toward self-discovery, the *Third Book* colloquium on marriage is so connotatively rich that we may easily read it without referring to structures of exchange or economic paradigms per se. Panurge himself, however, compares the time he is investing in his research to both a mystic cabal and monetary "capital" (*cabal* [*TB*, XV, 383]) that could be earning "interest" (*TB*, XV, 350). Pantagruel's assessment of investment as a balance between "cost" and "loss" on the negative side, and "welfare and profit" (*TB*, XVI, 351) on the positive side, reinforces the analogy. Much like would-be investors today who have little firsthand knowledge of the market, Panurge turns first to a friend for counsel: "My Lord," he begins, "you have heard me say I am determined to get married. . . . In the name of the love you have long borne me, I beg you to give me your advice" (*TB*, IX, 325). Panurge's choice of mentor is at once logical and ironic; for despite his book-learning, the prince is a motherless bachelor whose firsthand knowledge of matrimony is possibly inferior to that of Panurge. When his father presses him about his own marriage, he answers that he has "never given this business the slightest thought" (*TB*, XLVIII, 466). Partly because of his liberal education, Pantagruel advises his friend according to the Stoic principles that govern his own conduct. Panurge should marry or not marry, according to his own wishes, stoically accepting both the responsibility for his decision and the unforeseeable consequences that accompany it.

The advice is not to Panurge's liking for two reasons. First, it emphasizes qualities that are diametrically opposed to his character: at the age of 35, he remains irresponsible, bereft of self-knowledge, and afraid of his own shadow. Second, the dialogic risk management techniques proposed by Pantagruel are inconsistent with Panurge's goal, which is to eliminate risk entirely with a simple yes or no answer, based not upon past experience but upon his own personal future.

Outside Trading. If Pantagruel fails to give Panurge the answer he seeks, it is nonetheless he who handpicks the great majority of consultants to whom Panurge turns for advice, turning the marriage question into a forum for intellectual exchange and acquisition that is in part reminiscent of Pantagruel's own humanistic education. Like the Utopian giant in his youth, Panurge seeks instruction from knowledgeable people and ancient texts, consulting experts in the fields of medicine, theology, philosophy, and law whose disciplines all played a role in Pantagruel's education. His use of dice to select passages from Homer and Virgil recalls the games Gargantua played to hone his mathematical skills, and his consultation with the deaf-mute Nazdecanabre (Goatnose) at once echoes both his own dialogue with Thaumaste in the *Pantagruel* and Pantagruel's study of ancient languages and anticipates the *Fourth Book* quest for an immediate and transparent protolanguage. Less easy to explain in terms of the giants' education are the episodes involving dream analysis and consultations with a witch, a fool, and a necromancer, all alternative sources of knowledge that some humanists deplored and others explored freely. In his famous letter, Gargantua decries astrology and similar arts used for purposes of divination as "vanity and imposture" (*P*, VIII, 193), and interestingly enough, it is Epistemon rather than Pantagruel who introduces Panurge to Her Trippa, the astrologer whose real-life prototype was almost certainly Cornelius Agrippa, the well-known German philosopher. Pantagruel also condemns the use of dice in fortune-telling, citing the method's diabolic origins and his father's opposition to the practice (*TB*, XI, 331). After voicing these reservations, however, Pantagruel allows Panurge to throw the dice, "to give [him] satisfaction" (332).

Taking this foray into the occult a step further, Pantagruel himself counsels Panurge to consult a sibyl, whose art, according to Epistemon, is "forbidden by the law of Moses" (*TB*, XVI, 351). Defying the biblical taboo, however, the giant defends the forbidden consultation on the basis of both classical precedent and the freedom of scientific inquiry, which cannot progress efficiently when its field of investigation is restricted and when untested preconceptions are accepted as fact: "How do we know she isn't an eleventh sibyl, a second Cassandra? Even if she is neither, nor merits the name, what harm is there in consulting her about your problem? . . . Knowledge never harmed a man" (351). Edging away from the religiously based notion that certain forms of knowledge are forbidden, Pantagruel contends that truth, whatever its source or content, must be respected as the ultimate goal of human inquiry; while Pantagruel does not personally practice the occult arts, and even doubts their efficacity, he by no means excludes them from intellectual scrutiny. On the contrary, as a uomo universale he is fully conversant with the theories, methods, and major practitioners of these alternative sciences, which must be considered potentially valid until proven otherwise.

Interestingly enough, these unorthodox routes of inquiry are the first ones selected by Pantagruel and Epistemon. Witches and astrologers enjoyed a high degree of popularity in the Renaissance, and beginning a potentially dry symposium on marriage with a fortune-telling sequence is a consummate piece of showmanship on Rabelais's part, worthy of the carnival barker. Besides appealing to contemporary tastes, literary sibyls and necromancers such as Merlin were an integral part of the romance epic tradition espoused by Rabelais 14 years earlier.[8] Our familiarity with these intertexts helps generate an alternative grid of expectations for the *Third Book* that is transcendent instead of comic, satiric, or carnivalesque. Further, the opening fortune-telling sequence responds to the internal exigencies of the narrative itself. By refusing to opt for or against marriage until he knows whether he will be cuckolded, Panurge has boxed himself into a paralyzing dilemma that can only be resolved through divination. Whereas Gargantua and Pantagruel repeatedly make decisions based on probability and cost-benefit analysis, Panurge challenges the expanding limits of human knowledge—and the nature of textuality itself—by demanding prognostic or prophetic certainty prior to action. His bull-headed insistence upon seeing his own personal destiny implicitly rejects the predictive and pedagogical value of biblical and classical behavioral models upon which Pantagruel and other humanists base their conduct and make reasonable assumptions about the future. In their place, he ambitiously proposes a more exact science of living based on a knowledge of his own personal future. What he hypothesizes is not an absolute destiny, which would make his own decision-making quandary moot, but rather a future of alternative destinies, each of which can be activated or eliminated by choosing one course of action over another.

It is because Panurge wants to see his future, then, that Pantagruel points him first toward divination, introducing his friend to "fringe figures" or mediums—the equivalent of middlemen in commerce—who theoretically straddle the intersection between earth and eternity. In addition to the witch, deaf-mute, and necromancer, the potential mediums consulted by Panurge include a dead poet—Virgil—and a dying poet. Because of their intermediate status between sameness and otherness, between here and the beyond, Panurge hopes they can tell him a priori if he will be cuckolded, thereby resolving his matrimonial quandary. The commercial overtones of these transactions are reinforced by the tokens the "middlemen" are given for their efforts and by Pantagruel's contention that Panurge can "profit" from the encounters, deriving *(s)avoir* or "wealth" in the form of knowledge. Just as many investors diversify their interests in order to minimize risks and maximize gains, so Panurge inquires into many areas. Like many modern-day investors, Panurge does not commit all his eggs to a single basket but rather diversifies his portfolio, investing in multiple fields of knowledge, hoping at least one will be profitable.

In each instance, the locus of intellectual exchange is a set of tokens or symbols: Virgil's poetry, the oneiric symbols from Panurge's dreams, the witch's occult signs and the deaf-mute's sign language all constitute texts that Panurge must decipher in order to tap their resources. The otherness of this language is a stumbling block for Panurge, whose evaluation of the text-tokens differs from that of his comrades. Panurge interprets each of the three Virgilian lots, which are taken out of context from the *Eclogues* and *Aeneid*, in his own favor, disagreeing with his friends over the references, connotations, and general import of each quotation. A similar disagreement over signifieds hampers the Utopians' attempt to analyze Panurge's dream. In this dream, the rogue's wife laughingly places two horns on his head; then he is transformed into a drum and she into a screech owl.[9] To Pantagruel and his merry companions, the two horns clearly represent cuckoldry, in accordance with popular iconography, and they view the dual metamorphosis as a sign that Panurge will be beaten like a drum and robbed by a wifely "bird of prey." The dreamer himself reads the oneiric language more positively, however: "First, the horns my wife gave me were horns of plenty; abundance of good things rose about me, I assure you. Secondly, I shall be as joyful as a wedding tabor. . . . Third, my wife will be winsome and blithe as a pet madge owl" (*TB*, XIV, 345–46). Because this pattern of alternative interpretations recurs in each of the occult consultations, and because no single reading is convincing, the Utopians ultimately fail to reach a consensus regarding Panurge's matrimonial quandary.

The teasing jocularity with which Pantagruel discusses cuckoldry, in fact, and the farcical staging of the entire sequence, suggests that the consultations are partly ludic, a reading reinforced by the young men's leisured status and by the general affinity for intellectual gamesmanship among scholars and aristocrats of the era. The two protagonists' rival readings of the Virgilian texts constitute an exegetical tour de force that smacks of intellectual gamesmanship. Panurge may not relish the prospect of being cuckolded, beaten, and robbed, as Pantagruel predicts on the basis of Virgil's text (and all its successors), but the rogue's resourceful refutation of the exegesis suggests an even greater aversion to being beaten in a battle of wits.

Equally diverting, particularly to a band of leisured and aristocratic young men, are many of the consultants themselves, whose physical otherness, peculiarities, and marginal social status give them the allure of sideshow attractions. Surrounded by smoke and bent over her cauldron, the ragged and stereotypically toothless sibyl of Panzoust holds the Utopians mesmerized as she twists her spindle, twirls two skeinwinders, removes one shoe, drapes her apron over her head, takes a swig of Panurge's liquor, puts three coins in walnut shells, throws heather and laurel in the fire, and finally speaks in tongues. Reinforcing the spectacular, visual quality of this elaborately staged scene is an uncharacteristic intervention by the narrator, who assures us he "saw" (*je veidz* [OC, TB, XVII, 388]) the performance. Instead of reacting with awe, as did Aeneas before them, the Utopians experience the same mixture of titillation, wonder, and fear that accompanied Pantagruel's own introduction onto the carnival proscenium in 1532. The *Third Book*'s carnival overtones are further enhanced by the gold tokens that change hands before the consultation: "In this pouch of mine," claims Panurge upon meeting the sibyl, "I've a golden bough . . . but rounded in the shape of a ring. And I've some fine ringing golden coins beside it" (354). In this scene, the spiritual golden bough that gives Aeneas access to the underworld is transformed into a monetary price of admission. Equally important in building the mood of this scene are the phallic connotations of the golden bough mentioned by Panurge, in a scatological reference that resituates the epic intertext within the world of farce.

The combination of grossly exaggerated fear and off-color jokes with which Utopians greet the sibyl's strange ritual are reactions more consistent with the viewing of carnival oddities than oracles. Similarly, the deaf-mute's propensity for sign language in the region of his codpiece and the narrator's comparison of him to a goat who is miscarrying (*TB*, XX, 365) cause the scene to unravel into two grids, the one prophetic and the other farcical. In this scene, as in its predecessor, Panurge pays for his "fortune" in a manner more reminiscent of sideshows than the epic: upon

Nazdecanabre's arrival, "Panurge . . . gave him a fatted calf, half a hog, eighty gallons of wine, and a load of corn and thirty francs" (364). Here and in the golden bough exchange, where he refers so pointedly to the mercenary ethos of his culture, Rabelais effectively communicates the difficulty of uncovering transcendent signifieds in a world that prizes the signifier's material value, or "cents," over its mystical meaning, or "sense."

The fortune-telling sequence is not purely diversionary, however. While Pantagruel and his comrades entertain doubts about the validity of divination, or at least some of its forms, these ventures into the occult constitute for them an extension of the humanistic drive to know and an opportunity for epistemological exchange. The promise of divination, practiced by both the Greeks and Romans, resides in the otherness of its practitioners, who function as mediators between this world and the next. Positioned at the intersection between life and death, the Virgilian text holds the same promise as Virgil himself, who by virtue of his intermediate position between Roman and Christian civilization helped Dante hear the dead speak within the fiction of the *Divine Comedy*. Structurally similar to the Virgilian text, the dreams that Panurge suppressed during his waking hours constitute what according to the ancients is an intermediate link between human consciousness and that of God: "When . . . the body slept, the mind could absent itself and, until the body awakened again, could enjoy itself, revisiting its native land of heaven" (*TB*, XIII, 339). Citing Hippocrates, Plato, Plotinus, Aristotle, and a host of others, Pantagruel points out that "all these authors describe the conditions in which the soul, dreaming, may foresee what is to come" (338) by returning to a locus where "all time is the present, as the soul observes not only what has gone by, but also what is to come" (339). By deciphering the remnants of this oneiric text that seep through into the waking consciousness, the dreamer can theoretically catch glimpses of the future.

The sibyl of Panzoust and the astrologer Herr Trippa are also intermediate figures, the one living alone in a grotto cottage atop a mountain, on the frontier between the known world and the unknown, and the other on the insular Isle Bouchard. A similar principle applies to the deaf-mute, whose verbal skills resemble those of a newborn, suspended on the threshold between eternity and temporality. Living among humans but uncorrupted by the "ambiguities, obscurities and equivokes" of spoken language that cloud our (in)sight, the mute deaf from birth should, according to Pantagruel, be "more natural and sincere than one who has heard" (*TB*, XIX, 361). In economic terms, these fringe figures function as potential middlemen, whose Apollonian role as disseminators rather than creators of knowledge is equivalent to that of Alcofribas, who as an "abstractor of quintessence" communicates an "abstruse doctrine" and "deepest mysteries" (*G*, Prol., 5) to his reader.

Despite this promise of epistemological wealth, Panurge does not profit from the fortune-telling sequence, becoming ensnared instead in textual polyvalence that Pantagruel will later compare to a labyrinth: "You look like a mouse entangled in a snare," the prince observes. "The harder you try to emerge from the gin of perplexity, the more hopelessly you are caught" (*TB*, XXXVII, 430). Part of the blame may be laid at the feet of the consultants, who are not convincing prophets in the eyes of either Panurge or the reader. Panurge discredits the sibyl because she doesn't speak "Christian" (*TB*, XVII, 355), the dying poet because he curses the father who confesses him, and the astrologer for failing to divine his own wife's infidelity. Epistemon lends fuel to these arguments by suggesting that the era of oracles ended with the birth of Christ: "All these oracles and prophecies had grown as dumb as fish since the coming of the Savior King" (*TB*, XXIV, 381).

More important, Panurge's failure to profit from the consultations results from his own cognitive dysfunction. The lack of self-knowledge that prompts him to seek outside help in the first place also colors the way in which Panurge reacts to the consultants' prophecies: he fails to recognize his own personality traits in the weak and unloved husband that we and his friends see depicted. His inability to visualize himself as a battered cuckold stands in marked contrast to his friends' predisposition *toward* this reading, born of the objective realization that Panurge's own thievery, cuckolding tendencies, and abuse of women are likely to be reciprocated. Working in tandem with this lack of self-knowledge is the reluctant bridegroom's excessive self-love, which cripples his exegetical efforts and dooms his desire for productive exchange. Each time a friend or consultant predicts that he will be cuckolded, Panurge refutes the fortune with a favorable reading motivated less by reason than desire. In these readings, philautia acts as a subjective and protective filter that prevents him from seeing himself in a negative light. Ironically, it is Panurge's self-love more than anything else that augurs poorly for his marriage, which is itself a form of exchange. For if philautia blinds him to her-story, he is likely to be both cuckolded and unaware he is cuckolded, deluded into believing what his dream counterpart did: that the two protuberances on his head are "a bull's horns" (*TB*, XIV, 344), symbolizing virility rather than sexual and communicative inadequacy. While Panurge admits the possibility of just such a misreading, he remains true to form and recognizes interpretive error only in others. Blaming the bulk of these misreadings on women, whom he accuses of assigning erotic value to all signs regardless of their intended value, Panurge assimilates the textual other or reader to the sexual other: "Whatever women see, they never think, imagine or conceive it save in terms of the . . . deit[y] Ithyphallos" (*TB*, XIX, 362). The irony of this comment resides in its perfect applicability to Panurge's own reading of female discourse, to which he routinely assigns sexual connotations far removed from the text's denotative value.

Notwithstanding this irony, however, Panurge is right to suggest that the textual other or reader is inherently unfaithful to the locutor or writer, in part because different experiences produce different meanings, and in part because language has lost any claim to transparency. Pantagruel invokes this second argument at the beginning of the chapter, when he points out that sages far more knowledgeable than Panurge have been led astray by the ambiguous language of oracles: "Very often," reflects the prince, "men reputed to be the most learned and intelligent of their age, were deceived as much by ambiguities, obscurities and equivokes as by laconism" (*TB*, XIX, 361). Misunderstandings arise, if we follow the logic of Pantagruel, because words signify arbitrarily rather than naturally: "I believe it a gross error," he goes on, "to say there is such a thing as a natural language (361). Varying from culture to culture and from individual to individual, the majority of linguistic tokens have no universally recognized value and thus inevitably lend themselves to ambiguous interpretations. It is to transcend this ambiguity that Pantagruel urges his friend to consult a mute deaf from birth, whose sign language based upon physical similarities and natural analogies promises to narrow the gap between representation and reference. Though unsuccessful, this experiment in preverbal communication parallels Rabelais's fascination with premonetary and premarket economies, in which the thing itself rather than tokens of that thing changes hands and serves as currency.

Unlike the archetypal *verbum* or "word made flesh" sought by the Utopians, however, the deaf-mute's signs only approximate the thing itself. The resulting difference between signifiers and signified allows Panurge to contest what seems obvious to both his friends and many modern readers: "All truths agree and are one," declares Pantagruel.

"You will be . . . cuckold, beaten and robbed" (*TB*, XX, 367). Clearly
Rabelais steers us toward this interpretation by inscribing it within the
text not once but repeatedly and ascribing it to wise Pantagruel, whose
"authoritative" voice serves a normative function within the narrative:
by smoking out Panurge's far rosier counterreadings and drawing our
attention to subjective biases in these readings, Pantagruel awakens us to
the myriad contextual variables that affect the way we assign meaning to
symbols. This identification between author and character is only partial,
however, and does not necessarily imply that Pantagruel's own readings
of the prophecies are correct. When we compare his idiosyncratic interpretation of the Virgilian lottery to the Latin texts its purports to
explain, it becomes clear that Pantagruel is no more faithful to Virgil
than is Panurge.[10] And upon closer inspection, a similar pattern unfolds
in other divination scenes. Connotatively, the horn in chapter 14, the
dream episode, is no less a symbol of plenty than of cuckoldry, and the
sibyl's prophecy, written with a spindle on eight sycamore leaves that she
subsequently tosses in the wind, takes its apparently unfavorable meaning from the unauthorized syntax Utopians impose on it. Most important, Rabelais chooses not to resolve the exegetical disagreement by
actually narrating the future but leaves us instead with two parallel and
contradictory readings for each "prophetic" text.

    Inside Trading. The consultations themselves are not exclusively
divinatory but instead turn back from the outer fringes of society—its
islands and its grottoes—to seek the wisdom of insiders: a doctor, a
theologian, and a judge, whose rational thought processes counterbalance and complement the revelational tenor of earlier episodes. The
progression from revelation to reason might lead us to believe that
Rabelais, in keeping with humanistic values, is valuing the former over
the latter, were it not for the increasingly satiric nature of the "rational"
consultations, which culminate ironically with a fool. Clearly Epistemon
approves of the return to "normality," approving the new consultants
just as strenuously as he opposed the sibyl: "I don't think you could have
possibly chosen better throughout the whole country" (*TB*, XXIX, 402).
Much of the theologian Hippothadeus's advice is indeed sound, based
upon risk management techniques. If Panurge chooses a wife, and if he
himself sets a good example, he will minimize his risks of cuckoldry.
Hippathadeus does not, however, offer the *mot* or "one-word answer" that
Panurge is looking for, instead deferring Panurge's ultimate fate to an
"other" authority, God's will (*TB*, XXX, 404).

    Equally practical is Doctor Rondibilis, who suggests that Panurge's fear of cuckoldry in itself may be sufficient to contraindicate marriage. To circumvent the problem, Rondibilis prescribes five ways of sublimating the erotic impulses: wine, drugs, work, war, and the "act of copulation" (*TB*, XXXI, 409) itself. If Panurge is determined to marry, however, Rondibilis holds that cuckoldry is an inevitable risk, in part because woman is so capricious that her behavior cannot be predicted rationally, and in part because the female's sexual appetite is so voracious that no single man can satisfy her. As for the answer to cuckoldry, he encodes it in an allegory that at first glance seems no less hermetic than that of the sibyl. According to this allegory, the god Cuckoldry haunts the husbands who worship him and ignores those who ignore him, condemning this second group to a boring life without rivals. If we follow this line of reasoning, as does Panurge, the most foolproof method of guaranteeing wifely infidelity would be to forbid it; conversely, the best way to discourage infidelity would be to encourage it. The logic behind this paradox lies in the perceived otherness of woman, who is adjudged so unlike males in her modus operandi that she reacts by antiphrasis, craving what is forbidden and scorning what is permitted or encouraged. In itself, this discontinuity between male signifiers and female signifieds bodes ill for Panurge's matrimonial inquest, functioning as a metaphor of textual as well as sexual difference.

Our hopes for a rational solution to Panurge's dilemma recede even further with the appearance of Trouillogan (Skeinwinder), a skeptical philosopher who opines, far more obscurely than the deaf-mute and the sibyl, that Panurge should marry and not marry: "Panurge had put the question: should he marry or no? Skeinwinder had first replied that he should do both, then that he should do neither" (*TB*, XXXV, 421). Not a *mot* but a text, Trouillogan's advice makes sense only when deciphered by Pantagruel, who finds in the philosopher's conundrum a reflection of his own worldview, with its vertical system of allegiances in which woman's duties are to her husband, and the husband's to God and country. Marriage for Pantagruel entails possessing a wife without being possessed by her, a variation of the same taking without giving that informs Panurge's concept of marriage: "Having a wife," explains the prince, "means having the use of her in the way ordained by nature, namely for company, help, and pleasure. Not having a wife means [not] to loll and poltroon it uxoriously, tied to her petticoats" (421). As for the question of cuckoldry itself, Trouillogan also finds the answer not in human reason but in the same otherness invoked by the soothsayers, suggesting that the fidelity of his own wife depends on destiny, on whether or "not . . . it was fatally foreordained" (*TB*, XXXVI, 429).

Panurge's experiment with rational media of exchange reaches its nadir with the fourth professional consultant, Judge Bridoye, whose characterization as an "old friend" (*TB*, XXIX, 402) of Epistemon enhances his epistemological promise. Bridoye fails to appear at the colloquium with the other three sages, however, because he himself is being tried by Parlement for having erred in a recent decision. During the ensuing inquiry, it emerges that Bridoye, renowned for his judicious decisions, reaches them in two ways: first, he defers judgment until the conflict resolves itself; and second, he decides particularly thorny issues by rolling dice, in an ironic echo of Panurge. While the method can be justified ecclesiastically, as an example of Christian folly in which human judgment abdicates before divine providence, it runs counter to two of the basic tenets of Renaissance humanism: a belief in the primacy of human reason, and a respect for the past experiences of others as a guide to problem-solving in the present. Bridoye's inability to relate the universals of human experience and the generalities of Roman law to the singularity of individual cases ironically mirrors Panurge's own unwillingness to be guided by precepts and the experiences of others. In part a satire of the legal system, Bridoye's lengthy deliberations are also a microcosm of Panurge's suspension of judgment on marriage.

Inherent in the Bridoye episode, and indeed in Panurge's quest as a whole, is an interrogation of the written word or the book, a cornerstone of intellectual exchange in the Renaissance. Pantagruel's curriculum and Gargantua's optimism about the future were both made possible by the invention of the printing press and the ensuing information explosion, which, by placing quantities of information at man's disposal, theoretically provided him the means of judging more efficiently. Panurge's quest, however, is a sustained interrogation of Gargantua's "abyss" and of the validity of laws. As his experiences and that of Bridoye suggest, inflationary quantities of data may actually serve to complicate decision-making because of the opacity of texts and the tenuous rapport between the singularity of one individual's experience and that of others.

This recurring focus upon singularity, which is betrayed even by the universalizing principles of language, also finds expression in the prevalence of monsters in Renaissance art, so anomalous that they defy laws of nature and linguistic description, and of madness, which also lies outside the boundaries of linguistic and rational expression.[11] While Rabelais's interest in unreason is already evident in his first two books—not just in the giants themselves but also in such episodes as the Picrocholine War—madness emerges as a truly dominant theme only in the *Third Book*, where Panurge's consultations reach their apotheosis not with a sage but with a fool, Triboullet.[12] A well-known figure at the court of Francis I, Triboullet, by virtue of his alterity, is structurally and thematically related to the deaf-mute and the sibyl, both the occult consultants and woman, whose otherness constitutes at least the nominal object of Panurge's inquest. Though an indictment of rational routes to knowledge, Panurge's consultation with a fool is at the same time based on principles recognized by classical and Renaissance humanists alike: as a figure of alterity, the fool, like the sibyl, promised privileged access to the secrets of otherness. "A wise man . . . able to presage future events by divine inspiration," speculates Pantagruel, "is one who forgets himself, discards his own personality, rids his senses of all earthly affection, purges his spirit of all human care, neglects everything. All of which qualities are popularly supposed to be symptoms of insanity!" (*TB*, XXXVII, 431). Ironically, though, the fool not only suggests that Panurge will be cuckolded by a monk but also points the finger of madness at Panurge, at once reversing and enlarging our concept of both otherness and normality. As Panurge himself points out, "everyone [is] mad" (*TB*, XLVI, 462), but the worst madness is not to realize it.

While disagreeing about the sense of Triboullet's message and gestures, Pantagruel and Panurge agree that the fool's advice is superior to that of the earlier consultants. For the first time, claims the Utopian prince, we know *who* will cuckold Panurge: a monk, as indicated by the words *guare moine* or "beware the monk" (*TB*, XLV, 459). Panurge, on the contrary, reads the words as a charming but insignificant reference to a "sparrow [*moyneau*]" (*TB*, XLVI, 462) belonging to his future wife. He moreover follows the advice that he believes Triboullet has given him, organizing a trip to the Dive Bouteille (Divine Bottle), or Bacbuc, on the basis of the fool's parting gesture, the return of a bottle.

The fool's bottle, which at once echoes the text-cask of the prologue and anticipates the Divine Bottle of the *Fourth Book*, was originally a gift from Panurge, who sees in its return a prophecy of a prophecy, a sign that he will see his future in the oracle of the Divine Bottle. As readers, however, we cannot help but add our own interpretation of the bottle to those of Panurge and Pantagruel, who sees it as a sign that Panurge's wife will be a tippler (*TB*, XLVII, 463). In contrast to the "inexhaustible" cornucopia offered readers by the narrator in the prologue, the bottle-text that Triboullet returns to Panurge is an absence-abyss of meaning, rationality, and woman.

Pantagruel's virtual exclusion of female voices from his colloquium on marriage merits our attention. To be sure, the sibyl is a woman, but like the deaf-mute and the fool, she says little. Her first utterances are *mots barbares* (*OC*, 389) or "barbarous words" that prompt the polyglot Panurge to complain that she does not speak Christian (*TB*, XVII, 355). Clearly, however, the sibyl understands androcentric speech, for she listens to Panurge (354) and finally responds with 18 words in French, challenging him to read and understand her own language, which she inscribes with the stylus of female discourse: a spindle that she shares with the Fates. When the Utopians piece together the scattered text, Panurge and Pantagruel predictably disagree on the meaning, and perhaps because of this failure, Panurge declines an opportunity to consult a female deaf-mute immediately after the sibyl, claiming that male and female signifiers are distorted by the opposite sex. In keeping with Triboullet's advice, however, Panurge's ultimate consultation, always deferred, will be with the absence that is woman: the oracle of the Divine Bottle, who exists outside the margins of the text, near Cathay in Upper India (*FB*, I, 510). Because her-story will be doubly foreign, Pantagruel proposes that a sibyl "act as interpreter and guide" (*TB*, XLVII, 464), but Panurge resists the option of female exegesis in favor of his friend Xenomanes and a "learned lamp" (464) from Lanternland, whose grammatically feminine gender will be combined with male erudition.

The ideal of exchange with a woman—be it wife, witch, or sibyl— thus informs Panurge's quest from beginning to end, positing woman, like the fool, as the archetypal other. Panurge's quest to know her is, and will arguably remain, handicapped by linguistic barriers, androcentric biases, and his own lack of self-knowledge; indeed, one goal of the quest is to determine whether Panurge truly wishes to engage in exchange. In archetypal quests, ironically, this knowledge of self is gained only when the hero merges with otherness and sees himself objectively for the first time. The woman of the *Third Book*, in this sense, is structurally a mirror of Panurge, reflecting his thievery, abusiveness, and adultery. Moreover, because Panurge is characterized as a storyteller in the *Pantagruel* and a writer of wills in the *Fourth Book*, it is legitimate to read his communicative quandary, deferral of exchange, and fear of infidelity as a writer's fear of being misread, an inevitable result of textuality. Rabelais, however, builds the quest for otherness into his text: just as Panurge defers ultimately to Bacbuc to see his future-fortune, so Rabelais defers the reading of his text to a woman, ironically authorizing the otherness of sexuality and textuality.

Toward Cultural Exchange: The Praise of the Pantagruelion

The *Third Book* ends with a four-chapter *éloge*, "The Praise of the Pantagruelion," which structurally balances "The Praise of Debts" that opens the novel. Named for its discoverer, who is himself a uomo universale of multitudinous talents, the pantagruelion is an inauspicious-looking plant, now identified as hemp, that Pantagruel has put to hundreds of uses. In particular, it is fashioned into ropes and sails for the voyage and can be traded for staples at the ports of call the Utopians visit, as the intellectual exchange of the *Third Book* consultations gives way to the promise of geographical trade. The plant also lends itself to diverse culinary uses, reinforcing the theme of consumption; it is used in the construction of bags and baskets, or new container images, and, most important, can be made into paper, the "ropes and sails" of literary voyages.[13]

While these concluding chapters, with their masses of technical information and classical references, are often tedious for modern readers, they in fact constitute a microcosm of the Rabelaisian text. Like "The Praise of Debts," though perhaps less obviously so, "The Praise of the Pantagruelion" is paradoxical: not only is the object of praise lowly, but we shall see that its value is almost as ambivalent as Panurge's debts. At the same time, however, the plant's extraordinary functional stature clearly echoes the giganticism of Pantagruel himself. Moreover, as a vast compendium of practical knowledge on the medical, culinary, and technical uses of a botanical subspecies, the panegyric also brings to mind the popular sixteenth-century almanacs in which science was popularized for the masses, and in which Rabelais himself dabbled. Resembling a rhetorical copia in its amplitude and wealth of detail, "The Praise of the Pantagruelion" also contains page after page of semiotic theory revolving around the relationship between names and things. Partly as a result of this copia, the panegyric functions as an enigma similar to the one that ends the *Gargantua*: Rabelais never defines Pantagruel's miracle plant but instead teases us with cryptic hints about its identity.

If "The Praise of the Pantagruelion" ties up the *Third Book* structurally, with its reprise of the paradoxical encomium, it also facilitates the narrative transition to the *Fourth Book* ocean voyage by casting an eye toward progress and technology. True, many of the uses for hemp enumerated in these pages are extracted from Pliny's *Natural History*, already cited by the author in previous books, but the narrator emphasizes the progress modern man has made in relation to these classical models: "Indeed, I am amazed," he says, "that the discovery of this use remained so long hidden to the ancient philosophers, considering the inestimable benefit derived from it" (*TB*, LI, 480–81). As a tribute to human ingenuity, "The Praise of the Pantagruelion" seems to confirm the myth of man progressing set forth in Gargantua's ebullient letter to his son 14 years earlier. In addition to building upon classical models, which he transforms and surpasses, Pantagruel improves upon the inventions of Gargantua himself, substantiating the melioristic thesis implicit in his father's letter. For instead of applying many objects experimentally to a single task, like his father in the arsewipe episode, Pantagruel economizes the process by finding many uses for a single object. In addition to improving upon his father's methodology, Pantagruel will bequeath his own progress to a new generation in a continuation of Gargantua's progressive spiral: "Who knows," say the threatened gods in a burst of territorialism, "but Pantagruel's children will discover some herb equally effectual? Who knows but humans may, by its means . . . invade the regions of the moon, intrude within the territories of the celestial signs?" (481).

The pantagruelion also represents an investment for Pantagruel, echoing both the narrator's quandary about military commitment in the prologue and Panurge's reluctance to invest in a wife. Unlike his companion, who is unable to devote himself to a single activity or accept the responsibility of choosing a wife, Pantagruel makes a long-term investment in a lowly object of study, which in the long run yields great dividends. The episode further anticipates the *Fourth Book* theme of *mediocritas* (moderation) by suggesting that there is merit in cultivating one's own garden and "planting cabbages": with proper nurturing, creative grafts, and diligent cross-fertilization, one of these lowly plants may "[exceed] the length of a lance" (*TB*, XLIX, 471) and prove to be a wonder drug.

To read this panegyric monologically as a simple validation of human ingenuity, however, is to ignore the polyvalence of the cornucopian text.[14] On a purely aesthetic level, first of all, Rabelais's comic conclusion of the discourse prophesying humankind's ascent to Olympia gives the passage satirical overtones, inscribing within it the seeds of a parodical counterreading: once they arrive in Olympia, the conquering humans of this prophetic vision take up residence in celestial taverns, eat heartily, and bed the goddesses, infusing the panegyric's high style with an alternative grid of earthiness that produces guffaws in addition to awe. Second, the applications of the pantagruelion are clearly negative as well as positive: the ropes that are formed from it are used to hang the innocent as well as the guilty, and "if man . . . eats much and frequently of it, it will dry up the spermatic fluid" (*TB*, XLIX, 471). Capable of ending as well as enriching life, and of drying up generation and reproduction, this miracle plant ultimately doubles as the tree of knowledge and of life, whose reverse—like that of Gaster in the *Fourth Book*—is as dark as its obverse is luminous.[15] In its implicit advice to cultivate one's garden, finally, "The Praise of the Pantagruelion" not only announces the *Fourth Book* but also undermines part of the progressive myth it purports to praise: for the *abysme de science*, the universal man, has reduced the scope of his studies to a single plant, finding wealth not as a generalist but as a specialist.

Notwithstanding its introduction by a barker-bard, then, this masterpiece of erudition never leaves the world of exchange. From the paradoxical "Praise of Debts," which grafts the positive ideal of reciprocity onto the negative theme of debt, to "The Praise of the Pantagruelion," which paradoxically lauds human inventiveness, the *Third Book* unveils a spectacular parade of fools, freaks, and prodigies who are worthy of the carnival barker's proscenium. As an exercise in intellectual and matrimonial exchange, however, the characters' own quest—at once matrimonial and intellectual—is considerably less successful, handicapped by the paradoxical wealth of "answers" available, by the ambivalent value of the tokens transmitting this information, and by the specular nature of the evaluation process, which tends to confirm each reader's own self-image. Unable to recognize himself in these "prophetical" texts, and unwilling to commit himself to the uncertainty that is otherness, Panurge at book's end defers his "investment" one more time, proposing a visit to the oracle of the bottle. His indefinite postponement of commitment, and with it the realities of work and marriage, stands in direct opposition to the philosophy of Pantagruel, who has used his time differently during the quest: in developing the pantagruelion he has harnessed his own virtualities in a dramatic gesture of self-knowledge, tapped the modest resources around him for every drop of productivity they have to offer, and built his own destiny—for better or for worse—rather than waiting for it to be revealed.

Chapter Five
The *Fourth Book*

Rabelais's *Fourth Book*, the last complete novel attributed to him with any degree of certainty, chronicles a fantastic sea voyage in search of the Dive Bouteille (Divine Bottle), a flask-shaped oracle that, according to Panurge, holds the answer to his matrimonial quandary. Probably begun just after the *Third Book*'s censure in 1546, this vertiginous tale of peril on the high seas and "strange exchange" with insular cultures dates from a correspondingly turbulent period in the author's own life. With the burning of Etienne Dolet in 1546 and the reinstitution of France's inquisitional Chambre Ardente the following year, navigating the waves of public opinion was becoming increasingly perilous for traffickers in ideas like Rabelais. Accused of "various heresies" by "perverse readers" in the wake of his *Third Book*'s publication, the author nearly abandoned ship in midcourse, resolving to write no more (*FB*, Dedicatory Epistle, 491). Like a master navigator, however, he chose instead to steer clear of the storm's epicenter, lying low in Metz for two years before returning to the service of Cardinal du Bellay in 1548. It was at this juncture that an embryonic *Fourth Book*, consisting of 11 unpolished chapters and an embittered prologue on the negative returns of literary exchange, was published by Pierre de Tours in Lyon.

By the early 1550s, Rabelais had recouped his favored status with the crown and was ready to lift anchor again, casting his feather quill to the wind (*je mectz la plume au vent* [*FB*, Dedicatory Epistle, *OC*, 521])—in much the same way that the Utopians set sail (*feirent voile au vent OC, FB*, I,541). In 1552, a revised *Fourth Book* appeared, but despite the royal privilege that accompanied its publication, it is clear from the dedicatory epistle that Rabelais still felt beleaguered by "slanderers" such as Gabriel du Puy Herbault. And sure enough, the favorable winds that buoyed him in 1551 soon shifted. Like its predecessors, his *Fourth Book* was censored by the Sorbonne, and within two years of its publication, Rabelais himself was dead amid rumors of imprisonment and disgrace. As for the literary representation of his voyage, set adrift in a textual "vessel" resembling the bottle-encased will Panurge dreams of casting out to sea, its critical fortunes have been mixed. Probably the most difficult of Rabelais's novels, the *Fourth Book* encounters detractors even among devoted *pantagruélistes*, who see in its proliferating digressions, unstable symbolism, and inhuman oddities a literary monster, a cancerous explosion of nonsense.[1] It is precisely this freakishness, however, that links the *Fourth Book* to the huckster's caravan of Rabelais's earliest prologue, as bard and barker are once more conjoined in a carnivalesque, mercantile epic.

As a continuation of Panurge's matrimonial inquest in the *Third Book*, the *Fourth Book* revolves around commerce with otherness, but the locus of this alterity has shifted from European culture and its counterculture of fringe figures to the uncharted geographical beyond. Replacing the soothsayers and learned consultants of the *Third Book* are foreign ports of call, exotic fauna, and a fanciful menagerie of monsters that perpetuate the earliest novel's sideshow appeal, in a conflation of *foire* or "fair" and the similar-sounding *fors* or *forain*, both terms for "outside" that are etymologically linked to the English word "foreign." Appropriately enough, the first of the *Fourth Book*'s foreign civilizations is a fair site called Medamothi (*FB*, II), which establishes the commercial nature of the Utopians' odyssey from the outset. The extraordinary merchandise acquired by the sailors for virtually nothing and the goodwill they encounter among the citizenry at once reflect and satirize the high expectation for international and intellectual trade in the Age of Discovery. The idealized transactions at Medamothi, however, give way to an exploding seascape of (ex)changes and substitutions that subvert the Utopians' epistemological quest.

Inspired by Panurge's thirst for knowledge, the *Fourth Book* quest further unfolds under the emblem of consumption, symbolized by the optimistic association of drinking vessels and sailing vessels in chapter 1. Despite their high expectations, which recall the hopes of Rabelais and his fellow humanists a generation earlier, Utopian "drinkers" find their ingestion of data threatened by a devouring universe full of monsters and encounters with death. These risks, which enable the epic hero to test his mettle, run counter to the pointedly unheroic economy of survival outlined in the prologue, where Rabelais interrogates the cost-efficiency of humanistic greed, proposing in its place a low-risk work ethic that values health and life over wealth and knowledge, production over consumption, and moderation over excess.

The form of production that most interests Rabelais is art, a potential by-product of intellectual gluttony that ideally eases the artist's physical hunger, feeds the public's thirst for knowledge, and cheats the jaws of death of their prey by generating an immortal alter ego. Even more forcefully than its predecessor, the *Fourth Book* explores this ideal and the rents in its fabric, functioning as a metatext that reflects back on the processes of textuality, art, and representation in general, all forms of exchange in which tokens and facsimiles of the thing itself stand as substitutes for their models or prototypes. What the Utopians seek in the Divine Bottle is a transcendent and glass-clear representation, in which the proffered "word" or *mot* transparently reveals its inner truth. With a few exceptions, however, the Utopians encounter increasingly flawed forms of symbolic exchange over the course of their voyage, in which the distance or *différance* between truth and token results in flawed communication, misrepresentation, and misinterpretation.

Elements of Exchange in the Prologue

Only a trace remains in the *Fourth Book* prologue of the sideshow barker who has manipulated us over the course of three books. No longer hawking a product in 1552, he is a patent-medicine man grown old, donning glasses to see his patients better and inquiring after their health. In all likelihood, the narrator's preoccupation with health reflects Rabelais's own age-related infirmities, for he portrays himself as both doctor and patient, establishing a bond of identity between himself and the reader: "As for myself, I thrive by virtue of Pantagruelism. . . . Is it not the Bible which derides . . . the physician who neglects his own health? Does not the Holy Book say: 'Physician, heal thyself!'" (*FB*, Prol., 495). In contrast to young Alcofribas, the mature Rabelais offers no wonder drugs as an instant cure for his clients' ailments and his own. What he is peddling with new soft-sell techniques is a value system, born of his profession and advanced age, in which health equals wealth. This new economic paradigm, which reflects negatively upon the risky voyage Panurge is undertaking for epistemological profit, finds its logic in an inverted syllogism no less paradoxical than the Silenus box: if "health is our life" (496), then life without health is "no life" (496), or "an image of death" (497). That Rabelais views this as an economic equation is affirmed by his repeated references to deprivation and by his use of the word *eschange* or "exchange." Asclepiades, he tells us, exchanged life for death (*feist de vie à mort eschange* [*OC, FB*, Prol., 524]) when he fell "from the top of a defective, rotten staircase" (496), in a symbolic tumble from one extreme to the other that contraindicates the scaling of heights. Incompatible in the long run with extremism, health also functions within the prologue as a metaphor of *mediocritas* (moderation), a behavioral ideal resembling the golden mean, which was valued as "golden" and "precious" (*FB*, Prol., 497) by the ancients. Mediocritas for Rabelais is a relative measure defined by the avoidance of excess. Zachary, for example, who was "too small" (497) to see over the crowd, wanted "nothing more" (*rien plus* [*OC, FB,* Prol. 525]) than to see Christ, and his *médicore* or "moderate" (*FB*, Prol., 497) wish was granted. Similarly, the narrator tells us that gouty humanists who desire only good health, and "nothing more" (*rien plus* [*OC, FB,* Prol. 537] than health, stand a good chance of being requited if it "please[s] the Lord" (*FB*, Prol., 507), whereas those who scorn their physical well-being and seek only "profit" or "gain" (508) risk having "neither one nor the other" (*n'obtiennent l'un ne l'autre* [*OC FB*, Prol. 537]).

On the surface, this advocacy of modest or "moderate" goals flies in the face of Gargantua's advice in 1532 that his son should become an "abyss" of knowledge, learning everything there is to know. Because the abyss connotes vacuity as well as copia, however, there is some suggestion even in 1532 that inflationary ambitions carry with them the risk of deflated dreams and even perdition. More tragic than epic, the risk of nothingness or annihilation among characters who seek everything finds models in classical and biblical figures, such as Sisyphus, Prometheus, Lucifer, and Eve, all aspiring "humanists" who reach for too much and pay dearly. Within Rabelais's mythology, this loss of everything by humans who overstep their limitations hinges upon the hypothesis of a two-tiered economy organized by the gods and beyond man's ken. When humans attempt to overdraw their celestial "balance" by appropriating goods not intended for them, they are penalized within this new paradigm. Conversely, people like Couillatris who husband the blessings allotted them and ask favors sparingly of the gods may well accrue dividends beyond their original allotment.

The story of Couillatris, a woodcutter who loses his *coingnée* or "ax" and asks the gods to replace it, constitutes the narrative core of the *Fourth Book* prologue. As a test of the woodcutter's honesty and mediocritas, which stands in ironic contrast to the epic tests of heroism punctuating the body of the *Fourth Book*, the gods offer him a choice of three swords: "One made of gold, one of silver, and his own" (*FB*, Prol., 504). The justification for this test hinges upon the same inadequacies of linguistic exchange that Rabelais explores in the corpus of his novel. When Couillatris prays for the return of his ax, the phallic god Priapus points out that the word *coingnée* is connotatively polyvalent: like the ax it replaces linguistically, the verbal token's value depends upon its use or context. Defined not only as an "instrument used for cutting and splitting wood" (*FB*, Prol., 502), *coingnée* also refers colloquially and scatologically to trollops and the male genitalia. Given the word's ambiguity, Priapus jokingly wonders "just what sort of" (504) *coingnée* the woodcutter is seeking, a question that Jupiter attempts to resolve by offering Couillatris both the lost wooden ax and its two facsimiles.

Because Couillatris chooses his own humble blade, far more valuable than the gold and silver ones for his trade, the gods reward his honesty and modesty by giving "him the other two in the bargain" (*FB*, Prol., 504). Having no use for the shiny but untempered new axes, which are more suitable for display purposes than for felling trees, the woodcutter subsequently trades them for gold and silver coins, which make him the "richest man in the country" (505). But instead of hoarding his new wealth or consuming it unproductively like Panurge, his *Third Book* counterpart (*TB*, II), Couillatris invests the coins in a cornucopia of useful and productive commodities such as farms, barns, mills, and oxen (505). By way of contrast, the literary descendants of Picrochole, who attempt to emulate Couillatris's good fortune, going so far as to buy axes and lose them intentionally, pay for their greed with their lives: "Not a man but chose the golden," Rabelais tells us, "but as the fellow bent down to pick it up, Mercury . . . chopped his head off" (506). Interestingly enough, Rabelais expresses the entire sequence as an economic equation: "The number of severed heads," he tells us, "was exactly equal to the number of lost axes" (506).

This concluding equation of equality, representative of the world as it should be, at once rectifies and stands in marked contrast to the anecdote's opening sequence of imbalances and disproportions, characterizing the world as it is, which differentiates dramatically between the "poor" Couillatris with his "sorry livelihood" and the "prosperous master-woodcutters of the region" (*FB, Prol.*, 498). Even more than Panurge, the struggling woodcutter reflects the socioeconomic inequalities that subtend the social system in which he functions. Dependent for his livelihood upon the ax, without which "he would have met death . . . six days later" (498), Couillatris prizes the blade not for its market worth or "show" but rather for its use value to himself and his community, judging it "as precious and valuable . . . as a kingdom to a king" (502). For this reason, he can accept no substitutions. For the subsequent characters who "lose" their axes, however, it is the blade's exchange value and potential for profit that constitute its worth. Unlike

Couillatris, subsequent woodcutters quit their jobs, sell their property, and trade the tools of their craft to await windfalls from their investment, which they judge to be "cheap" (506) compared with the potential for gain.

Like the Picrocholine War, the fable of Couillatris implicitly criticizes France's precapitalistic economy and the changing value system that accompanied it. Clearly, the counterfeit woodcutters who literally and figuratively lose their heads refer contextually to the growing class of money-hungry speculators in Renaissance France, many of whom squandered patrimonies and sacrificed their honor in ill-conceived get-rich-quick schemes. By linking this rash of speculation specifically to woodcutting, Rabelais obliquely reiterates his concern, previously stated in the *Third Book*, over the decimation of France's forestland for heat-intensive industry and for the generation of capital.[2] In the fable of Couillatris, Rabelais poetically rights the wrongs of this market economy, where money is valued over morality and greed is a predictor of success, by reversing its amoral reward system and instituting what passes for a moral economy, in which earthly goods are redistributed by a syncretic deus ex machina according to merit. For his honesty and modesty, the hardworking Couillatris is lavishly rewarded, and conversely, his dishonest imitators pay a price far greater than the "small cost" of their original investment.

On the level of textuality or linguistic exchange, the counterfeit woodcutters are also penalized for misreading the fable of Couillatris and the test-text of the gods. Much like Panurge in the *Third Book*, the woodcutter's neighbors use all the exegetical skills they can muster to unravel the mystery of his wealth: "They bustled about, inquired here and there, put their heads together, pried high and low, seeking to discover the exact circumstances, time, place and motivation of his enormous treasure" (*FB*, Prol., 505). Notwithstanding their epistemological and speculative efforts, the metatext they reconstruct is marred by crucial gaps, owing in part to the second- and thirdhand nature of their information. Like Panurge, who seeks an answer to the "woman question" without serious input from women, the woodcutter's neighbors rely upon third-party glosses rather than interrogating Couillatris himself. As a result, they erroneously conclude that "the constellation of the firmament and the aspects of the planets are now such that whoever loses a hatchet gains a fortune" (506).

Upon imitating Couillatris and "losing" their own axes, the neighbors compound their unintended initial error of exegesis with the willful misreading of another text: the hatchet that is a token of their own worth. When asked to assess the symbol's value and their own by reappropriating their own blade from a field of three axes, the woodcutter's neighbors respond by gilding the proverbial lily with a rewritten and self-serving metatext. With the creative verve of fiction writers, they paint their wooden axes gold. From an aesthetic standpoint, the difference between their own axes and the upgraded version they claim is the locus of representation, a sine qua non of literary exchange. Within the moralistic parameters of the fable, however, this self-serving gap between reality and representation figures as an abyss of deception that merits damnation.

Like Panurge and Rabelais himself, the woodcutter's neighbors are "speculators" in the fullest sense of the word, which is derived from the Latin *speculatus*, meaning "observed" or "looked." Not only risking money in anticipation of the term's modern usage, the neighbors also engage in conjecture and speculative thought aimed at sorting out or "seeing" the mysteries of their universe. While Rabelais does not develop a specific vocabulary of seeing in connection with the woodcutters, the theme is of such crucial importance in the development of his thought that he opens both the *Third Book* prologue and its successor with discourses on the problematics of (in)sight. The light of gold ("twinkling of doubloons" [*TB*, Prol., 293]), he suggests in the earlier prologue, may well blind us to the "light of day" (293). This is what occurs in the case of the ersatz woodcutters, who both deal in and are false images, flawed by their very specularity: instead of revealing truth, their speculative efforts merely reflect their own greed.

In an ironic breach of his own opposition to excess, the narrator pursues his anatomy of greed outside the parameters of the fable through the rhetorical process of accumulation. Concluding the prologue are three additional examples of cupiditas, the first two involving Parisian beggars and the last involving Genoese bankers, all of whom share the extravagant dream of amassing gold coins or tokens. The first beggar, Rabelais tells us, "wished for as many crowns as had been minted, taken, received and otherwise exchanged in the city" (*FB*, Prol., 507), and the second "wished as many golden crowns as could be stuffed into as many bags as might be sewn by all [the] needles" (508) that could be crammed into the Cathedral of Notre Dame. The Genoese bankers, finally, who spend their mornings plotting schemes to swindle people in the afternoon, "want crowns minted by old Guadagno himself" (508), a rich Lyonese banker whose name in Italian means "gain." Included in this discourse is an admission that the worth of the coins is variable, a fact indicated by the first beggar's wish for his allotment of coins "in terms of the price, rate and value current at the peak of the best year" (507).

Far from gratuitous, the parallels between these unstable monetary tokens and the polyvalent linguistic currency introduced earlier in the prologue provide a key for understanding the *Fourth Book* voyage. Historical records indicate that most European bullion in the sixteenth century was obtained from New World sources. By extension, many geographical voyages of the era, prototypes for Rabelais's fictional odyssey, were motivated by the same greed for gold that is excoriated in the *Fourth Book* prologue. Instead of imbuing his own navigators with this thirst for monetary wealth, however, as the prologue might lead us to expect, the author modifies the content of the paradigm he has constructed by directing Panurge's greed toward intellectual wealth and linguistic rather than monetary tokens. As superior as this alternative form of wealth is held to be by humanists, Rabelais's analogy between the two kinds of tokens, both unstable in value, has profoundly negative implications for the Utopians' epistemological quest for the word, which reflects the linguistic greed of Renaissance scholars.

Far from leaving behind the world of exchange, as its lack of marketplace rhetoric might suggest, the *Fourth Book* prologue interrogates the intellectual hubris of Renaissance humanism and the greed of sixteenth-century hedonists from an economic perspective. The cost-benefit equation underlying his advocacy of *mediocritas*, which is based on the assumption that the risks of *superbia* (presumption) outweigh its benefits, at once recalls and reverses the sales pitch issued by Alcofribas two decades earlier, when he buoyantly claimed that the prowesses of Pantagruel, consubstantial with his own literary undertaking, would more than reward our investment of time and attention. Now aging and embattled, the barker-bard of earlier prologues has changed his tune, warning his readers *not* "to lay aside [their] business" (*P*, Prol., 161) to follow his humanistic giants but to "work" and "seek, rather, moderation" (*FB*, Prol., 507). Given the discrepancies between this advice and the voyage itself, it appears at first glance that the prologue or "billboard" and main text are diametrically opposed, related only by the Silenus principle of antiphrasis. As we look at the corpus of the *Fourth Book*, however, it becomes clear that echoes of the prologue permeate the voyage narrative itself. In the face of death, even Panurge will renounce the ambition that made him set sail. More important, the entire literary voyage functions as a test of voyaging: it is a text that tests textuality, an

artwork that explores the potentialities and limitations of art, an epistemological quest that simultaneously examines the very possibility of
knowing.

Exploring the Frontiers of Exchange

If the prologue retains few traces of the market, the body of the text
compensates by taking us first to the fairs of Medamothi, a Greek island
whose name means "nowhere." Semantically analogous to Utopia and
Thélème, which also means nowhere, Medamothi is at once a positive
and negative takeoff on both the expansion of maritime commerce in the
Renaissance and the expectations for further growth generated by geographical discoveries.

**Medamothi, Dindenault, and the Letters: Idealized and De-
formed Exchange.** Paying with "monkeymoney," or free and abundant leaves (*FB*, II, 512), instead of the costly gold upon which their own
economy is based, the Utopians purchase exotic "novelties" that are
ultimately reified fantasies. Among their purchases are marvelous animals, including three mythical unicorns that are so swift, according to
legend, that they can never be captured by hunters, and a tarand of the
sort described by Pliny, so adaptable that it mutates perpetually, changing colors with each new mood and situation. While the unicorn and
tarand find extratextual referents in the rhinoceros and reindeer, respectively, for Rabelais they are primarily literary fauna, magically reconstituted from words that come to life on the page.

In a similar vein, the Utopians purchase masterpieces of graphic art at
Medamothi that transcend the known limits of representation, miracu-
lously capturing and giving visible form to cosmic mysteries and abstrac-
tions. Among these mock-idealistic paintings are the ephemeral ideas of
Plato, the atoms of Epicurus, and the invisible Echo. Transcending the
partial perspective of conventional paintings, which myopically home in
on a single moment of history, the tapestries exhibited at Medamothi
very nearly capture his-story in its totality, depicting the life and feats of
Achilles from conception to afterlife. Rendered in 78 embroidered
panels, this massive undertaking further seeks to eliminate the partiality
of any one historian's account by drawing material from a plethora of
sources, including Statius, Ovid, Homer, and Euripides. Complement-
ing his-story is a visible rendering of the silence that is her-story:
"Panurge bought a large painting copied from the needlework done of

yore by Philomela to show her sister [how] Tereus had raped her and cut her tongue, lest she tell the shame of it" (*FB*, II, 512).

These sublime but fictional works of art reflect in large measure the mimetic and revelational ideals of Renaissance artists, who sought to unite history and philosophy, the temporal and the eternal, within their creations. Even as he espouses these ideals, however, Rabelais mocks his own aspirations and those of his contemporaries by cloaking the entire episode in paradox. For all his interest in her-story, Panurge by his very nature will never decipher it *her* way. Already, Philomela's tale, which she intends to be disseminated by her sister, is the *copy* of a representation, first glossed by the victim herself and then reglossed by an unknown painter, probably male. Inevitably Panurge will retell her-story as his-story, in a second violation of female textuality. A second paradox in the makeup of these artworks is the ironic void out of which they are created and which ultimately relegates them to fiction. Not only does the name Medamothi mean "nowhere," but its king is pointedly absent, and Echo, the ideas, and the atoms are all invisible. If visible, these representations deviate markedly from their referents, and if not, they are merely blank slates, no more enlightening than the verbal approximations they seek to improve upon. The reverse side of Medamothi's artistic copia is thus emptiness, and Rabelais has situated it where it must remain, in the fiction of never-never land.[3]

The idealized exchange postulated at Medamothi, where the Utopians acquire precious novelties for very little money, is counterbalanced in chapter 5 through 8 by Panurge's explosive encounter with the sheep merchant Dindenault (Dingdong), who is among a shipload of Frenchmen returning from and bearing news of Lanternland. Instead of exchanging information like their fellow travelers, Panurge and Dindenault first trade insults in a verbal dual revolving around cuckoldry that is triggered by Panurge's strange attire. In the *Third Book*, we may recall, Panurge removes his codpiece to signify his readiness for marriage and attaches spectacles to his cap, signifying his desire to see the future. Dindenault, however, assigns these sartorial indicators or tokens a different value, interpreting the absent codpiece as a sign of emasculation and the protruding spectacles as horns representing cuckoldry: "Here's a splendid portrait of a cuckold" (*FB*, V, 520), he concludes, hurling an insult that Panurge repays in full by threatening to cuckold the merchant personally.

This initial deformation of constructive exchange is followed by a second variation on the theme, when Panurge in a spirit of mischief asks to buy one of Dindenault's sheep. Instead of quoting a fair price like his predecessors at Medamothi, Dindenault feigns reluctance to sell, claiming his animals "are meat for only princes and kings" (*FB*, VII, 524). This rejection of a direct offer to buy, on the grounds that worthier customers exist elsewhere—in Rouen (*FB*, VI, 523) and Pygmyland (*FB*, VII, 526), for example—recalls the bakers of Lerné in *Gargantua*, who refuse to sell cakes to neighboring shepherds and instead seek to cart them off to a regional market. If the herdsmen in Rabelais's earlier novel symbolize prelapsarian moral economies, Dindenault the sheep merchant is at once the distorted twin and the direct descendant of uncorrupted Arcadian shepherds, who subsisted by means of hard work and barter with neighbors. By way of contrast, Dindenault repeatedly invokes distant markets: not just Rouen and Pygmyland, where his product is used, but also Leicester (*FB*, VI, 523), Segovia (523), Turkey (524), Munich (524), and the Abruzzi (524), which all produced goods prized and occasionally sold in France. On one level, this extended trade network reflects very real and not wholly positive changes in the economy of Renaissance France. The transport of local goods to regional and international markets at times resulted in shortages at home, and conversely, the increased influx in France of commodities imported from abroad taxed an already weak economy. More intriguingly, however, Dindenault's invocation of geographical distance parallels the vast stretch of rhetorical ground that he covers before agreeing to sell: the distance of hyping, haggling, and bargaining that extends and distends postlapsarian business transactions.

Even his reluctance to sell is a price-gouging tactic. By arguing that his lambs are a rare breed in high demand among connoisseurs, the merchant inflates the herd's value rhetorically, in an exhaustive and resourceful encomium of the sheep's myriad uses that constitutes an anatomy of both salesmanship and the beast: "Let me but duly praise my animals' internal members, their shoulders, their legs . . . their saddles, their breasts, their livers, their tripe. Let me sing their bladders, out of which men make footballs. Let me hail their ribs, which serve the warriors of Pygmyland as little crossbows. . . . Nor shall I ever tire of lauding their heads, which, if you add a touch of sulphur, produce a miraculous decoction to loose the bellies of constipated dogs" (*FB*, VII, 526). Curiously reminiscent of the pantagruelion, the *Gargantuine Chronicles*, and even the renaissance man in its varied functionality, this sheep for all seasons ironically echoes Panurge's own characterization as a jack-of-all-trades or *homme à tout faire*. As if in recognition of this fact, Dindenault begins his discourse by comparing Panurge and the sheep, going so far as to suggest that the husky animal is heavier and thus more valuable than the unimpressive specimen of humanity before him: "You, Robin Mutton, shall sit upon one scale; Robin Sheep, here, shall sit upon the other. I wager a peck of Arcachon oysters that he will outdo you in weight, price, and value" (FB, VI, 523). This scathing appraisal, which ranks the multitalented Panurge below sheep in market value and sheer usefulness, has implications that are patently antihumanistic.

In apparent confirmation of Dindenault's assessment, Panurge mutton-headedly allows himself to be fleeced by the merchant to the tune of "three Tours pounds" (FB, VII, 526), a price so inflated that it would buy him five or six sheep in Utopia. Rather than end his essay on exchange here, with the satiric bilking of the spendthrift Panurge at the hands of a stereotypically greedy salesman, Rabelais raises the stakes dramatically by adding one more "payback" to this spiraling series of transactions. Upon taking possession of his redefined "golden fleece," Panurge promptly "tossed his bleating purchase into the sea" (FB, VIII, 527), inciting the entire herd to follow their comrade overboard. As Panurge clearly plans, a distraught Dindenault pursues his fortune sheeplike into the ocean, ultimately wagering and losing his life in a struggle against prohibitive odds to save his herd. Within the inflationary economy of the episode, Dindenault's death is his payment for having cheated Panurge financially, an act that itself "repays" Panurge for verbally stealing the merchant's wife. As for the sum Panurge paid for the drowned sheep, he claims it was a bargain in terms of sheer entertainment value: "Have I not had more than fifty thousand francs' worth of amusement?" responds Panurge when Friar John chides him for giving money to a drowning man. "No man ever afforded me pleasure but I rewarded him. . . . By the same token, no man ever caused me grief without repenting" (FB, VIII, 528).

Panurge's assessment of the transaction in terms of its entertainment value is echoed by most readers, who view the derivative Dindenault frame, inspired by Folengo and the Farce of Master Pathelin (c. 1465), primarily as a semantically indifferent pretext enabling Rabelais to display his comic genius. Clearly, however, the episode in its entirety illustrates the ethos of mediocritas expounded by Rabelais's narrator in the prologue: "You are not the first man I know," says Panurge to Dindenault, "who, trying to get rich and be successful too quickly, sank back into poverty and even broke his neck in the fall" (FB, VII, 526). Because Dindenault attempts to extract an exorbitant sum from Panurge, he joins the dishonest woodcutters of the prologue in paying for his greed with his life. In a different and more troubling sense, Panurge is even greedier than his adversary, not so much for money as for oneupsmanship and pure entertainment, a hedonistic goal that he, like Dindenault, pursues at the expense of morality and life itself. Indeed Panurge survives the sheep-trading episode but in drowning Dindenault purely on a whim, he has wagered his immortal soul: "You are damning yourself," warns Friar John. "It is written: *Mihi vindictam* . . . Vengeance is mine" (*FB*, VIII, 528).

Separating the Medamothi and Dindenault episodes, both market-oriented, are two chapters about a different kind of exchange: Pantagruel's communications with his father back in Utopia during the course of the voyage. Unlike Dindenault, whose face-to-face discourse with Panurge is a masterpiece of distancing, the Utopian king and prince attempt to bridge the space that separates them by utilizing multiple and supplementary modes of exchange: letters, messengers, and a carrier pigeon, which "in less than two hours . . . covered a distance which had demanded three days and three nights of a ship at top speed" (*FB*, III, 514–15). Also instrumental in helping reduce the gap between father and son is memory, which supplements the written word or representation with sounds, images, and other sensory impressions from the past. Pantagruel, in fact, describes this mnemonic function as an idealized form of writing, "so deeply engraved upon the hindmost ventricle of my brain that I could conjure up your figure in its true, natural, living form" (*FB*, IV, 517).

In contrast to Dindenault, whose every word and gesture are geared toward selling, the Utopian communications revolve around giving and gifts. Dindenault's sale of an oriental sheep to Panurge is counterbalanced in chapter 4 by Pantagruel's gift to his father of the exotic tarand and three unicorns he purchased at Medamothi. This gift of livestock and the accompanying compendium of data about the animals make Pantagruel, no less than the merchant, a middleman in the dissemination of goods and information to consumers back home; but unlike Dindenault, the prince demands nothing in return. True, his own present to Gargantua is directly preceded by a gift from his father of "diverting books" (*FB*, III, 515), which increases the prince's sense of debt: "I am . . . overwhelmed by infinite obligations," he tells the king, "all of which arise from your vast bounty" (*FB*, IV, 517). Instead of attempting to repay this obligation, though, Pantagruel claims to be "wholly unable to make the slightest return" (517), in part because the debt is so vast, and in part because objects freely given cause the recipient to incur a moral as well as material debt, which endures even after being reciprocated. Within this idealized gift economy, however, the giver as well as the recipient benefits, deriving moral rather than monetary interest from the transaction in the form of unending gratitude from the recipient, who maintains the gift "in perpetual memory" (517).

The correspondence between Pantagruel and his father thus sets forth the ideal of a political, intellectual, and representational economy that is based upon generosity and sharing rather than greed and serves to minimize rather than maximize the distance between giver and recipient. Diametrically opposed to the worldview of Dindenault, this ideal is strengthened connotatively by the parent-child metaphor used to express it. Rather than acting solely out of duty or for self-serving motives, Gargantua showers gifts upon Pantagruel because of "the affection a father naturally bears a beloved son" (FB, III, 515). The mnemonic image of Gargantua inscribed in Pantagruel's brain is thus reciprocated: "You have never once," the king tells his son, "been out of my mind" (515). This familial model of giving and of representation is of such central importance in chapters 3 and 4 that Rabelais rearticulates it in the figure of the carrier pigeon, whose celerity and value as a messenger increase sharply "when it has eggs or young ones awaiting it in its nest" (514). Impelled forward by a "dogged concern for the presence and protection of its offspring" (514), the bird quickly bridges the distance between subject and object in an efficient act of communication.

The parental donor is also by definition a procreator whose archetype is God, an analogy that Rabelais makes clear at the outset of Gargantua's letter by referring to the grâces or "gifts" (FB, III, 515) that Pantagruel has received from heaven. Given the historical context, it is reasonable to assume that these "grace[s]" obtained "by divine election" (par élection divine [OC FB, III, 547]) refer in part to a state of theological grace. At the same time, though, this divine analogy enriches the metaphor of the giving parent by strengthening its representational implications. Both God and the other parent-figures of these chapters reproduce and hence represent children in their own image: like Rabelais, they are authors. Within the economy of literary exchange, however, the writer paradoxically figures as both son and father: the one sails away like Pantagruel from the literary ancestors to whom he is indebted, at once forging new ground and maintaining his textual progenitors—"our ancient writers" (FB, IV, 518)—"in perpetual memory"; and the other reproduces and represents himself both sexually and textually, consigning a shipload of "hope[s]" and "fear[s]" (FB, III, 515), wisdom and erudition ("Hesiod tells us" [515]), intertexts ("some diverting books" [515]) and contexts ("what has happened at my court" [516]), to a literary vessel that sails into the future without him, trying to reach new generations.

Ennasin, Cheli, and Chiquanous: Strange Exchange and Countereconomies. As far as we know, Pantagruel and his father never again make contact, and the next new world he visits, immediately after the Dindenault episode, is an island *without* conventional fathers and mothers, brothers and sisters, uncles and aunts. Formerly called Ennasin (noseless), in reference to the flat-nosed and red-skinned people who inhabit it, the Island of Alliances is the first in a trilogy of strange stopovers whose foreignness initially seems to offer different and potentially improved modes of exchange. In a variation on the world-upside-down topos, the only "father" that the culture recognizes is not an elderly male, symbolizing the past, but rather a "little [girl] of three or four" who addresses a "tall, snubnosed old man" (*FB*, IX, 530) as "daughter." Far from being a patriarchal or patrilineal culture, in the authoritarian mold of Utopia or Renaissance France, Ennasin has no genealogies, and the inhabitants' flat noses, shaped like an ace of clubs, figure as an inverse castration, signaling an apparent departure from filiation and phallocentrism. Replacing the diachronic and vertical genealogy of European civilization, with its restrictive definition of consanguinity, is a synchronic and lateral system of family ties in which "the islanders were all related to one another" (529), apparently by the same degree of kinship.

This creation of an entire society interrelated by familial bonds promises at first glance to restore and improve upon the moral economy outlined in chapters 3 and 4.[4] At the beginning of his *Third Book*, Rabelais proposes the simulation of familial nurturing as a way to establish peace and justice in Dipsody, and the correspondence between Gargantua and Pantagruel outlines a familial model of exchange resembling the perfect reciprocity of Thélème. Despite the absence of social hierarchies based on patriarchal bloodlines, however, Ennasin is by no means a strife-free or classless society. Its inhabitants include a "lady of high degree" (*FB*, IX, 531) and a toothless old man wearing high-heeled shoes who is described as *villain* (*OC*, 564), a word connoting base birth. Rabelais, in fact, builds up our expectations of reciprocity only to deflate them, concluding the chapter with a pointed return to Dindenault's market values, which are ironically rearticulated within the context of marriage: "I saw a sprig . . . marrying a sexagenarian," recounts the narrator in his closing anecdote. "We were told that he was not wedding her for her beauty, but through greed and avarice. He wanted the money in which she had been rolling" (533).

As important as the tension between avarice and altruism is within the novel, Rabelais ultimately devotes less attention in chapter 9 to monetary patterns of exchange and socioeconomic issues than to the linguistic process of reference and naming. The narrator's first allusion to nomenclature occurs at the beginning of the episode, when he informs us that the triangular body of land called Ennasin in the title is now known as the Island of Alliances. This shift from an old name whose etymology connotes lack and violence to a new and readily understandable appellation signifying peace and wholeness has many possible explanations. On a sociopolitical level, the token "alliance" communicates both the islanders' desire for constructive commerce with friendly visitors and their oneness of purpose in case of attack, improving immeasurably upon the wholly negative connotations of the old label, which alternately conjures up a tribe of savages slicing off noses and an army of emasculated cowards. From a purely domestic standpoint, moreover, the replacement of a name connoting absence and emasculation with a label signifying both marriage and the federation of households at once augurs well for social harmony and reproductive survival on the island and accurately reflects the unilateral bonds of kinship uniting the islanders.

This apparent effort to improve the representational accuracy of the island's name, by choosing one as closely "allied" as possible to its referent, sets the stage for a full-blown fantasy on the dynamics of onomastic exchange. Replacing family names and traditional kinship terminology on the island are families of *words* coupled not by vertically derived etymologies, the linguistic equivalent of genealogies, but rather by function and syntactical proximity. The epithets and endearments exchanged by Ennasin couples include the sexually evocative "oyster" and "shell" (*FB*, IX, 531), "glove" and "mitten" (531), "egg" and "omelet" (531). While this eccentric experiment in naming succeeds in dismantling both the genealogical biases and universalizing tendencies of conventional kinship terms, which equate pleasant elderly aunts with disagreeable young aunts, there is nothing to suggest that the islanders' overparticularized onomastic system, with its infinitely varied repertory of epithets, improves appreciably upon its European counterpart.

This is not to say that the Ennasin endearments and nicknames are signifiers without signifieds. Despite their ludic quality, it is likely that the epithets have private meaning for the couples who choose and use them, but their lack of universally understood symbolism makes them failures as linguistic tokens. As foreigners, the Utopians are stumped, in part because the onomastic currency is too "insular," and in part because they bring their own cultural biases to the exegetical process, attempting to decode the islanders' kinship terminology "with reference to [their] own customs" (*FB*, IX, 531). Even after being told that there are no mothers on Ennasin, the Utopians persist in using the term on the premise that the relationship it signifies is universal and that only the names for it differ. The Ennasin mayor disagrees: "What mother are you talking about? . . . Mothers belong to *your* world" (532). What the Utopians fail to contemplate is the vertiginous possibility that females do not give birth on Ennasin, and that they have truly entered a netherworld in which both the words *and* the reality subtending them are too strange to be assimilated and understood.

Rabelais twice uses the word *étrange* or "strange" in this part of his novel, and its various connotations help us understand the thread of conceptual unity tenuously linking the episodes of Ennasin, Cheli, and Chiquanous. Representing eccentric variations on the currency and rites of social exchange, the cultures of Ennasin and Chiquanous are specifically described as "strange" by the chapter headings, and the intervening visit to Cheli in chapter 10 completes the odd trilogy. "Strange" first of all means that the cultures differ noticeably from Utopia: while each is a distorted mirror of sixteenth-century France, with its euphemisms for sexual relationships, elaborate ceremonies, and pesky functionaries, the difference between the fictional "them" and "us" is sufficiently pronounced to make the "foreign" cultures exotic and entertaining. More than a mere source of diversion, the three fictional societies are also potentially instructive in that at the outset they appear to offer superior modes of exchange: Ennasin, as we have already seen, consists of a vast extended family; Cheli, whose name means "peace" in Hebrew, boasts fertile farmland capable of producing bountiful crops; and the Chiquanous subscribe to a work ethic capable of raising them to the forefront of industrial and/or agricultural production.

Upon closer inspection, though, the currencies and rites of social exchange in each society prove to be estranged from truth, a second connotation of the term *étrange*. To visit these three cultures is to enter a world of role-playing and substitutions. On the Island of Alliances, the otherness of the kinship terminology or onomastic currency, which at first promises a superior form of exchange, in general does nothing to alter the sameness of greed upon which social ties are founded. Similarly, on Cheli, which is ruled by King Panigon (Biscuit), the valuing of form or brilliant and copious compliments over meatier and more substantive greetings leaves at least one member of the Utopian crew famished.

Instead of lingering near the palace gate after his arrival to exchange kisses and small talk with ladies of the court, as "was the country's courteous custom" (*FB*, X, 534), Friar John slips off to the "magnificent kitchen," where "everything goes by the dozen and score" (534). What he eats is as copious as the feast of compliments that his fellow crew members are fed by the ladies, in a welcome ceremony whose hollowness is accentuated by the friar's infinitely more fulfilling reception from the cooks: "I understand better the customs and ceremonies of kitchens," explains the friar, "than all this crapocumshittening with these women, *magni magna*, bow to your partner, posture here, salute there, double bow, sweep, reverence, accolade, kiss the lady's hand" (534). The emptiness of these gestures, in which unproductive hands lift nothing but air, contrasts dramatically with Friar John's memory of the bustling kitchen, and with our own image of the monk's full hands as he gnaws a bone or lifts a bowl to his mouth.

For all its vaunted wealth, the currency of social exchange among the aristocracy at Cheli rings so hollow that Pantagruel finds an excuse (*fonda son excuse* [*OC, FB*, X, 566]) to set sail again the day of his arrival, and Rabelais likewise declines to linger poetically on the island, quickly abandoning his impoverished account of Panigon's court to embark on several spicier anecdotes and subnarratives. The first of these, recounted by Friar John, is an incident, like the Cheli narrative, involving token kisses, symbols of affection so inflated and devalued as signifiers that they are given and received indiscriminately among strangers. The ritual is so mechanical that the anecdote's protagonist, the Lord of Guercharois, blindly kisses an entire retinue of pages disguised as women before learning he has been tricked. This farcical assignment of signifiers to the wrong signified prompts the embarrassed nobleman to renounce kissing altogether, mistrusting both his own judgment and the reliability of face value in a world of mask and illusion.

The second subnarrative branching off from Cheli is an account of Epistemon's visit to Florence 20 years earlier, in the company of a group of travelers that included a monk named Bernard Lardon. After visiting monument after monument, and hearing his companions wax poetic about the splendid artwork, the monk begins to complain about the dearth of eating establishments on their itinerary: "In the length and breadth of this whole city," he laments, "I've not seen one single pastrycook's shop. . . . These porphyries and marbles are beautiful, I will not deny; but our Amiens cheesecakes are more to my taste" (*FB*, XI, 536). Linked to the main narrative by the satiric theme of monks in the kitchen, a theme that itself represents a rupture between the spiritual signifier "monk" and the material signifier "food," this anecdote quite forcefully restates Friar John's implicit objection to Cheli: there and in Florence, the most highly valued cultural manifestations and tokens of esteem are for show only, in contrast to the far higher use value of culinary art. The culture of Cheli is thus flawed on two counts: its gifts are useless, and its signs signify nothing.

Of the first four ports of call visited by Utopians, the strangest by far is a land called Procuration, inhabited by Chiquanous (Catchpoles), whose name, semantically similar to that of Panurge, means "capable of anything." Like the residents of Cheli, the Chiquanous offer hollow "bowing and scraping" (*FB*, XII, 538) in place of real food or sustenance ("they did not invite us to drink or eat" [538]), but in keeping with their names, they also volunteer to work for pay. Instead of embracing the kind of work ethic advocated by Rabelais in the prologue, however, the Chiquanous shun social responsibility by serving as proxies or professional substitutes, sacrificing their own identities, moral values, and health to represent others in volatile situations. "When a monk, priest, usurer or attorney wishes harm to some country gentleman," explains an interpreter, "he sends a Catchpole to him. The Catchpole proceeds to serve a summons upon My Lord, to insult and outrage him impudently, according to his power and instructions" (538). As a result, the outraged nobleman characteristically gives the proxy a sound beating, "whereupon Catchpole is . . . rich for the next four months" (539), living off both his reward from the "monk, priest, usurer or attorney" (539) and his damage settlement from the nobleman who attacked him.

Functioning as fanciful reflections of the process servers in sixteenth-century France, the Chiquanous also constitute a variation on the world-upside-down motif: they are not paid to harm others, like "the denizens of Rome" and the hired thugs today who "support themselves by poisoning, beating and killing people" (*FB*, XII, 538), but rather earn their living and support their families by "being beaten" (538). Sacrificing their health for monetary wealth, the strange Chiquanous become proverbial gluttons for punishment, driven by economic motives akin to those that prompted the dishonest woodcutters to claim swords other than their own. Unlike their ancestors in the prologue, however, the Chiquanous are damned if they do and damned if they don't: with each beating they risk their lives, but without beatings "the Catchpoles, their wives and children would die of starvation" (538). In this complicated world beyond the fable, the fine line between need and greed has become virtually indistinguishable.[5]

Like its predecessor, the Chiquanous episode branches off into two subnarratives, both involving role-playing and violent exchange. The first of these, recounted by Panurge, explains how the crafty Lord of Basché avoids being served with summonses and held liable for damages by the Chiquanous. Each time a Chiquanous visits him, Basché stages a fake wedding ceremony, which, within the economy of the novel, parallels the practical joke played on the Lord of Guercharois following the Cheli narrative. The ceremonial kisses of chapter 10, however, have been replaced by their antithesis at the castle of Basché, where the traditional custom among wedding guests of "exchang[ing] light fist-cuffs" (FB, XII, 540] in jest, similar to our own backslapping and high fives, has been rigged to maim the Chiquanous. Wearing steel gauntlets covered with kid, the wedding actors pummel the Chiquanous so severely that they can never return and do so in such a jovial manner that the professional proxy cannot collect damages. From Basché's viewpoint, which we as readers share, the symmetry of this scam is immensely satisfying: for to outwit the Church and government officials who use proxies to do their dirty work, the clever nobleman substitutes his own proxies, adding another degree of role-playing to the farce.

Within both the Cheli and Chiquanous episodes, the players are segregated along socioeconomic lines. Chapter 10 satirizes the theatrical affectations, counterfeit emotions, stylized social rituals, and elaborate costumes of the leisured classes, whose playacting for fun and show serves paradoxically as a source of group identity. It is by the behavioral and sartorial tokens they display that the Lord of Guercharois and his peers recognize each other, and his confidence in both the indicators and his own identity is shaken by the pages' success at cross-dressing, which transgresses social as well as sexual boundaries. "If pages disguised as women had deceived him," explains Rabelais, "then . . . how did he know these women here were not footmen and grooms?" (FB, X, 535). By way of contrast, the Chiquanous episode deals with role-playing for survival among the working classes. Not just the Chiquanous but most of Basché's actors as well are social dependents, such as cooks, grooms, valets, and porters, who profit marginally from their thespian undertaking and have no choice but to accept the commission. The masochistic confrontation that ensues between opposing proxies resembles a duel between seconds, one that bloodies and maims the paid agents of each principal while leaving the latter parties unscathed. "How much better," observes Epistemon, assessing blame on the principal rather than his proxy, "if that hail of glad gauntlets had fallen upon the fat prior" who hired the Chiquanous. "In comparison," he continues, "those Catchpoles (poor devils!) were quite innocuous!" (*FB*, XVI, 550). It is not a fat prior but rather a fat friar who gets his due in the second subnarrative, an anecdote about religious representation that the Lord of Basché recounts to his players on the eve of their second performance. The story focuses upon a rivalry between two different kinds of actors: on the one hand, a band of amateur thespians producing a passion play, and on the other hand, a mendicant friar who refuses to lend them the costume he uses to play God. This refusal to give and obsession with taking contrasts sharply with the moral economy outlined earlier by Pantagruel and Gargantua, making the friar an heir of both Dindenault and the bakers of Lerné. More important, the stance is radically at odds with the cleric's role as an agent of God, a posture that goes only as deep as his vestments. By way of contrast, the thespians who parade through the town as devils represent their prototype so convincingly that the friar dies of fright, in part because he "refused [the old peasant playing] God the Father a wretched cope" (*FB*, XIII, 543). The devils, who are urged by their leader Villon to "*live* [their] parts" (544), clearly tie in with the representational ideal of living art that Rabelais explores later in the Frozen Words episode. The friar, on the other hand, figures as their negative antipode, a false image of the deity whose blasphemous misrepresentation merits death.

Open Mouths and Bulging Bellies: The Dynamics of Consumption and Production

If role-playing and theatricality are integral forms of exchange in the *Fourth Book*, so is the telling of tales, a convention of the epic sea voyage rendered even more popular by the spate of *nouvelles* in sixteenth-century France.[6] In addition to their aesthetic function, Rabelais's tales serve a cognitive purpose: helping him explore the constant exchange with past experience that helps inform our present-day experiences, identity, and choices. While the stories interrupt the fictional and unilinear narrative, they realistically capture the multidimensionality of life and consciousness, which consists not just of events but of memories, shared experiences, analogies, and free association that often has only a peripheral connection with "objective reality."

Bringuenarilles, the Macreons, and the Storm: The Exchange from Life to Death. As an oral process, storytelling fits into the network of open mouths that punctuate the *Fourth Book*, often in tandem with bulging bellies. Following the Chiquanous episode is an account of Bringuenarilles, the giant who died after eating "every skillet, pot, kettle, cauldron and tureen in the whole land" (*FB*, XVII, 553). He is succeeded by figurative jaws of death during the tempest (*FB*, XVIII–XXIV), by the open orifice of the sea monster (*FB*, XXXIII–XXXIV), and eventually, by the rampant consumption of Messer Gaster (*FB*, LVII–LXII), in whom eating and speaking are conflated. On one level, these open abysses recall the predominantly positive oral imagery of the *Pantagruel*, where the newborn giant's ravenous hunger symbolizes growth, production, and the will to know. In the *Fourth Book*, this urge to consume still motivates the Utopians, who choose drinking vessels as their emblems (*FB*, I), indulge in banquets, and discourse repeatedly on cooking.

Grafted onto the joyous and productive consumption of the earliest novel, however, is the more negative symbolism of open mouths within the epic tradition, where they typically represent the threat of death. Panurge fears being swallowed by both the sea during the tempest scenes ("I sink, I drown, I perish!" [*FB*, XXI, 566]) and by the *physétère* or whale in chapter 33: "God's death, this is Leviathan," he exclaims; "that whale will swallow us up like so many pillules. . . . I vow it is the sea monster sent by Neptune to devour Andromeda" (*FB*, XXXIII, 593). In a more general way, the themes of death and negative consumption are omnipresent in the novel: the Macreons' civilization is in ruins—they discourse on the death of heroes—and the Frozen Woods preserve the cries of drowned voyagers. The *Fourth Book* is thus articulated as a tension between positive and negative consumption, between growth and decay.

Episodes involving negative consumption and death loosely mirror birth scenes and growth-oriented consumption in the first novel. The birth of a giant in 1532 is answered by the death of a giant 20 years later, and while overeating enhances Pantagruel's growth, it ultimately kills Bringuenarilles. The birth of a hero in the *Pantagruel* has moreover given way in the *Fourth Book* to the death of heroes, and the prodigies that augured the Utopian prince's birth have been replaced by proliferating monsters, which at once accompany and foretell the extinction of heroes. The phenomenon is at least partially explicable in terms of Rabelais's advanced years and the Renaissance's waning promise, factors that threatened to invert the original humanistic premises upon which the earlier novels were constructed. In contrast to Friar John's belief that heroes and demigods live forever, Pantagruel views their passing as part of an economic equation in which the proliferation of vice automatically triggers a reduction in the number of heroes (*FB*, XXVII, 580). Not insignificantly, his own heroics have disappeared along with his original gigantic stature.

The Utopians' extended discourse on the death of heroes occurs during their visit to the Sporade Islands, the land of Macreons (old people), who live on the outskirts of a vast "woods" or "wasteland" (*FB*, XXV, 576), which holds the souls of heroes and the ruins of "temples, obelisks, pyramids, monuments and ancient tombs" (576). The episode directly follows the tempest and death of Bringuenarilles, a logical progression within the syntax of both allegory and epic, as the crew's brush with death triggers a closer look at the human condition. The island's aged residents symbolize the physical decay facing all humans, Panurge and Pantagruel included, but more important, the dead heroes imply moral degeneration; the wasteland, agricultural inactivity; the ruins, cultural dilapidation; and the inscriptions on the ruins, representational and epistemological erosion. Not just a sign of agricultural inactivity, the reforested land of the Macreons further signifies epistemological confusion similar to that of Dante's pilgrim in the *Divine Comedy*: in contrast to the deforested farmland of Beauce, where the tree of knowledge is appropriated and humanized, the unruly forestland of the Macreons represents the unappropriated and labyrinthine masses of data uncovered by humanistic scholarship. The inscriptions, by extension, figure as potential symbols of truth embedded in the center of the labyrinth: written in foreign languages on decaying tombs in a deserted forest on a distant island, the inscribed letters and hieroglyphs constitute a text more remote than the twice-buried manuscript of *Gargantua*.

Intellectually and physically, the Utopians appear to have bitten off more than they, or at least Panurge, can chew. So frightened by the storm that he defecates in his pants and babbles, Panurge specifically links his predicament to overconsumption, a malady that killed Bringuenarilles in the preceding episode: "God help us," he cries, "we shall be drinking all too much as this ship goes down" (*FB*, XVIII, 557). In a variation on the *Pantagruel*, where the open-mouthed protagonist is urged to consume and interiorize an "abyss" of data, this new gulf that doubles as the jaws of death threatens to swallow up the thirsty protagonists. The threat of drowning, which results from excessive "appetite," causes Panurge to take stock of the disproportion between consumption and production in his own behavior. "Thrice-happy . . . the humble cabbage-planter," he laments (558), echoing the narrator's advocacy in the prologue of hard work and moderate wants. At the same time, however, Panurge shuns the entreaties of his hardworking comrades "to come and help [them]" (*FB*, XIX, 559) save the sinking ship, opting instead for *literary* production in the form of a will.[7]

Functioning simultaneously as the antithesis of production, this choice to write instead of fight echoes Panurge's role as a storyteller in the Dipsodian War, as well as the narrator's own decision in the *Third Book* prologue to roll his literary barrel rather than fortify walls and dig trenches. Rabelais mocks his own behavior even then, suggesting his art is in vain (*en vain-vin*), and this doubt about the funtionality of writing is resurrected during the tempest scene. For Panurge's will, more clearly than the narrator's barrel, is an empty one. With the exception of his title and a quantity of debts, he has nothing to bequeath. By the same token, he leaves no heirs to inherit this dubious legacy, and if his will is tossed out to sea, the chances of its ever being read are minimal.

Shrovetide, the Whale, and the Chitterlings: The Intersection of Consumption and Production. The description of Quaresmeprenant or King Lent, which immediately follows the tempest and death of heroes episode, further explores this tension between production and consumption. On one level, this tonsured demi-giant, who lives on Tapinois (Sneaks Island) not far from the Macreons, is a figure of abstinence and self-denial who directly opposes the immoderate appetites of Panurge. Not only does the name Quaresme or Carême mean "Lent," but its bearer *excretes* rather than consumes foodstuff, dresses only in gray, and is a mortal enemy of the Andouilles (Chitterlings) and Tripe ruled by Mardigras (carnival). Moreover, many of his body parts and mental traits resemble tools of production, including windmills (*FB*, XXX, 586), an auger (586), a shuttle (586), a mason's mortar (586), a pitchfork (587), a sickle (587), a trowel (587), and carpenter's planes (*FB*, XXXI, 588).

This pro-production and anti-consumption stance is only skin-deep, however: like most figures in Rabelais, Quaresmeprenant is so beset with ambiguities that he functions only partially as as figure of Lent, reflecting instead the ambivalence of the characters themselves.[8] This hybridity is already evident at the onomastic or linguistic level. While the term "Quaresme" by itself designates the period of austerity between Carnival and Easter—or, more specifically, the first Sunday in Lent—the combination "Quaresmeprenant" is popularly associated with carnival or Mardi Gras. In his austerity, moreover, the demi-giant is greedy, "a glutton for peas" (*FB*, XXIX, 584), and the larding sticks he produces connote the fat meat of carnival that he abjures. During a strictly observed Lenten season, of course, the sticks would be useless, a fact that further suggests that Quaresmeprenant is less productive than he first appears. Xenomanes, who describes the monster from afar rather than taking the crew to visit him, admits that "while working, he did nothing, and, doing nothing, worked" (XXXII, 590), a regimen recalling Gargantua's unproductive activities under the sophists. By the same token, Quaresmeprenant scorns reproduction by boycotting weddings (*FB*, XXIX, 584–85) and beating children (584); moreover, he shuns the kind of intercourse with others that would allow him to grow, refusing to interact with the Andouilles, who represent food, women, and his own sexuality. When he does marry, it is with Mid-Lent, another figure of abstinence, and together they produce replicas of their own sterility in the form of "local adverbs and certain double fasts" (*FB*, XXX, 587).

On one level, this tonsured monster who "swarms with pardons, indulgences, and stations" (*FB*, XXIX, 584) is clearly a figure of the clergy, not just Catholics like du Puy Herbault but "the Calvinist impostors" (*FB*, XXXII, 592) as well, whom Rabelais considered unnatural in their denial of basic human appetites and "hypocritical" (592) in their failure to practice what they preached. Within the syntax of the allegory, however, this anticlerical satire is secondary to Quaresmeprenant's primary function as the potentially corrective antipode of Panurge's appetite for knowledge and of humanistic overconsumption in general. That the Utopians have mentally moved in the direction of temperance, interrogating their own superbia, is suggested by Pantagruel's initial eagerness to visit the island (*FB*, XXIX, 584) and by his subsequent confusion with Quaresmeprenant, who like the Utopian prince is prone to sobriety and exceedingly large in stature. "You look nothing like King Lent, yet these worshipful Chitterlings might easily have taken you for him," points out the freewheeling Friar John to his more conservative companion (*FB*, XXXVI, 598). The resemblance is only partial, however; for unlike Pantagruel, Quaresmeprenant is so excessive in his fasting and so festive in his excretions that he figures as a monstrous and intemperate overcorrection of humanistic exuberance, far removed from the mediocritas that the narrator posited as a behavioral ideal in the prologue.

On Xenomanes' advice, the Utopians opt not to sail in the direction of Tapinois or Lent's kingdom, thereby rejecting out of hand the behavioral alternative of fasting, weeping, and renunciation that he offers. In what is almost a contrapuntal development, the episodes immediately following the Quaresmeprenant interlude mark at least a tentative return to consumption, which emerges as a necessary ingredient of survival in a world where one eats or is eaten. When the whale, a variation on the Lenten theme of seafood, threatens to swallow them in chapters 33 and 34, the Utopians turn the tables and consume him instead—not in a literal banquet, though indeed they feast after the kill, but rather by having the whale dissected and by selling the precious oil of its kidneys to line their pocketbooks (FB, XXXV, 596). Whether the Utopians use this money to buy food or actually eat part of the blubber is uncertain, but we do know that Quaresmeprenant's carnivalesque archrivals, the Andouilles, see them "examining whale urine" (FB, XLII, 613) and assume they are hostile Lenten forces.

Ironically, the Andouilles' own identity is no less ambivalent than that of the Utopians, for they figure as both friend and foe, male and female.[9] Xenomanes characterizes them specifically as "doubledealers" (FB, XXVI, 598), and the narrator defines them as both sausage and serpent, adding erotic and epistemological connotations to the appetite they represent: "The serpent who tempted Eve was the Chitterling called in Greek, Ithyphallus" (FB, XXXVIII, 604–5). As symbols of both the forbidden knowledge Panurge seeks and of the rich culinary and intellectual diet upon which Pantagruel was raised, the sausages are indeed "traitors" (FB, XXXVI, 598), albeit unwitting ones, when they attack the friendly Utopians, their most ardent devotees.

Figuring anew the dangers of overconsumption, the sausages are defeated not by consumers but producers, as an army of cooks armed with kitchen utensils (FB, XLI, 611) emerges from a "Trojan" sow to skewer the Andouilles. With a crew of cooks on hand, a battlefield strewn with sausages, and a battery of skillets and frying pans, the stage is painstakingly set for a carnivalesque banquet of Gargantuan proportions; yet the anticipated feast, in which the would-be consumers will be consumed, fails to materialize, as mustard emanating from Mardigras, the sausages' porcine god in the sky, resurrects the fallen, phallic Andouilles in a triumph of reproduction and regeneration. This sausage miracle, which improves upon Christ's miracle of the fishes, suggests that carnival even more than Lent is divinely ordained; but perhaps because they are still hedging their bets, the Utopians neither fete their victory nor accept the proffered tribute of Queen Niphleseth, who offers a lifetime supply of sausages to the Utopian court (FB, XLII, 613). Instead, consumption is deferred and displaced, as Gargantua sends his unwanted shipment of sausages to the King of Paris, where the symbols of knowledge promptly die, and Pantagruel opts for a different kind of exchange, one that is not culinary but erotic and epistemological. He gives the nubile monarch, whose name in Hebrew "means penis" (612), a phallic knife in exchange for information—or her story—about the flying hog.[10]

Ruach, Popefiggers, and Papimania: Spiritual Ports of Call

The decision on Pantagruel's part to consume epistemologically oriented data rather than the pork itself sets the stage for a series of spiritual stopovers, the first of which is Ruach, a word that means "spirit" in Hebrew. Subsisting not upon Utopian staples such as wine (*vin*) and meat (*viande*), but rather upon the similar sounding but semantically dissimilar *vent* (wind), the residents of this island feast not upon matter, such as the Andouilles, but rather upon "agitated air" (*FB*, XLIII, 616), in a conflation of eating and breathing. Like its predecessors, the episode is ambivalent in its symbolism, in part because the token "wind" has multiple and radically divergent connotations. On one hand, Aeolus's bag of wind and the breath of God have been assimilated to Rabelais's own cask of wine to generate an allegory of inspiration, aspiration, and expiration. With wind, the residents live, produce, and create; without wind, they become ill and die. On the other hand, this invisible source of life and creativity doubles as hot air or emptiness, the antithesis of art, and its manifestations are satirically anal as well as oral: in addition to gathering and storing atmospheric winds, the residents of Ruach also cultivate flatulence-producing "windflowers" that cause them to "[break] wind to good purpose" (614), constantly recycling and re-presenting their own inspiration.

On a moral level, Pantagruel's refusal to eat the Andouilles also stands in a relationship of antiphrasis to Bringuenarille's exploitative treatment of Ruach. Every year, the mayor of the wind eaters informs us, the neighboring giant comes to Ruach for a health cure and, unlike his higher minded Utopian counterpart, swallows "a great number of our windmills as you would a pill" (*FB*, XLIV, 618), depriving residents of a major source of food. By shifting here from micro- to macroeconomics, Rabelais allegorizes the interrelationship that necessarily links contiguous or overlapping economics, particularly when one is more powerful than the other. Because of his superior size and strength, and because he operates on market rather than moral principles, the bully Bringuenarilles routinely appropriates the commodities he needs to survive without addressing the deleterious effects of his gluttony upon others. Pantagruel, on the other hand, remaining true to the principles of caritas that have traditionally distinguished him from Panurge, refuses both the food and the fealty of Niphleseth, a relationship of dependency that, if enacted, would allow him to exploit her race with impunity. Ironically, the problems associated with market rather than moral systems of exchange also permeate the microeconomy of Ruach, where the rich hoard air in bags and the poor resort to stealing it (*FB*, XLIII, 615), in a reprise of Panurge's own deflationary trickery in the first novel. In addition to functioning on a political and material level, as an allegory of socioeconomic exploitation in which not just gold but even the air we breath is contested, the Ruach episode also figures the dialectics of literary inspiration, which, like these insular winds, may be either inherited or stolen, moribund or active, internal or external in origin.

Instead of focusing entirely upon aspiration or intake in these two chapters, Rabelais continues to unite consumption and production as a synergistic duo, as he does throughout the *Fourth Book*. Following in the footsteps of the Utopian crew in the tempest scene, of Pantagruel in his confrontation with the whale, and of the cooks in the sausage war, the residents of Ruach work resourcefully at sowing windflowers, devising fans, and setting up windmills for two reasons: to perpetuate the cycle of exchange that enables them to consume, and, equally important, to avoid *being* consumed. Their flatulent bodies, which consume and then recycle the windflowers they have produced by expelling wind for renewed consumption, allegorize the economic functions of a healthy body politic, which produces, consumes, and then produces again in a self-perpetuating and regenerative cycle.

The economic exploitation of these wind eaters by Bringuenarilles is mirrored in the relationship between the producers on the Island of Papefigues (Popefiggery) and the consumers of Papimania, which, like Ruach, are spiritual ports of call. For showing disrespect to the pope's image, a transgression figuring as their culture's original sin, the hardworking Papefigues of chapters 45 through 47 have been enslaved by the neighboring Papimaniacs, who idolize the Roman pontiff—or at least his picture, which they consider the "idea" of God—much as the Andouilles adore Mardigras or the Gastrolâtres (stomach worshipers) revere bellydom. As an "everlasting punishment" (*FB*, XLV, 620) for their ancestors' irreverence, the formerly wealthy Papefigues are visited by "plagues" and "famines" (620) that seem to emanate from God as part of a divine economy of retribution. As the episode progresses, however, we learn that devils, not gods, are perpetrating these scourges. This first slippage of the allegory's meaning, in which the agents of retribution remain metaphysical, inevitably suggests a second possibility: that the "devils" who have wasted the Island of Papefigues, bringing death and famine to its shores, are in fact human emissaries of Papimania, who have caused figurative and entirely man-made storms and plagues to be visited upon their independent-minded neighbors.

Much like the Papimaniac clergy who feed off parishioners, using their "voluntary contribution[s]" for "good drinking" and "good eating," (*FB*, LI, 634), or like the Roman see, which "draw[s] yearly from France . . . four hundred thousand ducats or more" (*FB*, LIII, 641), the devils who beleaguer the Papefigues aspire to profit without producing in the manner of absentee landlords, collecting a hefty share of the revenues from each crop at harvest time without lifting a finger to help the farmers. "We will divide the land's yield in two parts," dictates a young devilkin to a struggling farmer. "I choose for my portion what lies underground; you may have everything above earth's surface. . . . Meanwhile, do your duty: work away, churl, work away" (*FB*, XLV, 621). Unable to read and write, however, the ignorant young devilkin is so uninformed about production that he repeatedly chooses the part of each crop that is least in demand—wheat roots and beet leaves—and sells nothing at market, while the farmer reaps a handsome profit.

This lack of experience in production extends to reproduction as well, suggesting an ironic analogy between the devils and the priesthood: the resourceful Papefigues ultimately rid themselves of their dim-witted extortionist—who in frustration has proposed a scratching duel between himself and the farmer—when the farmer's wife convinces the devil that female genitalia, the locus of reproduction, are actually a wound created by male strength. In economic terms, moreover, she has sold him a line, using marketplace craftiness to inflate the value of her husband's fingernails and devalorize the devil's claws. This triumph of female ingenuity lends an intriguing symmetry to the episode, reminding us that a woman's breach of epistemological taboos is the biblical source of original sin. Wilier and less pious than her husband, who chooses to pray and pay penance rather than fight, this new Eve uses the "fruit" of her apostasy—an agile mind—to outsmart the devil, thereby saving her family and removing the yoke of intellectual repression.

Both damned and apparently delivered by their wits, the Papefigues seem to operate within an economy of survival common to the disenfranchised, combining the hard work of Couillatris with astuteness and occasional trickery. With characteristic ambivalence, however, Rabelais divides these traits between the Papefigue husband and wife, whose radically divergent approaches to salvation, the one pious and the other hubristic, engender two different grids of meaning. Clearly the wife's ingenuity appears to save her family from the devil, but Rabelais's inclusion of a burlesque devotional scene prior to the scene of her prowesses sets in place an alternative but weaker hypothesis: that the wife's victory is God's way of answering the farmer's prayers. The entire episode is thus structured around two different economies of survival, which are ultimately conflated rather than conflicting: ultimately, the Papefigue couple optimize their chances for survival by diversifying their "salvational portfolio," investing in three possible routes to salvation and survival rather than relying on work, worship, or wits alone.

The Papimaniacs' salvational strategy is also economic in nature, but unlike that of the Papefigues, it hinges upon ecclesiastically defined "works" rather than upon secular labor and productivity. The island's wealth consists of nonmonetary tokens—an image of the pope and a set of holy writs called the *Decretals*—that are displayed rather than circulated or exchanged. According to the Papimaniac bishop, whose name is Homenaz (Stoutmoron), those who "give themselves up" (*vous adonnans* [*OC, FB*, LIII, 687]) to the documents through study and worship are guaranteed both earthly success and salvation in exchange for their investment: "By devoting yourselves to the sole study of these sainted *Decretals*, you will become wealthy and honored in this world [and] in the next . . . will infallibly be saved" (*FB*, LIII, 644). Similarly, those who gaze upon the pope's portrait "gain not only complete remission of all [their] remembered sins, but also one-third of all the sins [they] have overlooked, plus eighteen times forty for good measure" (*FB*, L, 632).

Weakening Homenaz's case, however, is the one-dimensionality of his worldview and the insularity of his "singular" economy, which ignores the multicultural macrocosm of the *Fourth Book*. From the reader's global perspective, for example, the bishop's portrait of the Unicque or his culture's "idea" of God—whom the Utopians identify as "some pope" (*FB*, L, 632)—ironically figures as one in a series of godlike representations in the novel, joining the ranks of Niphleseth's hog god and the "ventripotent" Messer Gaster or "divine belly" (*FB*, LIX, 656), who "insists that he is no god, but rather a poor, base, miserable creature"

(*FB*, LX, 660). Even more subversively, the two theatrical "gods" in the Villon subnarrative (*FB*, XIII) infect all their successors with the specter of misrepresentation.

Similarly, Homenaz contends that his culture's holy writs, penned not by man but "by a cherub" (*FB*, XLIX, 630), are singular in their representation of divine truth. When Panurge claims to have seen *Decretals* "in vast quantities" (630) elsewhere, obviating the necessity of further study, the bishop scoffs at the very thought of a comparison: "I swear you never saw any *Decretals* penned by angels," he retorts. "Those of your land are but transcripts of ours" (631). What Homenaz forgets, however, is that representation itself is inherently mediated, dependent upon linguistic or graphic symbols that are the locus of difference. Any claim the *Decretals* might have to linguistic transparency is belied by the vast quantities of time Papimaniacs take to decipher them. At the same time, the much touted singularity of the *Decretals'* truth is necessarily compromised by translation into a common medium, just as the singularity of their pears is distorted and misrepresented by the universalizing word that denotes them: "They are a singular variety," claims Homenaz; "you will not find them elsewhere." Yet when Pantagruel asks for their "special name," the bishop responds that "they have no other name than you have heard": "We call figs, figs; plums, plums; and pears, pears" (*FB*, LIV, 645).

Lest we fail to catch the irony at work in Homenaz's myopic praise of the *Decretals'* singularity, Rabelais inserts a reminder of pluralism into the heart of the bishop's linguistic abyss, confusing "Decretalist" with the humanistic decretist who "follows the *Decrees* of Gratian" (*FB*, LIII, 643). With this play on words, Rabelais creates a rent in the encomium's fabric that causes it to deconstruct. Homenaz's use of the word *adonnans*, meaning both "devoting oneself" and "(over)indulging," further suggests that his single staple diet, which contrasts dramatically with the Utopians' literary fare, is an addiction (*adonnement*) or mania that distorts his perception of reality, causing him to twist and bend the Utopians' negative anecdotes about the *Decretals* to accord with his own worldview. When informed that children using the *Decretals* for masks have been disfigured, Homenaz shouts, "O miracle, miracle!" (*FB*, LII, 640). By enumerating deleterious effects such as these, which counterbalance Homenaz's encomium, the Utopians construct an antipanegyric that is a negative mirror of Alcofribas's first sales pitch: instead of healing the gouty and syphilitic as the *Great Chronicles of Gargantua* and *Pantagruel* do, the *Decretals*, according to the Utopians, produce hemorrhoids, boils, ulcers, and sheep rot in previously healthy people. That they are flawed tokens or representations is suggested by two of these negative anecdotes. In the first, Ponocrates tells of a monk who tried to beat out gold coins between the pages of high-quality *Decretals*. But "no piece he struck ever turned out properly. One and all were chipped or broken" (638). In the second anecdote, Gymnastes reinforces the theme of misrepresentation by suggesting that *Decretals* are always off the mark: when they are used as targets, arrows invariably "shift" and "go shy" (639) of the bull's-eye. With its promises of spiritual and material wealth, then, Homenaz's inflated abyss of rhetoric ultimately serves to fleece followers who buy its message. In exchange for his shining but empty words, the bishop emerges from mass with a basketful of gold that he uses to fund a banquet to satisfy his physical appetites (*FB*, LI, 634). Appropriately enough, the meat served at the banquet is not solid but abundantly filled with *farce magistral* or "farcical, magisterial" stuffing (*OC, FB,* LI, 676).[11]

The Frozen Words, Gaster, Chaneph, and Ganabin: Linguistic Exchange and Counterfeiting

The Utopians' difficulty in finding a satisfactory *mot*, their own version of the Unicque, is due in part to the inherent limitations of linguistic exchange, which functions as both the medium and a major theme of the Pantagrueline Tales. From the opening pages of *Pantagruel*, in such episodes as the encounter with the Limousin schoolboy, the case of Baisecul and Humesvesne, and Panurge's dialogue with Thaumaste in sign language, Rabelais counterbalances a critique of language with a quest for an originary word or language, an ambivalence that continues in the *Fourth Book*. The entire voyage is motivated by and structured around the search for a transcendent and transparent *mot*. While the open mouths of the thirsty Utopians and the monsters they encounter signify consumption, they are also the locus of speech. Likewise, the omnipresent winds that propel the ships forward have traditionally been associated symbolically with the breath of God or divine inspiration.[12] As the ambivalent winds of Ruach indicate, however, it is often difficult to distinguish between inspiration and hot air. On two occasions the Utopians encounter what promises to be the word of God; the Papimaniacs' written truths are rendered suspect by the specter of mediacy, however, and Gaster's sign language in chapters 57 through 62 proves to be inspired by his stomach.

Between the Papimaniacs and Gaster is a far more promising experiment in linguistic exchange, borrowed from Petronius by way of Castiglione: the myth of the Frozen Words.[13] Like travelers in the desert who glimpse a mirage, the Utopians "out at sea" suddenly hear disembodied words, which the fearful Panurge initially attributes to "foes" who "lie in ambush for us" (*FB*, LV, 647). Pantagruel, on the other hand, compares the phonemes to those emanating from Petron's "dwelling of Truth, where dwelled words, ideas, copies and likenesses of all things past and future." "At very great intervals," he continues, "parts of these words, ideas, copies and likenesses would fall upon humankind like vapors. . . . Thus they would be preserved for the future" (648). As an alternative, he suggests that this is the locus of Plato's philosophy, frozen in time like words in Arctic winters, which will finally thaw and fully yield their secrets. The pilot, who has heard of the words before, corrects the prince's transcendent hypothesis with a related but more earthbound explanation: the sounds are the thawing vestiges of cries emitted during a shipwreck that took place the previous winter (*FB*, LVI, 649).

That the words can be preserved intact through time and then be reconstituted, not just as sounds but as images, too, would appear to make them an ideal vehicle of linguistic exchange, allowing them to bridge the usual gap between signified and signifier. Indeed, their communicative promise is so enormous that Panurge compares them to the visible voices by which God transmitted the law to Moses: "I remember having read," he cries, "that the people actually *saw* voices" (*FB*, LVI, 649; emphasis mine). Further, the listener-reader's active role in reconstituting the words, by rubbing them between his or her hands, posits the Frozen Words episode as an idealized metaphor of cooperative textuality. In response to Panurge's literal request that he be "given" some frozen words to thaw (*requist Pantagruel luy en donner* [*OC, FB*, LVI, 693]), Pantagruel responds that "giving words is an act of lovers" (*donner parolles estoit acte des amoureux* [693]). What emerges is an implicit analogy between sexual and textual exchange reminiscent of the debate on marriage and cuckoldry in the *Third Book*; the additional resonance here of "giving [one's] word" articulates the exchange process as an act of faith that may be kept or broken in a gesture of fidelity or infidelity. Taking his friend's refusal to "give" words literally, Panurge adds a further twist when he offers to buy the words ("Well then, sell me some" [*FB*, LVI, 650]), as if they were commodities. Even as he points out the analogy between financial and linguistic exchange, Panurge reminds us that the use value of words—which more often serve as vehicles of

personal gain than of transparent communication—often outweighs
their truth value. Lawyers, for example, traffic in words as if they were
jewels: "To sell words is a lawyer's job," observes Pantagruel; "I would
rather sell you silence" (650).

This indictment of the truth value of language does not reflect directly
on the Frozen Words, whose proximity to the moment of death lends
them an aura of veracity and authenticity beyond that of everyday
discourse. As expressive as they are, however, the Frozen Words fall short
of the Utopians' communicative expectations, primarily because they fail
to understand the foreign dialect: "We could hear [the words] clearly,"
says the narrator, "but we did not understand them, for they were in
barbaric idiom" (FB, LVI, 650). To be sure, the physical and connotative
"color" of the reconstituted words, which are red, blue, green, black, and
gold, helps bridge this linguistic barrier by communicating the mood of
the original speaker: bloody words emanate from persons who had their
throats slit, for example, and swear words are physically "unpleasant to
behold" (650). But even though the images increase the words' communicative potential, the reconstructed phonemes only partially close the
gap between representation and reference.

In the two episodes following the Frozen Words, the myth of perfect
linguistic exchange is further eroded. Rabelais uses Messer Gaster, whose
sign language is "all for the gut," to redefine linguistic communication
and indeed all human creativity within the context of economic and
agricultural exchange. For the paunchy monarch and his Ventriloques
(Engastrimythes), who are literally "talking bellies," the truth value of
language is ultimately subordinate to its use as an economic tool.
"Invariably reality seemed to escape him," says Rabelais in reference to
the evil spirit Cincinnatulo, who was thought to speak from the belly of
the famous Italian ventriloquist Jacoba Rodogina. "He told untruths, he
flatly confessed his ignorance" (FB, LVIII, 655). The Ventriloques'
mendacity, similarly, derives from the stomach-oriented ethos they share
with the Gastrolâtres, who sacrifice everything, even truth, to the
demands of the gastric divinity.

Far from being transparent representations of truth, then, the tokens
used in linguistic exchange in Gaster's allegorical land double as counterfeit or as misrepresentations motivated by greed or physical hunger.
The Utopians learn about a second kind of linguistic counterfeit off the
island of Chaneph, which means "hypocritical." Professing to be "poor
people," the religious recluses who people Chaneph exact a sizable toll or
"alm," (FB, LXIV, 669) from passing sailors; despite their claims to

chastity, they have repopulated the formerly desert island with a copia of *petitz hypocritillons* or "little hypocrites" (*OC, FB*, LXIV, 717).

Ganabin, the last island in this allegorical progression, introduces a third kind of linguistic counterfeit related to the creative duel between imitation and invention. Physically resembling the mountain site of Parnassus (*FB*, LXVI, 675), or the mythical source of poetic inspiration, the island of Ganabin, or "Anti-Parnassus," is populated by "thieves, bandits, brigands, murderers and assassins" who "are fiercer than cannibals" (675). While on one level this scene reflects the growing number of brigands in sixteenth-century France—who, displaced from the land and unable to find work in the cities, resorted instead to pillaging for survival—on an allegorical level these brigands and assassins do violence not to the physical body but rather to the literary corpus of other writers. As an external obstacle to the writer's literary odyssey, this "test" may refer in part to the critics and censors who butcher the Rabelaisian text in the name of right religion and propriety, taking words out of context and twisting them for their own nefarious purposes. At the same time, however, these brigands who appropriate the language of others allegorize humanistic "borrowing" from the ancients and, in a more general way, the derivative nature of all linguistic exchange. Instead of representing our own thoughts and ideas exactly, the common linguistic tokens that we use are necessarily stolen from others and therefore can only approximate any singular or individual reality.

The *Fourth Book* ends not with the *mot* but rather in media res—amid a sea of conflicting words that are alienated from the truths they purport to represent. As an allegory of reading and writing, the voyage perilous bodes ill for Panurge's epistemological quest by suggesting that signs are twice removed from the thing itself: first by the locutor, whose tokens may be counterfeit, and then by the reader, who misevaluates them. The text is thus autoreferential, referring not only to Rabelais's struggle for physical survival in a world of shifting allegiances and political as well as religious factionalism, but also to his quest for literary survival and integrity. For though he markets his representation as new and different, similar in its novelty to the tarand at Medamothi, ultimately the Rabelaisian text, too, for all its experimentalism, grapples with the inevitability of hypocrisy, mendacity, and plagiarism. Like the kinship terminology of Ennasin, Rabelais's own "strange exchange" attempts to improve upon traditional signifier-signified relationships by forging new representational routes, but the copia of his writing self-consciously remains a copy, which modifies rather than transcends the tokens of literary exchange. The trajectory itself of the voyage confirms this representational crisis: while it begins at Medamothi, apparently a utopia of free trade and transparent representation, the voyage ends at Ganabin, a patently un-utopic island given over to socioeconomic and literary theft.

Whether Rabelais intended to leave the voyage unfinished, and at its nadir, is uncertain. The *Fifth Book*, which may be based upon sketches found among Rabelais's papers at the time of his death, clearly hypothesizes a kind of apotheosis, as the crew reaches the Dive Bouteille and receives the divine *mot*, which is "drink." Remarkably Rabelaisian in its polyvalence, the "transcendent" Word of the Bottle echoes Pantagruel's own advice near the end of the *Fourth Book*: he promises a solution to all doubts and questions *after* the crew has feasted (*FB*, LXIII, 668). While this promise has New Testament resonances, recalling Christ's last supper with the apostles, it also has purely biological overtones: as Panurge points out, his "doldrums have vanished" (*FB*, LXV, 673) with his hunger, and his last word, which closes the novel, is "Beuvons!" ("Let us drink!" [*FB*, LXVII, 681]).[14]

The Pantagrueline Tales thus end much as they began, with a glorification of consumption. But the new banquet, unlike its youthful prototype, is steeped in mediocritas: retaining little of its earlier hubris, drink in 1552 is arguably, more than anything else, a simple strategy for survival, reconfirming the wisdom of cabbage planting and anticipating Candide's garden.

Chapter Six
Conclusion

Like the ambiguity it generates, exchange is coterminous with the communication process and figures inherently in all written texts. To write is to encode reality and represent consciousness by means of graphic signifiers or substitutes for the thing itself, resembling monetary tokens, and this common currency in turn serves as a medium of commerce between the author and his or her audience. By linking both language and number to semiotics, patristic and medieval theorists, including Augustine and Nicole d'Oresme, helped lay the groundwork for this analogy between words and money; it supplements a classical tendency to view reading, rational discourse, and the acquisition of knowledge as a nonmaterial form of commerce. Both traditions converged in the sixteenth century and were rearticulated as signifiers of intellectual, linguistic, and economic ferment by a host of humanistic writers who routinely used monetary and trade-related terms in discourses about language and learning. Erasmus and Budé, both influential in Rabelais's formation, refer to fame as "credit," describe intellectual acquisitions in terms of "profit" and "wealth," classify writing as an "expenditure," and argue over the relative merits of linguistic moderation and prodigality.

Given this "monetized" backdrop, along with the mercantile ambiance of Lyon and the economic importance of bookmaking there, it is no surprise that Rabelais should graft these contemporary structures of exchange onto the commerce with otherness that is an integral part of the epic. What results is not so much a mercantile epic, in the manner of Boccaccio, as a freewheeling essay in and on exchange, encompassing topics as diverse as literary debt, sociopolitical reciprocity, intellectual commerce, and literary production. Once we recognize the variety of exchange-related structures in Rabelais, and the common currency of economic metaphors in the Renaissance, the market atmosphere of the prologue to *Pantagruel* no longer seems unrelated or even marginally related to the corpus of the text. Instead, it serves as an antechamber to the entire saga, providing a unifying and meaningful frame for the variations on exchange that ensue. Instead of disappearing after his opening discourse, the huckster of that first prologue permeates the text from start to finish with his monetary concerns, countercultural perspective, and fascination with the mechanics of exchange. In subsequent prologues, the barker with his patent medicine remains in place but is metamorphosed, reappearing as a philosopher-pharmacist in *Gargantua*, as a barker-bard in the *Third Book*, and as a medicine peddler turned physician in the *Fourth Book*.

Each book is structured around and offers new permutations on the theme of exchange. Inscribed within economic cycles of production and consumption, the *Pantagruel* at first glance seems oriented toward the rarefied spheres of intellectual "profit" and linguistic wealth glorified by humanists and outlined by Gargantua in his letter. This superlative goal, however, is paradoxically devalued by its very inflation, much like the French monetary supply of the sixteenth century, as abysses of epistemological, moral, and socioeconomic poverty emerge like rents in the cornucopian text. In this folkloric and humanistic antiepic, the upstaging of a large prince named Pantagruel by a small pauper named Panurge, both variations on the uomo universale, sets the stage for an upside-down netherworld in which the rich and poor, heroes and antiheroes, trade places.

While less overtly market-oriented than its predecessor, the *Gargantua* opens with an extended interrogation of face value in which the discontinuous relationship between package and product, cover and contents, is examined. This exercise in weighing and assessing serves to hone the reader-buyer's judgment and parallels the hero's own education and maturation process, which progresses by trial and error from self-absorption toward commerce with alterity and social responsibility. The young Gargantua's struggle between inner and outer, self and other, is externalized allegorically in the Picrocholine War, a market-based dispute between old allies that finds temporary resolution on a sexual level in the perfect reciprocity of males and females at Thélème.

Rabelais returns to the same economic model in his *Third Book*, replacing the wise hero Gargantua with the antihero Panurge in a second and far more complicated essay on commerce with alterity. While Panurge voices the desire for perfect reciprocity twice, first in his paradoxical praise of debts and secondly in his quest for a perfect marriage with a woman, the prototypical other, his own philautia precludes the realization of these ideals in what amounts to a negative rewriting of Thélème. Reluctant to invest in matrimony—an unabashedly economic undertaking in the Renaissance—without knowing its outcome, Panurge seeks to read his fortune in a series of occult and learned consultations that are a cross between the philosophical symposium and a carnival sideshow. What results is an inflationary maze of data reminiscent of Gargantua's *abysme de science*, proffered by untrustworthy middlemen whose judgments, already tarnished by the mercenary "gifts" that buy them, are expressed in verbal tokens that both differ from and defer the truth they purport to represent.

Panurge's failure in the *Third Book* to read the future, or to settle his matrimonial dilemma, yields a new attempt at commerce in the *Fourth Book*, as the Utopians set sail for ports unknown in search of the oracular Word of the Bottle. At tale's end, their quest is unresolved, and the foreign islands they visit—rife with greed, theft, and misrepresentation—propel them further and further away from the linguistic transparency, epistemological clarity, and socioeconomic reciprocity they seek. Moreover, the ethics of mediocritas posed by the narrator in the prologue, and seconded by Panurge during the storm, constitutes an economy of survival totally at odds with the hubristic economy of excess, *superbia*, and *curiositas* that we associate with the humanistic hero. The latter's appetite for knowledge, figured by the baby giants' open mouths in the early novels, comes directly into conflict in the *Fourth Book* with the jaws of death, as the growth-oriented consumption of the 1530s gave way in the 1550s to a fear of being consumed and a revaluing of small-scale productivity.

If we accept the *Fifth Book*'s authenticity, the Word of the Bottle with which it concludes seems to bring the saga full circle, returning us to the joyous golden age of humanistic gluttony that fueled the first two books. Upon closer inspection, however, the message "drink" or *trinch* fails to overcome the ambiguity inherent in verbal exchange throughout Rabelais, wavering between philosophical truth and Christian fideism, physical replenishment and world-weary escapism in its symbolism. Figured as female in gender, the oracle reinforces rather than bridges sexual as well as symbolic difference by answering the androcentric "woman question" with an enigma.

While the saga thus defies closure, eluding us with its protean allure and multiple faces, a few general patterns nonetheless emerge from the maze. From start to finish, first of all, the themes and structures of exchange in Rabelais are infused with negativity: communication is repeatedly botched, marriage indefinitely deferred, and wealth distributed unevenly. Throughout the four authenticated books, the world of Rabelais's fiction is in fact polarized along socioeconomic lines. Begin-

ning with the introduction of Panurge, and continuing through the
netherworlds, the Picrocholine War, "The Praise of Debts," and the
dyadic couples of the *Fourth Book*, the Pantagrueline Tales unfold as a
tension between haves and have-nots, consumers and producers, givers
and takers, oppressors and the oppressed. This tension has led a number
of readers, and particularly those who view Panurge as the novel's life
force, to label Rabelais the voice of popular culture or an early proponent
of class struggle. That he was acutely conscious of contemporary poverty
and socioeconomic disparities is clear, as is his denunciation of greed, his
fundamental advocacy of caritas, and his basic ambivalence toward the
increasingly mercenary culture in which he lived. Whether this enhanced sensitivity stemmed primarily from personal poverty, familiarity
with contemporary peasant revolts, or evangelical theology, however, is
a question to which the text yields no answers. Indeed, it is difficult to
pin any ideological tag on Rabelais without doing violence to the
polyvalence of his text, which reflects the many countercurrents of his
culture.

Far more crucial for an understanding of his work in its entirety is an
understanding of the original market setting's importance as a generative metaphor, which not only lays the groundwork for sociological
tensions in Rabelais but also serves as a unifying frame for the saga's
principal action, themes, and tropes. Episodes as diverse as the giants'
education, the Picrocholine War, the two paradoxical encomia,
Panurge's marriage consultations, and the geographical voyage are
united under the umbrella of exchange, as contemporary economic
considerations such as profit and loss, risk and investment, inflation and
devaluation, consumption and production are fused with ideals of humanistic commerce.

More intriguingly, this economic frame also merges with the rhetorical figures of copia and *accumulatio* to figure a linguistic crisis with
profoundly negative epistemological implications. For Rabelais's famous
abyss—his plentiful storehouse of learning and words representing the
intellectual and linguistic wealth of French Renaissance humanism—
ultimately proves no less inflationary than the monetary currency of the
era. In addition to using this economic paradigm to question the
ultimate value of humanism's increased intellectual wealth, the Rabelaisian narrator and sometime peddler also wields words like monetary
tokens, which are at once unstable in value and two-sided in structure.
The result is a cornucopia of ambiguity and polyvalence, alternately
joyous and vertiginous, that at once interrogates and assays the possibil-

ity of knowing and communicating in a fragmented, polyphonous world. Paradoxically, however, Rabelais succeeds in representing this crisis of representation as well as any writer of his generation, leaving us a richly nuanced and pluralistic portrait of an era in the throes of change. That we continue to study this portrait even today, in spite of its difficult prose style and its antifeminist rhetoric, is in part a mark of the fundamental similarity between Rabelais's world and our own. Our most authentic heroes, like his, are flawed, self-searching figures. Likewise, the technological advances and information explosion with which Rabelais wrestled ambivalently, in alternating bursts of elation and confusion, optimism and skepticism, all strike a familiar note with children of the atomic age, the computer revolution, and Einsteinian relativity. The good doctor's growing intuition that increased learning does not always bring certainty, that progress brings destruction as well as construction, that quantity and quality are not coterminous, and that improved modes of dissemination do not guarantee communication, is a fundamental lesson of the maturation process on this the eve of the twenty-first century. The inflationary tendencies of the Rabelaisian text, which reflect a financial as well as linguistic crisis in Renaissance France, have dramatic corollaries within our own culture, where devalued currencies and economies with double-digit inflation coexist with pretentious, circuitous, and semantically bankrupt rhetoric reminiscent of the Limousin schoolboy.

Because of the inherent tension between signifier and signified that informs the Pantagrueline Tales, finally, they lend themselves particularly well to modern strategies of reading suggested by recent criticism. As a result of the polyvalence inscribed within it, the text in a sense is self-deconstructing, its meaning often deferred as it awaits the "other" perspective of a reader who is always different. Readings that explore these alternative meanings complement the many fine historical analyses that have helped elucidate the Pantagrueline Tales over the years, as we continue to enlarge upon the myriad ways in which Rabelais reflects his environment. Ultimately, it is this polyphony and openness to alterity that guarantees the text's freshness four and a half centuries after its composition, as Rabelais continues to engage each of his readers in intellectual and literary exchange.

Notes and References

Chapter 1

1. Unless otherwise noted, all quotations of Rabelais in English are from *The Five Books of Gargantua and Pantagruel*, trans. Jacques LeClercq (1936; reprint, New York: Modern Library, 1944). Quotations in French, where necessary for clarification and amplification, are from *Oeuvres complètes*, 5 vols., ed. Jacques Boulenger and Lucien Scheler (Paris: Gallimard, Bibliothèque de la Pléiade, 1955); hereafter cited in the text as *OC*.

2. The term "cornucopian text" is borrowed from Terence Cave, *The Cornucopian Text: Problems of Writing in the French Renaissance* (Oxford: Clarendon, 1979).

3. The judgments of Rabelais are cited in notes to *Gargantua*, ed. Jean-Christian Dumont (Paris: Nouveaux Classiques Larousse, 1972), 167–68.

4. For a discussion of the *Fifth Book*'s authenticity, see Alfred Glauser, *Le Faux Rabelais, ou L' Inauthenticité du "Cinquiesme Livre"* (Paris: Nizet, 1975); and Mireille Huchon, *Rabelais grammarien: De l'histoire du texte aux problèmes d' authenticité* (*Etudes Rabelaisiennes* 16) (Geneva: Droz, 1981).

5. See Rosalie Colie, *Paradoxia Epidemica: The Renaissance Tradition of Paradox* (Princeton: Princeton University Press, 1966).

6. Mikhail Bakhtin expounds this theory in *Rabelais and His World*, trans. Hélène Iwolsky (Bloomington: Indiana University Press, 1984).

7. See Mikhail Bakhtin, *The Dialogic Imagination: Four Essays*, trans. Caryl Emerson and Michael Holquist (Austin: University of Texas Press, 1981).

8. Numerous scholars have noted the importance of economic elements and structures of exchange in Rabelais. See, for example, Guy Demerson, *Rabelais: Une vie, une oeuvre, une époque* (Paris: Balland, 1986).

9. That this analogy between coins and words was widespread in the sixteenth century is demonstrated by Danielle Trudeau, "Langue et monnaie au 16e siècle," *Stanford French Review* 7 (Spring 1983): 37–55. In Rabelais's case, the analogy is clearly operative in the printer's salutation preceding the expurgated *Gargantua* and *Pantagruel* of 1542, where readers are urged to distinguish between *la faulse monnoye* or "false money" of Dolet's pirated text and *la bonne monnoye* or "good money" of the authorized edition. See Michael B. Kline, *Rabelais and the Age of Printing* (*Etudes Rabelaisiennes* 4) (Geneva: Droz, 1963). Within the body of the text, references to money and coins include *écus, marcs d'or* (*G*, XLVI, 135), *moutons à la grand laine* (*G*, VIII, 30), *unzain* (*G*, XXV, 80), *bezans d'or* (*G*, XXXI, 94; *G*, LI, 146), *philippus* (*G*, XXXII, 95), *sou* (*G*, XXXIII, 98), *carolus* (*G*, XLVI, 133), *saluz* (*G*, XLVI, 134), *ducatz* (*G*, XLVI, 135; *P*,

XXI, 263, 264), *seraphs* (P, XIV, 229), *teston* (P, XVI, 242), *denier* (P, XVII, 244), *liards* (P, XVII, 244), *fleurins* (P, XVII, 245), *francs* (P, XVII, 247), and *gettons* (P, XXI, 263).

10. The reference to du Bellay, quoted by Trudeau, "Langue et monnaie" (49), is taken from *Deffence et illustration de la langue françoyse*, ed. H. Chamard (1549; Paris: Didier, 1966), 196–97. Textual citations of the correspondence between Erasmus and Budé refer to the French translation by Marie-Madeleine de la Garanderie, *La Correspondance d'Erasme et de Guillaume Budé* (Paris: J. Vrin, 1967).

11. R. Howard Bloch, *Etymologies and Genealogies: A Literary Anthropology of the French Middle Ages* (Chicago: University of Chicago Press, 1983), 168.

12. Ibid., 168–69.

13. See R. J. Knecht, *French Renaissance Monarchy: Francis I and Henry II* (London: Longman, 1984), 5–7; and J. H. M. Salmon, *Society in Crisis: France in the Sixteenth Century* (New York: St. Martin's Press, 1975), 27–57.

14. From *The Travel Journey of Antonio De Beatis*, ed. J. R. Hale (London: The Hakluyt Society, 1979), 165, quoted in R. J. Knecht, *Francis I* (Cambridge: Cambridge University Press, 1982), 305.

15. For a discussion of the Avignon connection, see Franco Simone, *The French Renaissance: Medieval Tradition and Italian Influence in Shaping the Renaissance in France*, trans. H. Gaston Hall (New York: Macmillan, 1969), 37–78.

16. See Elizabeth Eisenstein, *The Printing Press as an Agent of Change: Communications and Cultural Transformations in Early Modern Europe*, 2 vols. (Cambridge: Cambridge University Press, 1979).

17. The biographical data included here generally follow the outline of Jean Plattard, *The Life of François Rabelais*, trans. Louis P. Roche (London: Frank Cass and Co., 1968).

18. Ibid., 111–12.

19. The *livre tournois* or "Tours pound" was France's official money of account in the sixteenth century and originally was worth a pound (*livre*) of silver. In Rabelais's day, the livre was not coined at Tours, as it had been through the thirteenth century, but functioned instead as an ideal or imaginary standard that was equivalent to 20 *sous* (shillings) or 240 *deniers* (pence) and was payable in ever-decreasing quantities of "real" coins, including the *écu* (crown). For more information on coinage and monetary values in the age of Rabelais, see Martin Wolfe, *The Fiscal System of Renaissance France* (New Haven: Yale University Press, 1972), 293–94; and Frank C. Spooner, *The International Economy and Monetary Movements in France, 1493–1725* (Cambridge, Mass.: Harvard University Press, 1972). The real buying power of these currencies and of Rabelais's stipend is more difficult to assess. We know that the barber-surgeon at the Hôtel-Dieu received the same salary as his more illustrious supervisor (Plattard, *Life of Rabelais* [112]), and that half that amount was received by a typical Paris-area vineyard worker in 1510 (F. P. Braudel and Frank P. Spooner, "Prices in Europe

from 1450 to 1750," in *The Cambridge Economic History of Europe*, vol. 4, ed. E. E. Rich and C. H. Wilson [Cambridge: Cambridge University Press, 1967], 374–486). The difference between the two stipends diminishes considerably when we factor in the effects of devaluation over a 22-year period and the barter goods that typically augmented agricultural wages. Not surprisingly, Plattard concludes that Rabelais's salary was little more than an honorarium.

20. "L'Italie n'a nulle plante, nul animal, que je n'eusse vu et noté auparavant" (*OC*, 972).

21. "Je suis contrainct de recourir encores à vos aulmosnes, car les trente escus qu'il vous pleust me faire icy livrer sont quasi venus à leur fin, et si n'en ay rien despendu en meschanceté ny pour ma bouche" (*OC*, 986).

22. See Richard Cooper, *Rabelais et l'Italie* (*Etudes Rabelaisiennes* 24) (Geneva: Droz, 1991), 61–78, 183–223.

Chapter 2

1. In his *Irony and Ideology in Rabelais: Structures of Subversion* (Cambridge University Press, 1990), Jerome Schwartz distinguishes between Rabelais's "ideological discourse" and his "counterdiscourse." As for the *abysme de science*, Thomas Greene glimpses a "chasm of folly" beneath it in his *Rabelais: A Study in Comic Courage* (Englewood Cliffs, N.J.: Prentice-Hall, 1970), 29. See also Alfred Glauser, *Fonctions du nombre chez Rabelais* (Paris: Nizet, 1982), 75–76.

2. Donald M. Frame, *François Rabelais: A Study* (New York: Harcourt Brace Jovanovich), 27. Gérard Defaux argues that Panurge is a sophist in his *Pantagruel et les sophistes: Contribution à l'histoire de l'humanisme chrétien au XVIe siècle* (The Hague: Nijhoff, 1973).

3. For a discussion of Rabelais's marketplace and carnivalesque rhetoric, see chapter 2 of Bakhtin, *Rabelais and His World*, as well as Carol Clark, *The Vulgar Rabelais* (Glasgow: Pressgang, 1983).

4. Edwin M. Duval discusses the fratricidal origins and lapsarian implications of the "year of gross medlars" and race of giants in his *The Design of Rabelais's "Pantagruel"* (New Haven: Yale University Press, 1991), 18–28. For a more general discussion of the negative connotations of giants in literature prior to Rabelais, see Walter Stephens, *Giants in Those Days: Folklore, Ancient History, and Nationalism* (Lincoln: University of Nebraska Press, 1989).

5. The translation of *torchecul* as "arsewipe" is that of John Michael Cohen in *Gargantua and Pantagruel* (Harmondsworth, England: Penguin, 1955).

6. For example, Gerard Brault, "'Ung abysme de science': On the Interpretation of Gargantua's Letter to Pantagruel," *Bibliothèque d'Humanisme et Renaissance* 28 (1966): 615–32. See also Defaux, *Pantagruel et les sophistes*, 59–68.

7. "Qui fit, tiraquelle doctissime, ut in hac tanta seculi nostri luce, quo disciplinas omneis meliores singulari quodam deorum munere postliminio receptas videmus, passim inveniantur, quibus sic affectis esse contigit, ut a densa

illa gothici temporis caligine plus quam Cimmerie ad conspicuam solis facem
oculos attollere aut nolint, aut nequeant? . . . An vero quod ea vis est tene-
brarum hujuscemodi, ut quorum oculis, semel insederint, eos suffusione im-
medicabili perpetuo sic hallucinari necesse sit, et caecutire." (*OC*, 954)

8. Michael A. Screech, *Rabelais* (Ithaca: Cornell University Press, 1979),
89–90.

9. Duval argues that the wall "is not . . . an affront to the female sex"
but a "willful degradation of a Spartan and Utopian ideal, in which the citizens'
valor and courage . . . are shown to count for less than" their genitalia (94).

10. In her *Father Figures: Genealogy and Narrative Structure in Rabelais*
(Ithaca: Cornell University Press, 1991), Carla Freccero gives voice to the
alternative and more traditional hypothesis that the "haughty lady" is merely
hypocritical (32). While Rabelais by no means excludes this possibility, the
fascination of the scene resides in this very convergence of alternative meanings.

11. In his "The Evolving Attitude toward Material Wealth in Rabelais's
Oeuvres" (*Stanford French Review* 9 [Winter 1985]), Richard Berrong says that
this "indifference toward material possessions could be explained in part by
Rabelais's years as a Franciscan, which order was distinguished by its vow of
poverty and its rejection of worldly wealth" (304). As an alternative hypothesis,
he proposes that this "very un-capitalistic attitude toward money/goods/prop-
erty" (304) in the first novel expresses "the sixteenth-century 'indigens' point of
view" (306).

12. The roguish Cingar, whose name means "zingaro" or "gypsy" in the
Lombard dialect, is characterized in book 4 of *Baldus* as a liar, a cheat, and a thief.
For more on parallels between the two mock-epics, see Marcel Tetel, "Rabelais
et Folengo: *Patria Diabolorum*," in *Rabelais en son demi-millénaire*, Actes du
Colloque International de Tours (*Etudes Rabelaisiennes* 21) (Geneva: Droz, 1988),
203– 11.

13. In his *Design*, Duval suggests that this antiheroic inversion in Epistemon's hell is part of a revolutionary antiepic pattern, based upon the tenets of
Christian humanism, that conquers "the very idea of Hero, Empire, and Epic"
(107) in favor of pacifism and "brotherly love" (111).

14. See Erich Auerbach, *Mimesis: The Representation of Reality in Western
Literature*, trans. Willard Trask (Garden City, N.Y.: Doubleday/Anchor Books,
1957), 229–49.

Chapter 3

1. For a traditionalist interpretation of the word *oeconomique* in Rabelais,
see Jean Bichon, "Rabelais et 'La Vie Oeconomique,'" *Etudes Rabelaisiennes* 7
(1967): 107–26. Concurring with Brunetto Latini's definition of "economy" as
the "part of philosophy regarding the government of a family" (108), Bichon
further contends that Rabelais "never speaks concretely about commerce and
finance," and that "there is nothing analogous [in his writings] to the preoccu-

pations of Copernicus" (117) about the depreciation of inflationary money supplies. As we hope to show, this overly literal reading of the Pantagrueline Tales ignores Rabelais's verbal inflation, which parallels monetary inflation in Renaissance France.

2. Duval reduces the play of this paradox in his "Interpretation and the 'Doctrine Absconce' of Rabelais's Prologue to *Gargantua*," *Etudes Rabelaisiennes* 18 (1984): 1–17. For a different approach, see Richard Regosin, "The Ins(ides) and Outs(ides) of Reading: Plural Discourse and the Question of Interpretation in Rabelais," in *Rabelais's Incomparable Book: Essays on His Art*, ed. Raymond La Charité (Lexington, Ky.: French Forum, 1986), 59–71.

3. In a stimulating discussion entitled *Language and Meaning in the Renaissance* (Princeton: Princeton University Press, 1987), Richard Waswo hypothesizes that this myth of linguistic transparency, of perfect continuity between sign and meaning, was frustrated in the Renaissance by the beginnings of a shift from referential to relational semantics.

4. According to Ricardo Quinones (*The Renaissance Discovery of Time* [Cambridge, Mass.: Harvard University Press, 1972]), time was becoming increasingly important as a commodity and material of production in the time of Rabelais (187–203).

5. See Screech, *Rabelais*, 132–34, for a purely historical look at the legal status of ten- and eleven-month pregnancies.

6. Cave discusses the positive and negative copia of the Rabelaisian codpiece, first Gargantua's and later Panurge's, in his *Cornucopian Text*, 183–222.

7. This, at least, is the contention of Boulenger in his notes to the *Oeuvres*, 27.

8. According to Greene, Rabelais "is in effect rejecting an arbitrary system of medieval symbolism for an interpretation rooted in universal tradition ('ius gentium'), in human physiology, and the nature of things" (*Rabelais*, 38).

9. Again, Waswo's theory about the tension between referential and relational semantics in the Renaissance is extremely pertinent in this episode and its predecessor on color symbolism, where the narrator's attempt to restore the lost continuity between sign and meaning, a vestige of referential semantics, is directly followed by a refragmentation of referentiality by relational variables.

10. In his "Rabelais et les cloches de Notre-Dame" (*Etudes Rabelaisiennes* 9 [1971]: 1–28), Gérard Defaux also recognizes the ambiguity and educational value of this episode but finds its *altior sensus* or "higher meaning" in the identification of the bells with two contemporary theologians.

11. For a discussion of the importance of wine in Rabelais, see Florence M. Weinberg, *The Wine and the Will: Rabelais's Bacchic Christianity* (Detroit: Wayne State University Press, 1972).

12. For a different reading of Gargantua's gifts, one that focuses upon the relationship between power and money, see Daniel Ménager, "La Politique du

don dans les derniers chapitres du *Gargantua*," *Journal of Medieval and Renaissance Studies* 8 (1978): 179–81. Enlarging upon the same topic, Berrong in his "Material Wealth" agrees that Grandgousier is essentially "buying off" the impoverished enemy (308) and goes on to suggest that Rabelais's esteem for material goods increases in his second novel.

13. Less a reflection of real progress in society than a critique of existing problems, the utopian genre by nature is unstable, imaginary, and implicitly satirical. See Jean Servier, *Histoire de l'utopie*, Collection Idées (Paris: Gallimard, 1967); Massimo Baldini, *Il Linguaggio delle utopie. Utopia e ideologia: Una rilettura epistemologica* (Rome: Edizioni Studium, 1974); Claude-Gilbert Dubois, *Les Problèmes de l'utopie* (Paris: Archives des Lettres Modernes, 1968).

Chapter 4

1. Because it is offered freely, the cask of the *Third Book* also figures as a gift recalling the "present" of the utopian Abbey of Thélème in *Gargantua*. The idea of the book as gift or common property is discussed by Natalie Zemon Davis in "Beyond the Market: Books as Gifts in Sixteenth-Century France," *Transactions of the Royal Historical Society*, 5th ser., 33 (1983): 80–81.

2. See Freccero, *Father Figures*, 63; François Rigolot, *Le Texte de la Renaissance: Des rhétoriqueurs à Montaigne*, (Geneva: Droz 1982), 123–35; and Regosin, "The Ins(ides) and Outs(ides)."

3. Specifically, Panurge's justification of debt in chapter 3 in terms of brotherly love and his allusion to "faith, hope, and charity" (*TB*, III, 311) recall the Pauline imperative of caritas in 1 Corinthians 12–13. Panurge further links borrowing and lending to Plato's harmony of the spheres: "Just imagine another world, where all men borrowed and all lent. . . . Oh, what a harmony would attend the regular motions of the heavens! I think I can hear it as plainly as Plato" (*TB*, IV, 312). The categories of "commutative" and "distributive" justice in commerce cited in chapter 2 (306) are from Aristotle's *Ethics* (V, 4). The mock-encomiastic genre itself recalls both Erasmus's *Praise of Folly* and the Lucianic panegyrics of the fly and parasite that help inform it. Rabelais's specific decision to praise debt may have been influenced by Francesco Berni's (1497–1535) *Capitolo del debito* (Chapter on Debt), which found a later corollary in Ortensio Lando's *Paradossi* (Paradoxes). First published in Lyon in 1543, only three years prior to Rabelais's *Third Book*, this volume of "sayings contrary to public opinion" contains a paradoxical praise of debt. See Colie, *Paradoxia Epidemica*, 462–63.

4. In his *Rabelais au futur* (Paris: Seuil, 1970), Jean Paris points out the economic link between the *Third Book* "Praise of Debts" and the marriage theme that follows, citing Marcel Mauss's analogy between the circulation of wealth and the circulation of wives or women (185). For a far more traditional treatment of the matrimonial theme in the *Third Book*, see Michael A. Screech, *The*

Rabelaisian Marriage: Aspects of Rabelais's Religion, Ethics, and Comic Philosophy (London: Arnold, 1958).

5. See Daniel Russell, "Panurge and His New Clothes," *Etudes Rabelaisiennes* 14 (1977): 89–107.

6. In her "Damning Haughty Dames" (*Journal of Medieval and Renaissance Studies* 15 [Spring 1985], Carla Freccero rightly points out the "parody of Petrarchan and Platonic motifs" (60) in Panurge's interaction with the Parisian lady in chapter 21 of *Pantagruel.*

7. During the sixteenth century, the ambivalent medieval attitude toward women continued. In the Middle Ages, the fabliaux illustrated the harsh, belittling opinion of women while the romances idealized woman. During the Renaissance, the ideological and literary struggle continued. The Platonic argument of idealization finds a supporter, among others, in Antoine Héroët's *Parfaicte Amye* (The Ideal Lady) (1542), and the opposite current produces, with ironic undertones in the titles, Thomas Sebillet's *Louenge des Femmes* (In Praise of Women) (1551) and Bertrand de la Borderie's *L'Amye de court* (The Court Lady) (1542). For a more detailed account of the "woman question," see Constance Jordan, *Renaissance Feminism: Literary Texts and Political Models* (Ithaca: Cornell University Press, 1990), 86–94; Screech, *The Rabelaisian Marriage,* 5–13; and Emile V. Telle, *L'Oeuvre de Marguerite d'Angoulême, reine de Navarre, et la querelle des femmes* (Toulouse: Lion, 1937), 9–68.

8. On the subject of witchcraft and the occult in the Renaissance, Harry A. Miskimin (*The Economy of Later Renaissance Europe 1460–1600* [Cambridge: Cambridge University Press, 1977] observes:

> Witchcraft proliferates when fundamental premises are challenged and society itself appears unstable; it is thus no accident that the later Renaissance witnessed a profusion of witches. By definition, witches are supernatural creatures who exist beyond and in defiance of the laws of nature. They have the capacity to alter regular and expected patterns, to affect the cycles of fertility and regeneration, and to assume unnatural forms and powers. So long as witches are present, the homogeneity of experience is moot; the value of previous empirical observation is dubious; and the possibility of creating rational, scientific hypotheses on the basis of an orderly and immutable set of natural laws is questionable. Witchcraft, then, perhaps unfortunately, is antithetical to the more mundane craft of the modern economist. (2)

9. In "The Dream of Panurge" (*Etudes Rabelaisiennes* 7 [1967]: 93–103), N. L. Goodrich rightly contends that the two interpretations of Panurge's dream represent both a wish and a fear.

10. For an interesting account of Pantagruel's errors in reading Virgil and

166

RABELAIS REVISITED

the other *Third Book* texts, see Richard Berrong, *Every Man for Himself: Social Order and Its Dissolution in Rabelais* (Saratoga, Calif.: ANMA Libri, 1985), 30–36.

11. For a stimulating account of monsters and oddities in the Renaissance, see Jean Céard, *La Nature et les prodiges: L'Insolite au XVIe siècle en France* (Geneva: Droz, 1977).

12. In his *Praisers of Folly: Erasmus, Rabelais, Shakespeare* (Cambridge, Mass.: Harvard University Press, 1963), Walter Kaiser provides an excellent analysis of the multiple forms of folly—and different kinds of fools—that are present in the *Third Book*, interacting dialectically to generate and subvert the work's meaning.

13. That the pantagruelion is used in papermaking is clearly indicated in the text, where the narrator contends that without this plant, "paper . . . would not exist" and "the art of printing would perish from the earth" (*TB*, LI, 480). Kline develops this analogy briefly in his *Rabelais and the Age of Printing*, 29.

14. In his poetic and detailed discussion of the pantagruelion, François Rigolot takes into account the plant's *effets nocifs* or "negative effects" (145) and its "ambivalence" (149). See his *Les Langages de Rabelais* (*Etudes Rabelaisiennes* 10) (Geneva: Droz, 1972), 144–53.

15. For more on the multiple connotations of the pantagruelion, and the question of its relationship to the tree of knowledge, see Kline, *Rabelais and the Age of Printing*, 60; and Michael A. Screech, "L'Enigme du Pantagruelion," *Etudes Rabelaisiennes* 1 (1956): 48–72.

Chapter 5

1. See Paul J. Smith, *Voyage et écriture: Etude sur le "Quart Livre" de Rabelais* (*Etudes Rabelaisiennes* 19) (Geneva: Droz, 1987), 10–14.

2. See Michel Devèze, *La Vie de la forêt française au XVIe siècle*, 2 vols. (Paris: Ecole Pratique des Hautes Etudes, 1961).

3. For a discerning look at the dynamics of representation, exchange, and filiation in the Medamothi episode, see Alice Fiola Berry, " 'L'Isle Medamothi': Rabelais's Itineraries of Anxiety (*Quart Livre* 2–4)," *PMLA* 106 (October 1991): 1040–53.

4. In his *Every Man*, Berrong suggests that Ennasin figures as an "ideal society" whose universal kinship, military readiness, and mutual defense system directly oppose Panurge's selfish resistance to military service for the common good (52).

5. For a slightly different reading of the Chiquanous episode, see Lawrence Kritzman, "Rabelais's Comedy of Cruelty: A Psycho-Allegorical Reading of the Chiquanous Episode," in La Charité, *Rabelais's Incomparable Book*, 141–54: "Rather than assuming a mode of direct self-expression, the Rabelaisian subject transcribes the 'real' world allegorically through a rhetorical 'coun-

terfeiting' in which the texts point to social circumstances and power relationships that both shape and inhibit the politics of representation" (141). Kritzman views the episode as "a narrativized staging of repressed fantasies" that in their theatricality and contestation of the "system" are closely linked to carnival. A revised version of this essay appears in Kritzman's *The Rhetoric of Sexuality and the Literature of the French Renaissance* (Cambridge: Cambridge University Press, 1991), 187–201.

    6. See Abraham C. Keller, *The Telling of Tales in Rabelais: Aspect of His Narrative Art* (Frankfurt am Main: Klostermann, 1963).

    7. Berrong, in his *Every Man*, makes the point that Panurge's refusal to work and help his comrades during the tempest solidifies the rogue's role as a threat to social order and harmony (54–57). For more on the tempest, see Dorothy Gabe Coleman, "Rabelais: Two Versions of the 'Storm at Sea' Episode, *French Studies* 23 (1969): 113–30; Frank Lestringant, "La Famille des 'tempêtes en mer': Essai de généalogie (Rabelais, Thevet et quelques autres)," *Etudes de Lettres* 2 (1984): 45–62; and Florence M. Weinberg, "Comic and Religious Elements in Rabelais's 'Tempête en mer,'" *Etudes Rabelaisiennes* 15 (1980): 129–40.

    8. For a discussion of Quaresmeprenant's ambiguity, see Samuel Kinser, *Rabelais's Carnival: Text, Context, Metatext* (Berkeley: University of California Press, 1990), 69–92.

    9. Ibid., 93–124.

    10. In her article "La Guerre des Andouilles, Pantagruel, IV, 35–42" (*Etudes seiziémistes offertes à V.-L. Saulnier* [Geneva: Droz, 1980], 119–35), Françoise Charpentier reads the feminizing bisexuality of the phallic Chitterlings as a threat to male supremacy, in the form of an all-female society, which the Utopians systematically resist.

    11. As Screech points out in his *Rabelais*, the word *farce* in French denotes both a comic play and stuffing, an ambiguity that enriches Rabelais's satire in the *Fourth Book* (446–47).

    12. See Smith, *Voyage et écriture*, 83–109.

    13. See Gérard Defaux, "Vers une définition de l'herméneutique rabelaisienne: Pantagruel, l'esprit, la lettre et les paroles gelées," *Etudes Rabelaisiennes* 21 (1988): 327–37; Jean Guiton, "Le Mythe des paroles gelées (Rabelais, *Quart Livre*, LV–LVI)," *Romanic Review* 31 (1940): 3–15; and Michel Jeanneret, "Les Paroles dégelées (Rabelais, *Quart Livre*, 48–65)," *Littérature* 17 (1975): 14–30.

    14. In his *Voyage et écriture*, Smith's chapter entitled "Au large de Chaneph: Eucharistie et interprétation" (193–205) addresses the religious connotations of the *Fourth Book*'s concluding banquet. For a different view of the banquet, see Michel Jeanneret, *A Feast of Words: Banquets and Table Talk in the Renaissance*, trans. Jeremy Whiteley and Emma Hughes (Chicago: University of Chicago Press, 1991).

Selected Bibliography

PRIMARY SOURCES

Important Editions of Rabelais's Works

Oeuvres, Edition Variorum. 9 vols. Paris: Dalibon, 1823–26. Noteworthy for its critical comments by scholars up to that time.

Oeuvres. Edited by Charles Marty-Laveaux. 6 vols. Paris: Lemerre, 1868–1903. The standard edition of the nineteenth century.

Oeuvres. Edited by Abel Lefranc, Robert Marichal, et al. 7 vols. Paris and Geneva: Champion and Droz, 1912–55. A basic tool for Rabelais studies, a model critical edition. The first three books were published under the editorship of Abel Lefranc (1912–31), and the first seventeen chapters of the *Fourth Book* under Robert Marichal (1955).

Pantagruel. Edited by Verdun-Louis Saulnier. Geneva: Droz, 1946, 1965. This edition profits from scholarship done since the critical edition.

The "Quart Livre." Edited by Robert Marichal. Geneva: Droz, 1947. An important work at the time, but a new edition is now needed.

L'Abbaye de Thélème. Edited by Raoul Morçay. Geneva: Droz, 1947. More important for its introduction than the text.

Oeuvres complètes. Edited by Marcel Guilbaud. 5 vols. Paris: Imprimerie Nationale, 1957. A standard edition in modernized French.

Oeuvres complètes. Edited by Jacques Boulenger and Lucien Scheler. Paris: Gallimard, Bibliothèque de la Pléiade, 1955. A standard and compact edition with a very adequate critical apparatus. A new edition edited by Mireille Huchon is forthcoming.

Oeuvres complètes. Edited by Pierre Jourda. 2 vols. Paris: Garnier, 1962. A useful edition equal to the one in the above Pléiade collection.

Le Tiers Livre. Edited by Michael A. Screech. Geneva: Droz, 1964. A timely work that takes into account scholarship since the last critical edition.

Gargantua. Edited by Ruth Calder, Michael A. Screech, and Verdun-Louis Saulnier. Geneva: Droz, 1970. A very useful edition.

Oeuvres complètes. Edited by Guy Demerson. Paris: Seuil, 1973. Collection "l'Intégrale." A bilingual edition (modern and original French) that offers a very good critical apparatus.

Standard Translations

The Five Books of Gargantua and Pantagruel. Translated by Jacques LeClercq. New York: Random House/Modern Library 1936, 1944.

Gargantua and Pantagruel. Translated by Sir Thomas Urquhart and Peter Le Motteux. Chicago: Encyclopedia Britannica, 1955. The first translation of Rabelais's works into English. Urquhart translated the first two books in 1653 and the *Third Book* in 1693. Le Motteux translated the *Fourth Book* and the *Fifth Book* in 1694.

Gargantua and Pantagruel. Translated by John Michael Cohen. Harmondsworth, England: Penguin Books, 1955.

Gargantua and Pantagruel. Translated by Burton Raffel. New York: Norton, 1990. A highly readable and generally faithful translation into modern English.

Complete Works. Translated by Donald M. Frame. Foreword by Raymond La Charité. Berkeley: University of California Press, 1991. Also highly readable and faithful.

SECONDARY SOURCES

Books

Antonioli, Roland. *Rabelais et la médecine. Etudes Rabelaisiennes* 12. Geneva: Droz, 1976. A well-balanced and illuminating account of medical elements in Rabelais.

Bakhtin, Mikhail. *The Dialogic Imagination: Four Essays.* Translated by Caryl Emerson and Michael Holquist. Austin: University of Texas Press, 1981. Insightful essays on the characteristics and generative principles of dialogic forms in literature.

———. *Rabelais and His World.* Translated by Hélène Iwolsky. 1968; Rpt. Bloomington: Indiana University Press, 1984. Notwithstanding its sparse documentation and tendency to overgeneralize, this seminal work on popular culture and dialogism in Rabelais offers critical insights into the binarity of his text.

Baraz, Michaël. *Rabelais et la joie de la liberté.* Paris: José Corti, 1983. A valuable study of polyvalence in Rabelais that unites bipolarities under the unifying umbrella of philosophical liberty and joy.

Beaujour, Michel. *Le Jeu de Rabelais.* Paris: Editions de l'Herne, 1969. Building upon the theses of Bakhtin, this study focuses upon narrative ambivalence and ludic structures in the Rabelaisian text.

Berry, Alice Fiola. *Rabelais: "Homo Logos."* Studies in the Romance Languages and Literatures. Chapel Hill: University of North Carolina Press, 1979. An insightful study of the quest for a transcendent signifier and the inadequacy of language in Rabelais.

170

Bloch, R. Howard. *Etymologies and Genealogies: A Literary Anthropology of the French Middle Ages.* Chicago: University of Chicago Press, 1983. Contains an important chapter, "The Economics of Romance" (159–97).

Boulenger, Jacques. *Rabelais à travers les âges.* Paris: Le Divan, 1925. A rapid overview of opinions on Rabelais from the sixteenth through the nineteenth centuries, including a study on portraits.

Bowen, Barbara. *The Age of Bluff: Paradox and Ambiguity in Rabelais and Montaigne.* Urbana: University of Illinois Press, 1972. Useful comments on ambiguity in Rabelais.

Brown, Huntington. *Rabelais in English Literature.* Cambridge, Mass.: Harvard University Press, 1933. Competent and needed study, though the emphasis is on post-seventeenth-century literature. A new study of the subject by Ann Prescott is forthcoming from Yale University Press.

Busson, Henri. *Le Rationalisme dans la littérature française de la Renaissance.* Paris: Vrin, 1957. A basic study on the subject of freethinking writers in which the position toward Rabelais (157–78) is justifiably ambiguous.

Carpenter, Nan Cooke. *Rabelais and Music.* Chapel Hill: University of North Carolina Press, 1954. The only book on the subject.

Cave, Terence. *The Cornucopian Text: Problems of Writing in the French Renaissance.* Oxford: Clarendon, 1979. Successfully combines Renaissance rhetorical theory with modern criticism in an important look at the polyvalence of copia in masterworks of the period, including Rabelais (183–222).

Chesney (Zegura), Elizabeth A. *The Countervoyage of Rabelais and Ariosto: A Comparative Reading of Two Renaissance Mock Epics.* Durham: Duke University Press, 1982. Compares bipolarities and structural anomalies in Ariosto and Rabelais.

Clark, Carol. *The Vulgar Rabelais.* Glasgow: Pressgang, 1983. Studies the popular background of Rabelais's world, including the mountebank tradition.

Coleman, Dorothy Gabe. *Rabelais: A Critical Study in Prose Fiction.* Cambridge: Cambridge University Press, 1971. Closely analyzes the narrator and narrative structure of the Pantagrueline Tales.

Colie, Rosalie. *Paradoxia Epidemica: The Renaissance Tradition of Paradox.* Princeton: Princeton University Press, 1966. A classic study of paradox and ambiguity in major Renaissance texts.

Concordance des Oeuvres de François Rabelais, ed. J. E. G. Dixon and John L. Dawson. *Etudes Rabelaisiennes* 26. Geneva: Droz, 1992. An invaluable lexical tool for serious students of Rabelais.

Cooper, Richard. *Rabelais et l'Italie. Etudes Rabelaisiennes* 24. Geneva: Droz, 1991. A thorough analysis and exhaustive documentation of Rabelais's contacts with Italy in his lifetime.

Defaux, Gérard. *Pantagruel et les sophistes: Contribution à l'histoire de l'humanisme chrétien au XVIe siècle*. The Hague: Nijhoff, 1973. An ingenious reading of the entire first novel as an essay in and critique of sophism.

De Grève, Marcel. *L'Interprétation de Rabelais au XVIe siècle*. Geneva: Droz, 1961. Interesting insights into Rabelais's reception by his contemporaries.

Demerson, Guy. *Rabelais: Une vie, une oeuvre, une époque*. Paris: Balland, 1986. A broad-based introduction to the life, text, works, and critical fortunes of Rabelais containing salient comments on the importance of exchange.

Dieguez, Manuel de. *Rabelais par lui-même*. Paris: Seuil, 1960. An excellent little study that emphasizes the evolution of Rabelais's language.

Dontenville, Henri. *La Mythologie française*. Paris: Payot, 1948. The best work available tracing the legend of Gargantua in popular tradition.

Dubois, Claude-Gilbert. *Les Problèmes de l'utopie*. Paris: Archives des Lettres Modernes, 1968. An essay on the paradoxality of utopian thought that poses important questions pertaining to Thélème.

Duval, Edwin M. *The Design of Rabelais's "Pantagruel"*. New Haven: Yale University Press, 1991. Through parallels with the New Testament and the *Aeneid*, endeavors to prove that the earliest novel is a Christian antiepic.

Eisenstein, Elizabeth. *The Printing Press as an Agent of Change: Communications and Cultural Transformations in Early Modern Europe*. 2 vols. Cambridge: Cambridge University Press, 1979. Provides important insights for understanding the early age of printing and the economic, epistemological, and linguistic crisis that accompanied it.

Febvre, Lucien. *The Problem of Unbelief in the Sixteenth Century: The Religion of Rabelais*. Translated by Beatrice Gottlieb. Cambridge, Mass.: Harvard University Press, 1982. Originally published as *Le Problème de l'incroyance au XVIe siècle: La Religion de Rabelais* (Paris: Albin Michel, 1942). Rebuts Lefranc's portrait of an atheistic Rabelais on the spurious grounds that unbelief was unthinkable in the Renaissance.

Françon, Marcel, ed. *Les Croniques admirables du puissant roy Gargantua*. Rochecorbon (Indre-et-Loire): C. Gay, 1956. One of the *Gargantuan Chronicles*.

Freccero, Carla. *Father Figures: Genealogy and Narrative Structure in Rabelais*. Ithaca: Cornell University Press, 1991. Views the hesitation between paternal authority and filial rebellion as a structuring principle of Rabelais's fiction.

Frye, Northrop. *Anatomy of Criticism*. Princeton: Princeton University Press, 1957. Contains pungent pages (232–36, 308–13) on satire and structure.

Gebhart, Emile. *Rabelais, la Réforme et la Renaissance*. Paris: Hachette, 1904. Points out medieval aspects of Rabelais, then puts him in a reasonable light. The storm over Lefranc's atheistic Rabelais soon drowned out this study.

Glauser, Alfred. *Rabelais créateur*. Paris: Nizet, 1966. Focuses on the literary artistry of Rabelais.

Gray, Floyd. *Rabelais et l'écriture*. Paris: Nizet, 1974. Concentrates on the

172

experimental and interrogative nature of Rabelais's writing, which the author views as a self-searching dialogue between origins and originality, the visual and the aural.

Greene, Thomas M. *Rabelais: A Study in Comic Courage.* Englewood Cliffs, N.J.: Prentice-Hall, 1970. A cogent and incisive introduction to Rabelais.

Huchon, Mireille. *Rabelais grammairien: De l'histoire du texte aux problèmes d'authenticité. Etudes Rabelaisiennes* 16. Geneva: Droz, 1981. On the problem of the *Fifth Book*'s legitimacy.

Huguet, Edmond E. A. *Etude sur la syntaxe de Rabelais, comparée à celle des autres prosateurs de 1450 à 1550.* Paris: Hachette, 1894. An essential but quite dated study on the subject.

——*Dictionnaire de la langue française au 16e siècle.* Paris: Champion, 1925. Though incomplete, this dictionary of sixteenth-century French is an indispensable tool for Rabelais studies.

Jeanneret, Michel. *A Feast of Words: Banquets and Table Talk in the Renaissance.* Translated by Jeremy Whiteley and Emma Hughes. Chicago: University of Chicago Press, 1991. Originally published as *Des mets et des mots: Banquets et propos de table à la Renaissance.* (Paris: José Corti, 1987). A masterful study ranging from antiquity to the Renaissance on the interplay of the banquet and narration.

Jordan, Constance. *Renaissance Feminism: Literary Texts and Political Models.* Ithaca: Cornell University Press, 1990. Excellent pages (191–99) on the *Third Book* marriage question from an economic standpoint.

Juillière, Pierre de la. *Les Images de Rabelais.* Halle: N. Niemeyer, 1912. A catalog of the imagery in Rabelais, but with no aesthetic approach.

Kaiser, Walter. *Praisers of Folly: Erasmus, Rabelais, Shakespeare.* Cambridge, Mass.: Harvard University Press, 1963. An important study on the polyvalence of Renaissance folly, including a salient chapter on Panurge.

Keller, Abraham. *The Telling of Tales in Rabelais: Aspects of His Narrative Art.* Frankfurt am Main: V. Klostermann, 1963. An insightful study within its self-limited scope.

Kinser, Samuel. *Rabelais's Carnival: Text, Context, Metatext.* Berkeley: University of California Press, 1990. Focuses upon the ambiguity of carnival elements in the *Fourth Book*.

Kline, Michael B. *Rabelais and the Age of Printing. Etudes Rabelaisiennes* 4. Geneva: Droz, 1963. Situates Rabelais in the making of books in the Renaissance.

Krailsheimer, Alban J. *Rabelais and the Franciscans.* Oxford: Clarendon Press, 1963. A fresh and sensible approach to many questions facing Rabelais scholarship.

Kritzman, Lawrence. *The Rhetoric of Sexuality and the Literature of the French Renaissance.* Cambridge: Cambridge University Press, 1991. Includes sections on Rabelais (especially 29–44, 171–213) focusing on the representation of male subjectivity and the literary acting out of aggressions.

La Charité, Raymond C. *Recreation, Reflection, and Re-creation: Perspectives on Rabelais's "Pantagruel."* Lexington, Ky.: French Forum, 1980. Finds the unity of *Pantagruel* in the work's repetitive and re-creational structure.

Lefranc, Abel. *Rabelais. Etudes sur Gargantua, Pantagruel, le Tiers livre.* Paris: Albin Michel. 1953. A posthumous collection of introductions to the editions Lefranc edited. Contains the controversial essay on Rabelais's freethinking tendencies and suspected atheism.

Lote, Georges. *La Vie et l'oeuvre de François Rabelais.* Paris: Droz, 1938. Good introductory work; both content and style receive ample treatment.

Masters, Mallary. *Rabelaisian Dialectic and the Platonic Hermetic Tradition.* Albany: State University of New York, 1969. Reads the quest within a Platonic framework.

Paris, Jean. *Rabelais au futur.* Paris: Seuil, 1970. Addresses the semantic openness of the Rabelaisian text.

Plattard, Jean. *L'Invention et la composition dans l'oeuvre de Rabelais.* Paris: Champion, 1910. A basic tool to any specialized approach to Rabelais.

———. *The Life of François Rabelais.* Translated by Louis P. Roche. New York: Knopf, 1931; London: Frank Cass and Col., 1968. Originally published as *La Vie de François Rabelais.* (Paris and Brussels: Van Oest, 1928). The standard biography.

Quinones, Ricardo. *The Renaissance Discovery of Time.* Cambridge, Mass.: Harvard University Press, 1972. Perceptive comments on the concept of time in Rabelais and other major writers of the period.

Quint, David. *Origins and Originality in Renaissance Literature: Versions of the Source.* New Haven: Yale University Press, 1983. A stimulating discussion of the tension between origins and originality in the Renaissance, focusing on a theological approach to Rabelais.

Rigolot, François. *Les Langages de Rabelais. Etudes Rabelaisiennes* 10. Geneva: Droz, 1972. A sensitive and far-reaching treatment of Rabelais's use of language.

Sainéan, Lazare. *L'Histoire naturelle et les branches connexes dans l'oeuvre de Rabelais.* Paris: Champion, 1921. The only study on the natural sciences in Rabelais's books.

———. *La Langue de Rabelais.* 2 vols. Paris: E. De Boccard, 1921. A fundamental work on the language, though unfortunately in catalog form. Includes imagery, proverbs, sources of words.

———. *L'Influence et la réputation de Rabelais.* Paris: J. Gamber, 1930. Opinions on and influences of Rabelais in France and abroad; complements Boulenger's *Rabelais à travers les âges.*

Saulnier, Verdun-Louis. *Le Dessein de Rabelais.* Paris: Société d'Edition d'Enseignement Supérieur, 1957. Especially important for its approach to the *Third Book* along quest-for-happiness lines.

———. *Rabelais I and II: Rabelais dans son enquête.* 2 vols. Paris; Société d'Edition d'Enseignement Supérieur, 1982, 1983. A magisterial and balanced study of Rabelais's five books.

Schwartz, Jerome. *Irony and Ideology in Rabelais: Structures of Subversion.* Cambridge: Cambridge University Press, 1990. A noteworthy study of the way in which counterdiscourse subverts the ideological discourse and generates polyvalence in Rabelais.

Screech, Michael A. *L'Evengélisme de Rabelais.* Geneva: Droz, 1959. Rabelais situated in a pre-Reformation context.

————. *The Rabelaisian Marriage: Aspects of Rabelais's Religion, Ethics, and Comic Philosophy.* London: Arnold, 1958. Studies the *Third Book* and the woman question within the framework of Paulinism.

————. *Rabelais.* Ithaca: Cornell University Press, 1979. A study rich in historical documentation.

Sébillot, Paul. *Gargantua dans les traditions populaires.* Paris, 1883; Rpt. Paris: Maisonneuve, 1967. Complements the Dontenville book but is also superseded by it.

Smith, Paul J. *Voyage et écriture: Etude sur le "Quart Livre" de Rabelais. Etudes Rabelaisiennes* 19. Geneva: Droz, 1987. A discerning reading of the *Fourth Book.*

Stephens, Walter. *Giants in Those Days: Folklore, Ancient History, and Nationalism.* Lincoln: University of Nebraska Press, 1989. Illuminating study of the multiple "giant" traditions in circulation at the time of Rabelais.

Telle, Emile V. *L'Oeuvre de Marguerite d'Angoulême, reine de Navarre, et la querelle des femmes.* Toulouse: Lion, 1937. Important for its discussion of the "woman question" in the Renaissance.

Tetel, Marcel. *Etude sur le comique de Rabelais.* Florence: L. Olschki, 1964. A study of the comic primarily from the stylistic point of view.

————. *Rabelais et l'Italie.* Florence: L. Olschki, 1969. How Rabelais pervades Italian literature from the Renaissance to the twentieth century.

Waswo, Richard. *Language and Meaning in the Renaissance.* Princeton: Princeton University Press, 1987. Studies shift from referential to relational semantics in Renaissance literature.

Weinberg, Florence M. *The Wine and the Will: Rabelais's Bacchic Christianity.* Detroit: Wayne State University Press, 1972. The theme of wine within the context of Christian evangelism.

Articles and Parts of Books

Auerbach, Erich. "The World in Pantagruel's Mouth." In *Mimesis: The Representation of Reality in Western Literature,* trans. Willard Trask, 262–84. Garden City, N.Y.: Doubleday/Anchor Books, 1957. A perceptive look into Rabelais's conception of reality.

Berrong, Richard. "The Evolving Attitude toward Material Wealth in Rabelais's *Oeuvres.*" *Stanford French Review* 9 (Winter 1985): 301–19.

Details the shifts in Rabelais's attitude toward money, goods, and property.

Berry, Alice Fiola. "'L'Isle Medamothi': Rabelais's Itineraries of Anxiety (*Quart Livre* 2–4)." *PMLA* 106 (October 1991): 1040–53. A perceptive look at problems of exchange, representation, and filiation in the *Fourth Book*'s opening chapters.

Guiton, Jean. "Le Mythe des paroles gelées (Rabelais, *Quart Livre*, LV–LVI)." *Romanic Review* 31 (1940): 3–15. Classic study of the Frozen Words.

Jeanneret, Michel. "Les Paroles dégelées (Rabelais, *Quart Livre*, 48–65)." *Littérature* 17 (1975): 14–30. A thought-provoking analysis of the dialectic between the material and ideal, the literal and figurative, the visual and aural in the last 20 chapters of the *Fourth Book*.

Kritzman, Lawrence. "Rabelais's Comedy of Cruelty: A Psycho-Allegorical Reading of the Chiquanous Episode." In *Rabelais's Incomparable Book: Essays on His Art*, ed. Raymond La Charité, 141–54. Lexington, Ky.: French Forum, 1986. A psychoanalytical approach to the Chiquanous episode.

Lanham, Richard A. "The War between Play and Purpose: *Gargantua and Pantagruel*." In *The Motives of Eloquence*, 165–89. New Haven: Yale University Press, 1976. A thought-provoking study that situates the tensions and apparent inconsistencies in Rabelais within the theatrical and ludic tradition of "rhetorical narrative."

Regosin, Richard. "The Ins(ides) and Outs(ides) of Reading: Plural Discourse and the Question of Interpretation in Rabelais." In *Rabelais's Incomparable Book: Essays on His Art*, ed. Raymond La Charité, 59–71. Lexington, Ky.: French Forum, 1986. An important essay on the plurality of meaning in Rabelais.

Spitzer, Leo. "Rabelais et les 'Rabelaisants.'" *Studi Francesi* 4 (September–December 1960): 401–23. Takes issue with the historically based Abel Lefranc school of criticism and advocates a more aesthetic approach.

Tetel, Marcel. "Carnival and Beyond." *L'Esprit Créateur* 21 (1981): 88–104. How the *Fourth Book* begins and is propelled to its mirrored ending.

Weinberg, Bernard. "Rabelais as an Artist." *Texas Quarterly* 3 (1960): 175–88. A succinct and valuable contribution to the subject.

Zegura, Elizabeth Chesney. "Toward a Feminist Reading of Rabelais." *Journal of Medieval and Renaissance Studies* 15 (Spring 1985): 125–34. Woman as both the unfaithful other and a satiric mirror of the same.

Specialized Bibliographies

Cioranescu, Alexandre. *Bibliographie de la littérature française au 16e siècle.* 17933–18789. Paris: Librairie C. Klincksieck, 1959.

Cordié, Carlo. "Recenti studi sulla vita e sulle opere di François Rabelais, 1939–1950." *Letterature moderne* 1 (1950): 107–20.

La Charité, Raymond C. *A Critical Bibliography of French Literature: The Sixteenth Century*, nn. 1144–1263A. Syracuse: Syracuse University Press, 1985.

Plan, Pierre-Paul. *Bibliographie Rabelaisienne: Les éditions de Rabelais de 1532 à 1711*. Paris: Imprimerie Nationale, 1904.

Rackow, Paul. "Der gegenwärtige Stand der Rabelais-Forschung." *Germanisch-romanische Monatschrift* 18 (1930): 198–211, 277–90. Rabelais studies up to 1930.

Saulnier, Verdun-Louis. "Dix années d'études rabelaisiennes." *Bibliothèque d'Humanisme et Renaissance* 11 (1949): 104–28. Rabelais studies from 1939 to 1949; covers the same period of time as Cordié's article.

Schrader, Ludwig. "Die Rabelais-Forschung der Jahre 1950–1960: Tendenzen und Ergebnisse." *Romanistisches Jahrbuch* 11 (1960): 161–201. Rabelais studies in the 1950s.

Important Periodicals

Revue des Etudes Rabelaisiennes (1903–12). This journal, though no longer devoted solely to Rabelais but to the Renaissance as a whole, continued under the following titles: *Revue du Seizième Siècle* (1913–32), *Humanisme et Renaissance* (1934–40), *Bibliothèque d'Humanisme et Renaissance* (1941 to the present), and *Nouvelle Revue du Seizième Siècle* (1983 to present).

Bulletin de l'Association des Amis de Rabelais et de la Devinière (1951 to the present).

Etudes Rabelaisiennes (1959 to the present). A publication in which volumes appear as books on a specific topic or as collections of essays.

Symposia, Collected Essays, and Commemorative Volumes

François Rabelais: Ouvrage publié pour le quatrième centenaire de sa mort. Geneva: Droz, 1953.

Rabelais. In *Cahiers de l'Association Internationale des Etudes Françaises* 30 (May 1978).

Renaissance et nouvelle critique: Quatrième Symposium sur la Renaissance. New York: Modern Language Association of America, 1978.

A Rabelaisian Symposium. Special issue of *L'Esprit Créateur* 21 (1981).

Rabelais in Glasgow: Proceedings of the Colloquium Held at the University, December 1983. Edited by J. A. Coleman and C. M. Scollen-Jimack. Glasgow: Dept. of French, Univ. of Glasgow, 1984.

Rabelais. Special issue of *Etudes de Lettres* (Lausanne) (April-June 1984).

Rabelais's Incomparable Book: Essays on His Art. Edited by Raymond C. La Charité. Lexington, Ky.: French Forum, 1986. An important collection of studies on Rabelais incorporating a variety of contemporary methodologies.

Rabelais en son demi-millénaire. Actes du Colloque International de Tours. *Etudes Rabelaisiennes* 21. Geneva: Droz, 1988. A broad sampling of critical approaches are represented.

Index

Abyss, 45, 51, 61; between reality and representation, 123; definition of, 37; interrogation of, 37, 42, 110; of learning, 11, 35, 37, 40, 42, 86, 110, 115, 155; negativity of, 23, 44, 120, 154; netherworlds as, 50; open mouth as, 138; of Panurge's finances, 93; sea as, 139, Utopia as, 25

Accumulatio (Accumulation), 30, 37, 78, 123, 156. *See also* Copia, Inflation

Aeneas, 4, 104

Aesop, 33

Affaire des Placards, 8

Agrippa of Nettesheim, Cornelius, 101

Alcofribas, journey in Pantagruel's mouth of, 51; disappearance of, 85. *See also* Narrator

Allegory, as counterfeit, 166–67n5; of cuckoldry, 109; in *Fourth Book*, 139, 143–45, 150; in *Gargantua*, 154; mockery of, 57; in netherworlds, 51–52; popularity of, in Renaissance, 3; of reading, 83, 151

Alliances, Island of, 131–33, 150

Ambiguity, of Andouilles, 142; of *coingnée*, 120; of *Decretals*, 147; in economic rhetoric, 37; effort to transcend, 40, 107; as function of exchange, 153, 155–56; as function of syncretism, 10; linguistic, 70; narrative, 23; nature and scope of, ix–x, 1–3, 7, 10, 22; of Pantagruelion, 114–15; of Panurge's costume, 97; political expediency of, 14; of prophecies in *Third Book*, 103, 106–8; of Prophetic Enigma, 83; of Sileni metaphor, 57; of wind at Ruach, 143

Amy, Pierre, 14

Anarchus, King, 48

Andouilles (Chitterlings), 140–43, 167n10

Androgyne, 2, 63, 96

Antiphrasis, 62, 91, 109, 124, 143

Antiquity, commerce with, 9–10

Appropriation, process of, 66, 68. *See also* Theft

Ariosto, Ludovico, 10; *Orlando Furioso*, 26

Aristotelianism, 1

Aristotle, 93, 94, 105, 164n3

Arsewipe. *See* Invention

Art, functionality of, 134; ideal of, 118–19, 125–26, 137

Asclepiades, 119

Astrology, 35, 101

Auerbach, Erich, 162n14

Augustine, Saint, 153

Avignon, 9

Bacbuc (Dive Bouteille), 111–13

Bacchic furor. *See* Inspiration

Bade, Josse, 14

Badebec, death of, 5, 30, 31

Baisecul (Kissarse), 5, 39, 42, 43, 45

Bakhtin, Mikhail, ix, 159n6–7, 161n3

Baldini, Massimo, 164n13

Barbarossa, Sultan Kheir-ed-Din, 17

Basché, Lord of, 136, 137

Beda, Nicola, 10

Berni, Francesco, 164n3

Berrong, Richard, 162n11, 164n12, 166n10, 167n7

Berry, Alice Fiola, 166n3

Bloch, R. Howard, 160n11

Boccaccio, 9, 153

Bodin, Jean, 6

Books, as commodity in Renaissance, 12, 27; value of, interrogated, 38, 42, 62, 110; as vehicle of intellectual commerce, 12

Borderie, Bertrand de la: *L'Amye de court*, 165n7

Botticelli, Sandro, 9

Bouchard, Amaury, 14

The Authors

Elizabeth Chesney Zegura teaches French and Italian at the University of Arizona and is the author of *The Countervoyage of Rabelais and Ariosto (1982)*.

Marcel Tetel is a professor of French and Italian at Duke University and the author of *Etude sur le comique de Rabelais* (1964) and *Rabelais et l'Italie* (1969).